P9-AOW-341

THE CHOICE OF LIFE

THE CHOICE OF LIFE

Samuel Johnson and the World of Fiction

Carey McIntosh

New Haven and London, Yale University Press

1973

Library of Congress catalog card number: 73-77160
International standard book number: 0-300-01571-2

Designed by John O. C. McCrillis and set in Baskerville type.
Printed in the United States of America by The Vail-Ballou Press, Inc., Binghamton, N.Y.

Published in Great Britain, Europe, and Africa by Yale University Press, Ltd., London.
Distributed in Latin America by Kaiman & Polon, Inc., New York City; in Australasia and Southeast Asia by John Wiley & Sons Australasia Pty. Ltd., Sydney; in India by UBS Publishers' Distributors Pvt., Ltd., Delhi; in Japan by John Weatherhill, Inc., Tokyo.

For Nadia,
Rustin, and Thaniel

Contents

Preface

Johnson was not a novelist, and except for *Rasselas* no single work of fiction by Johnson is of great consequence today. Until we stop to count, however, we do not realize how many short fictions he wrote. (When we do stop to count, we shall not soon agree on exact figures, since some of the tinier anecdotes or "characters" are scarcely recognizable as "fiction.") About 143 of the 325 essays by Johnson in *The Rambler, The Adventurer,* and *The Idler* resort to fiction of some kind. There are also two political satires from 1739, one from 1756, a humorous letter to *The Public Ledger* (1760), "The Vision of Theodore," "The Fountains," a chapter in Charlotte Lennox's *The Female Quixote,* and *Rasselas.* Collected, it is a respectable body of narrative.

The importance of this respectable but small and heterogeneous body of narrative is the access it provides to new perspectives on Johnson as a writer, as an artist in prose. Viewed through the lens of his own fiction, Johnson displays qualities and affinities that are not apparent from other perspectives. Perhaps a brief review of major topics in the six chapters that follow will clarify some of my intentions.

Chapter 1 examines Johnson's ideas on fiction-in-general: basic axioms that help to justify his notorious lack of enthusiasm for certain kinds of narrative, his generous appreciation of works like *Don Quixote,* and his writing the kinds of fiction he did. In chapters 2–5 I confine myself largely to the periodical-essay fiction, not only because it has received far less attention than the criticism or than *Rasselas,* but also because in effect it gives Johnson's inventive faculties about 150 chances to exercise themselves in almost perfect freedom: nothing constrained him to paint precisely the "pictures of life" we see in *The Rambler* and its successors; they may be read therefore as a map of the world of his imagination. Chapter 2 deals with the "choice of life" as a central theme. The phrase comes from *Rasselas,* but the problem of deciding what activity or profession or position in society to devote one's talents to dominates the periodical-essay fiction also and serves as a harbor where most of the topics floated in subsequent chapters find a fairly comfortable berth. Chapters 3 and 4 focus on the distinctive qualities of Johnson's performances in three of the most popular genres in periodical-essay fiction: satire, oriental tale, and allegory. Johnson's special achievements here are analyzed in terms of prose style, irony, vivid pictorialisms, and dark pessimism. Chapter 5 puts Johnson's periodical-essay fiction in a specific literary-historical context, by plunging into the swamp of journalistic fiction (where armies whole have sunk) between *The Spectator* (1711) and *The Rambler* (1750). Here, for a while, I shake free of the generic approach (which is not always easy to do in treating periodical-essay fiction, since so many of these shreds and patches of narrative conform to type) by defining three "voices" that may be said to have established three more or less distinct sets of narrative conventions in eighteenth-century journalism; Johnson's aptitudes and liabilities show up very clearly in this context. Chapter 6 is devoted to *Rasselas.* Why do we feel that the book as a whole is a far more powerful (and personal) affirmation than the periodical-essay fiction taken singly or in a lump? Genre has something to do with it; and style, which undergoes significant mutations as the "voices" of the narrator shift from irony, to pathos, and to sublimity; structure also, a qualitative difference between events in the first half of the story and those that follow chapter 30; and context: this is a philosophic voyage; and so to understand what it means in the eighteenth century to be "philosophic" we turn to selected texts from and critiques of the European Enlightenment.

Johnson's fiction, though limited, poses a variety of critical problems. It is circumstantial but not always plausible; its narrator has several different voices and prose styles; some of the narrative traditions it relies on are not well known, but it intersects at crucial points with major currents in the history of the novel. In every chapter I have used concise comparisons to enlarge contexts. The notes carry much of the burden of allusion and brief reference; they are intended, nevertheless, to be suggestive rather than exhaustive.

Research for this study began in 1963. Some of it has been supported by grants from the Kendall and the Canaday Humanities Funds of Harvard University, and by a Summer Fellowship from the University of Rochester. Without the encouragement and guidance of Professor W. J. Bate at the beginning and long afterward, I would almost certainly have foundered some years ago. At various stages along the way I have received useful assistance from Professors Allen T. Hazen, David Jeffrey, J. W. Johnson, Paul Korshin, and Robert Mayo. The manuscript in what I thought when I sent it to them was its complete and final form was read by Professors Robert Folkenflik, Paul Fussell, and Howard Weinbrot; I am most grateful to them for helpful suggestions.

C. M.

Rochester, New York
January, 1973

Short Titles

Adventurer: Samuel Johnson, *The Idler and The Adventurer.* Yale Edition of the Works of Samuel Johnson, vol. 2. Edited by W. J. Bate, John M. Bullitt, L. F. Powell. New Haven, 1963.

Boswell: *Boswell's Life of Johnson.* Edited by G. B. Hill, revised by L. F. Powell. 6 vols. Oxford, 1934–50.

Censor: Lewis Theobald, *The Censor* (London, 1715 and 1717). Cited from reprint edition. 3 vols. London, 1717.

Citizen of the World: Oliver Goldsmith, *The Citizen of the World,* in *Collected Works,* vol. 2. Edited by Arthur Friedman. Oxford, 1966.

Dictionary: Samuel Johnson, *A Dictionary of the English Language.* 2 vols. London, 1755. Facsimile reprint New York, 1967.

Free-Thinker: Ambrose Philips, *The Free-Thinker* (London, 1718–21). Cited from folio edition and from reprint edition. 3 vols. London, 1723.

Guardian: Richard Steele, *The Guardian* (London, 1713). Cited from reprint edition in *The British Essayists.* Edited by Alexander Chalmers. 45 vols. London, 1802–03.

Hazen: *Samuel Johnson's Prefaces and Dedications.* Edited by Allen T. Hazen. New Haven, 1937.

Idler: Samuel Johnson, *The Idler and The Adventurer.* Yale Edition of the Works of Samuel Johnson, vol. 2. Edited by W. J. Bate, John M. Bullitt, L. F. Powell. New Haven, 1963.

Lay-Monk: Richard Blackmore, *The Lay-Monk* (London, 1713–14). Cited from edition of 1714 reprinted as *The Lay-Monastery.*

LCL: Loeb Classical Library.

Letters: The Letters of Samuel Johnson. Edited by R. W. Chapman. 3 vols. Oxford, 1952.

Lives: Samuel Johnson, *Lives of the English Poets.* Edited by G. B. Hill. 3 vols. Oxford, 1905.

Lover: Richard Steele, *The Lover* (London, 1714). Cited from *Richard Steele's Periodical Journalism 1714–16.* Edited by Rae Blanchard. Oxford, 1927.

Miscellanies: Johnsonian Miscellanies. Edited by G. B. Hill. 2 vols. Oxford, 1897.

Plain Dealer: Aaron Hill and William Bond, *The Plain Dealer* (London, 1724– 25). Cited from edition "now first Collected into Two Volumes." London, 1730.

Rambler: Samuel Johnson, *The Rambler.* Yale Edition of the Works of Samuel Johnson, vols. 3–5. Edited by W. J. Bate and Albrecht B. Strauss. New Haven, 1969.

Rasselas: Samuel Johnson, *The Prince of Abissinia.* Edited by R. W. Chapman. Oxford, 1927.

Spectator: Joseph Addison, *The Spectator* (London, 1711–12 and 1714). Cited from edition edited by Donald F. Bond. 5 vols. Oxford, 1965.

Tatler: Richard Steele, *The Tatler* (London, 1709–10). Cited from reprint edition in *The British Essayists.* Edited by Alexander Chalmers. 45 vols. London, 1802–03.

Universal Spectator: Henry Baker, *The Universal Spectator and Weekly Journal* (London, 1728–46). Cited from folio edition and from reprint edition. 2 vols. London, 1747.

Works (1825): Samuel Johnson, *The Works of Samuel Johnson.* 9 vols. Oxford, 1825.

Works (Yale): Samuel Johnson, *Johnson on Shakespeare.* Yale Edition of the Works of Samuel Johnson, vols. 7–8. Edited by Arthur Sherbo. New Haven, 1968.

1 A Useful Luxury

> Nay, lat hym telle us of no ribaudye!
> Telle us som moral thyng, that we may leere
> Som wit, and thanne wol we gladly heere.
>
> Chaucer

The consistency with which Johnson maintains priorities, and subordinates lesser values to greater, is one of his distinctive strengths as critic and moralist. To understand his opinions on any issue, we must understand its relative importance within the largest possible context. "Sir," he told Boswell, "there is no settling the point of precedency between a louse and a flea," intending a judgment not only on lice and fleas but also on trivial comparisons. What seems to be prejudice in his writings and even in his conversation is usually based on principle if we follow it back far enough. I shall begin by asking how Johnson's attitudes to fiction fit into a large framework of general assumptions about life and art.

A powerful sense of priorities does not necessarily imply philosophical consistency. Johnson doubted whether a completely systematic philosophy, in which "by long circumduction, from any one truth all truth may be inferred," was possible, and apparent contradictions within his own writings are sufficiently well known. By temperament and by allegiance he was a divided man, attracted to conflicting goods, brought up on Renaissance hierarchies but influenced by the realistic humanitarianism of the Enlightenment. Nevertheless, on single issues, and especially where he must evaluate, Johnson operates on the basis of consistent assumptions about what is truly important.[1]

1. For some apparent contradictions in Johnson, see W. K. Wimsatt, Jr., and C. Brooks, *Literary Criticism: A Short History* (New York, 1957), ch. 15; Paul Fussell, *Samuel Johnson and the Life of Writing* (New York,

Johnson assigns priorities in terms of necessity, utility, and luxury. He recognizes two kinds of necessity: conditional, that without which a thing is not; and contractual, implying ultimate (religious) obligation. (1) The physical facts of human existence establish certain necessary conditions to valuableness of any sort. Baldly stated, this is not a revolutionary postulate, but in Johnson's hands it hews down forests of casuistry—as, for example, in his description of a degree of poverty in which "want of necessaries" makes even elementary moral obligations difficult if not impossible to meet. (2) The spiritual facts of human existence, the facts of Christianity, prescribe a universally necessary obligation to cultivate the favor of God. No experience is so odd, and no topic so abstract, as to be wholly exempt from obligations, proximate or remote, to Christianity. All Johnson's opinions are delimited and anchored by an awareness of necessary conditions, what is essential to a given operation, and necessary obligations, the indispensable duties of a Christian.

But society in any degree elevated above savagery progresses "from Necessities to Accommodations," and beyond this there is only a finite distance "from Accommodations to Ornaments." "The mind set free from the importunities of natural want, gains leisure to go in search of superfluous gratifications," under which heading falls every elegance of civilized life, conversation and cupolas, fine eating, fine arts, landscaping, and learned societies. There is a sense in which all such external goods, all ornament and luxury, are "counterfeit advantages," "treacherous phantoms in the mist," the pursuit of which is tragically delusive. There is another sense, however, in which luxuries are necessary. This is not a paradox, but, again, a matter of priorities: "to man, as a member of society, many things become necessary, which, perhaps, in a state of nature are superfluous." "The time of listlessness and satiety, of peevishness and discontent must come at last, in which we shall be driven for relief to shows and recreations," to artificial activities and refinements. "The cure for the great-

1971), pp. 8, 43, 62, 81–83, 157–80. Boswell, in the long Character that concludes the *Life,* emphasizes Johnson's consistency; see Boswell, 4 : 429.

est part of human miseries is not radical, but palliative." [2]

A distinction between the "Necessaries" and the "Superfluities" of life was very much in the air in the eighteenth century, and served a number of moralists as a base for attacks on luxury.[3] But those who espoused this simple dichotomy were liable to find themselves forced to classify everything that is not essential to self-preservation as superfluous and luxurious; on these grounds it is hard to justify any of the civilized amenities, or much of what we now call culture. Johnson's trichotomy is more flexible. We sense it at work behind some of his most pregnant spur-of-the-moment remarks (e.g., "Publick affairs vex no man"); and it is the bedrock upon which many of his most authoritative judgments are founded.

Language, like other "works of men," may conduce to rudeness, convenience, or pleasure. While still in his thirties, Johnson wrote for Robert Dodsley a preface to a collection of school texts called *The Preceptor,* intended "not to deck the Mind with Ornaments, but to protect it from Nakedness; not to enrich it with Affluence, but to supply it with Necessaries."

2. *Review of a Free Enquiry,* in *Works* (1825), 6 : 54; Hazen, p. 197; *Adventurer* 111; *The Vanity of Human Wishes,* line 9; *Adventurer* 119; *Ramblers* 167, 32.

3. Joseph Butler: "The Labour of one Man, or the united Labour of several, is sufficient to procure more *Necessaries* than he or they stand in need of, which it may be supposed was, in some Degree, the Case, even in the first Ages; this immediately gave Room for Riches to arise in the World. . . . And, by Degrees, these secondary Wants, and Inventions for the Supply of them, the Fruits of Leisure and Ease, came to employ much of Men's Time and Labour. Hence *a new Species of Riches* came into the World, consisting of things which it might have done well enough without, yet thought desirable, as affording Pleasure to the Imagination, or the Senses. And these went on increasing, till, at length, the *Superfluities* of Life took in a vastly larger Compass of things, than the Necessaries of it. Thus Luxury made its Inroad, and all the numerous Train of Evils its Attendants; of which Poverty, as bad an one as we may account it, is far from being the worst" (Sermon 17, 1740, in *Fifteen Sermons Preached at the Rolls Chapel . . . To which are added, Six Sermons Preached on Publick Occasions.* 4th ed. [London, 1749], pp. 345, 347). See also Warburton, *The Alliance between Church and State* (1736), in *The Works of William Warburton* (London, 1788–94), 4 : 22–27, and Adam Smith, *The Wealth of Nations* (London, 1776), bk. 3, ch. 1, par. 2.

Johnson introduces each subject of study in turn—dispassionately, since all the splendors of learning in all its branches "are merely temporary Benefits, except as they contribute to illustrate the Knowledge, and confirm the Practice of Morality and Piety, which extend their Influence beyond the Grave, and increase our Happiness through endless Duration." Among these splendors, literature has a place of honor, for "*Rhetoric* and *Poetry* supply Life with its highest intellectual Pleasures." Thirty years later, Johnson honored an epic poem with "first place . . . among the productions of the human mind." Nevertheless, poetry cannot discover truth, only recommend it, and the highest truth transcends ornament; poetry is therefore in one sense "merely a luxury." [4]

Fiction, considered either as a particular stratagem of the artistic enterprise or as invented narrative, is even less "necessary" than poetry. "The truth is, that very few have leisure from indispensable business, to employ their thoughts upon narrative or characters." In a world bursting with sin and sorrow, "the luxurious wonders of fiction" are simply not very important. And yet they have their place, limited, but valid within those limits, as a medium of aesthetic pleasure. The vacancies of life must be filled up, and "nothing detains the reader's attention more powerfully than deep involutions of distress or sudden vicissitudes of fortune"; the "business" of "writers of fiction" is "to furnish that entertainment which Fancy perpetually demands." [5]

The same system of priorities that generates the famous Johnsonian hostility to fiction, then, permits a vigorous appreciation of fiction embodied in particular works of art. As a critic, with serious responsibilities to his readers, Johnson denounced romances; as a traveler, with several hours of bouncing inactivity on his hands, and a current interest in Italian to cater to, he clambered into the coach carrying not Dante but *Il Palmerin d'Inghliterra*. As a boy, according to his old friend Dr. Percy, "he was immoderately fond of read-

4. *Idler* 63; Preface to *The Preceptor* (1748), in Hazen, pp. 179, 186, 183; *Lives,* 1 : 170; Boswell, 2 : 351–52.

5. *Rambler* 118; *Idler* 102; Hazen, p. 163.

ing romances of chivalry, and he retained his fondness for them through life; so that spending part of a summer at my parsonage-house in the country, he chose for his regular reading the old Spanish romance of Felixmarte of Hircania, in folio, which he read quite through."[6] What evidence there is suggests that Johnson had read widely in fiction of every kind.

Even within the realm of literary criticism, itself a "subordinate" art, Johnson frequently thinks in terms of priorities; and since the only necessary condition of artistic excellence is the capacity to please ("that book is good in vain which the reader throws away"), he can afford a larger tolerance and wider range than most critics—certainly than most of his colleagues in neoclassicism, formalists like Voltaire, and connoisseurs in the School of Taste like Boileau. "The roads of science are narrow, so that they who travel them, must either follow or meet one another; but in the boundless regions of possibility, which fiction claims for her dominion, there are surely a thousand recesses unexplored, a thousand flowers unplucked, a thousand fountains unexhausted."[7]

The Insipidity of Truth

Hawkins claimed that Johnson "could at any time be talked into a disapprobation of all fictitious relations, of which he would frequently say they took no hold of the mind."[8] This is at first blush a surprising statement, since Johnson is ordinarily not malleable in his opinions but dogmatic, even pugnacious, and elsewhere he does not underestimate the attractiveness of "fictitious relations." This is a useful statement in that it suggests the complexity of Johnson's attitude to fiction. In *Rambler* 4 he acknowledges that fiction can "take possession of the memory by a kind of violence," but he does not like to have his mind possessed by any form of untruth.

For Johnson, as for his contemporaries, the word *fiction* refers not merely to narratives and novels, but to any de-

6. Boswell, 3 : 2, 1 : 49.

7. *Rambler* 208; *Lives,* 1 : 454; *Rambler* 121.

8. Cited by Irving Babbitt, "The Problem of the Imagination: Dr. Johnson," *On Being Creative* (New York, 1932), p. 84.

parture from literal truth, hence to some figures of speech and literary conventions as well as to all invented episodes. The term is in many contexts as neutral as more familiar critical categories, like *fable* or *diction*. In 1744, Johnson announces that the "descriptions" of his friend Savage "are striking, his images animated, his fictions justly imagined, and his allegories artfully pursued"; in 1765 he praises *Macbeth* "for the propriety of its fictions"; in 1781 he recommends Gilbert West's imitations of Spenser for "the metre, the language, and the fiction." A fiction is any "thing feigned or invented," whether it be drawn out to two volumes, or spliced into the narrative of a true event, or compressed into a conceit. Certain fictions become fashionable, are imitated, and harden into generic conventions: "accordingly we find, that . . . there has prevailed in every age a particular species of fiction. At one time all truth was conveyed in allegory; at another, nothing was seen but in a vision; at one period, all the poets followed sheep, and every event produced a pastoral; at another they busied themselves wholly in giving directions to a painter." [9]

Every poet, then, is "an author of fiction," and imaginative literature has Johnson's positive permission to traffic in untruth—not, however, irresponsibly; Johnson demands that fiction maintain some meaningful relation to the world of everyday experience, and discriminates sharply between "natural" fictions ("unaffected; according to truth and reality") and mere fantasy. "The most artful tale raises little curiosity when it is known to be false." [10]

This is one reason why Johnson so frequently castigates pastoral and mythological fictions: not only are they "easy" and "puerile" and "pedantic" (Prior was "trying to be amorous by dint of study; . . . his fictions therefore are mythological"); they are untrue to life. Of "Kensington Gardens," by Thomas Tickell, "the fiction [is] unskilfully compounded of Grecian Deities and Gothick Fairies. Neither of these exploded beings could have done much; and when they are brought

9. *Lives,* 2 : 433; *Works* (Yale), 8 : 795; *Lives,* 3 : 332; *Dictionary,* s.v. "fiction"; *Lives,* 2 : 338, 1 : 28; *Rambler* 121.

10. *Dictionary,* s.v. "poet," "natural"; *Idler* 84.

together they only make each other contemptible." Philips's pastorals "exhibit a mode of life which does not exist, nor ever existed." The same objection can be made to the metaphysical poets: "they cannot be said to have imitated any thing"; and to *Gulliver's Travels,* "a book written in open defiance of truth." It is greatly to Shakespeare's credit, on the other hand, that he peopled his theater with genuine lovers, and abandoned those romantic conventions which constrain most playwrights to "entangle" their male and female leads

> in contradictory obligations, perplex them with oppositions of interest, and harrass them with violence of desires inconsistent with each other; to make them meet in rapture and part in agony; to fill their mouths with hyperbolical joy and outrageous sorrow; to distress them as nothing human ever was distressed; to deliver them as nothing human ever was delivered.[11]

If fictions which are unreal in this sense cannot compel belief, they certainly cannot move the passions. Young's rigidly dignified heroic tragedy *Busiris* seemed to Johnson "too remote from known life to raise either grief, terror, or indignation." "What I cannot for a moment believe, I cannot for a moment behold with interest or anxiety." "Where there is leisure for fiction, there is little grief." [12]

It is important to keep in mind that however memorable Johnson's contempt for some pastoral, mythological, romantic, metaphysical, and heroic fictions, he does not condemn all such fictions out of hand. He disparages "Lycidas" and "The Bard" because they seem to him unattached to real experience or real emotion. And yet he is quite willing to praise pastoral and mythological fictions properly used—that is, as "just representations" of real life, and as effective instruments of instruction. "The images of true pastoral have always the power of exciting delight"; a skillful imitation of an action or passion "by its effects upon a country life" (which is *The Rambler*'s definition of pastoral) calls up in the reader emotions asso-

11. "Easy": *Rambler* 37, *Adventurer* 92, *Lives,* 2: 204; "puerile": *Lives,* 2 : 294, 3 : 225; "pedantic": *Lives,* 2 : 202, 204, 211, 283. Other quotations in this paragraph: *Lives,* 2 : 311, 3 : 324, 1 : 19, 3 : 38; *Works* (Yale), 7 : 63.

12. *Lives,* 3 : 397, 2 : 16, 1 : 163.

ciated with "peace, and leisure, and innocence: and therefore we readily set open the heart" to it. If the gross untruthfulness of myths (they were "exploded" by Christianity) is firmly borne in mind, they may be enjoyed as literary allusion *and* as delightful fictions; for example, in *Paradise Lost,* where Ovid is safely swaddled in a biblical story and a puritan atmosphere, they "contribute variety to the narration, and produce an alternate exercise of the memory and the fancy." Similarly, it is not the meetings and partings, raptures and agonies of romantic stage lovers per se that evoke Johnson's eloquent scorn, but the uniform and reduplicated triteness with which love stories were commonly presented on stage. He found the catastrophe of *Romeo and Juliet* "irresistibly affecting." [13]

Johnson's passion for truth intrudes on his theories of fiction at every turn. Where there is any question of "just representation," wherever literature pretends to imitate the real world, Johnson sweeps aside convention and calls for accuracy, truth. "Poets, indeed, profess fiction, but the legitimate end of fiction is the conveyance of truth." [14]

Truth, however, like nature, is not just a matter of fact, it is also a matter of morality, and if the two conflict, if a chronicle of what is, does not somehow teach us what ought to be, Johnson grows uneasy, sometimes seems to hedge, and sometimes leaves himself open to charges of inconsistency. *Rambler* 4 faces the problem squarely:

> It is justly considered as the greatest excellency of art, to imitate nature; but it is necessary to distinguish those parts of nature, which are most proper for imitation: greater care is still required in representing life, which is so often discoloured by passion, or deformed by wickedness. If the world be promiscuously described, I cannot see of what use it can be to read the account; or why it may not be as safe to turn the eye immediately upon mankind, as upon a mirror which shows all that presents itself without discrimination.

But *Rambler* 4 is only one skirmish in the intermittent feud between naturalism and moralism in Johnson's writings.

13. *Ramblers* 36, 37 (Johnson knew Virgil's *Eclogues* by heart—see Boswell, 1 : 160, n. 2—and praises them in *Adventurer* 92); *Lives,* 1 :178–79; *Works* (Yale), 8 : 956.

14. *Lives,* 1 : 271.

Surely these are two of the presiding powers in his literary criticism, and as a consequence the problem of poetic justice continued to be difficult for him. He defended the ending of Addison's *Cato* against readers indignant at the death of a virtuous hero, but he also defended Tate's revision of *Lear,* in which the good old king is revived and rewarded. A review of his responses to tragedy suggests that in the end, and after a struggle, he was always "better pleased" by "the final triumph of persecuted virtue" than by heroic agony, however authentic.[15]

The problem of attractive villains also involves a conflict between accuracy and morality. Again *Rambler* 4 takes a hard line, against the portrayal of men "splendidly wicked, whose endorsements threw a brightness on their crimes." "Vice, for vice is necessary to be shewn, should always disgust." Nothing could be more decisive; yet Johnson's responses to particular characters are not always as stern as this. One passage in his edition of Shakespeare exhibits him in the very process of sorting out his standards. We can watch him (in the general observation on *Henry IV*) exult over Falstaff, "unimitated, unimitable," see him wind up for applause, and then check himself, gather his morality about him, and plunge stalwartly into an analysis of pleasing vice:

> But Falstaff unimitated, unimitable Falstaff, how shall I describe thee? Thou compound of sense and vice; of sense which may be admired but not esteemed, of vice which may be despised, but hardly detested. Falstaff is a character loaded with faults, and with those faults which naturally produce contempt. He is a thief, and a glutton, a coward, and a boaster, always ready to cheat the weak, and prey upon the poor; to terrify the timorous and insult the defenceless. At once obsequious and malignant, he satirises in their absence those whom he lives by flattering. He is familiar with the prince only as an agent of vice, but of this familiarity he is so proud as not only to be supercilious and haughty with common men, but

15. See J. E. Brown, *The Critical Opinions of Samuel Johnson* (Princeton, 1926), s.v. "Drama: Poetic Justice." Note the ingenuity with which Johnson finds faults in Oedipus (J. E. Brown, s.v. "Sophocles") and in Clarissa (*Miscellanies,* 1 : 297), as if to justify their suffering. For Johnson's "naturalism" see René Wellek, *A History of Modern Criticism,* vol. 1 (New Haven, 1955), ch. 5.

> to think his interest of importance to the duke of Lancaster. Yet the man thus corrupt, thus despicable, makes himself necessary to the prince that despises him, by the most pleasing of all qualities, perpetual gaiety, by an unfailing power of exciting laughter, which is the more freely indulged, as his wit is not of the splendid or ambitious kind, but consists in easy escapes and sallies of levity, which make sport but raise no envy. [*Works* (Yale), 7 : 523]

In spite of Johnson's affection for Falstaff, he concludes this little essay rather sternly: "The moral to be drawn from this representation . . ."—he is making a final adjustment of priorities.

The subservience of fiction to truth raises certain problems, because of idiosyncrasies in Johnson's ideas on how human nature responds to truth. "Just representations" please many and please long, but moral or philosophical truth in its "naked dignity" is "not often welcome" to ordinary readers. A man who, in *Rambler* 162, has "banqueted on flattery" shies away from "the harshness of remonstrance," naturally enough, but Johnson carries it one step farther, makes him unable to bear even "the *insipidity of truth*"—a beautiful phrase, at once simplistic, utilitarian, and austere; it reappears in the preface to Shakespeare; it means that compared with "the luxurious wonders of fiction" and the pleasing inventions of flattery, truth is plain, dowdy, and unglamorous, even when it is not painful. In the battle between Truth and Falsehood of *Rambler* 96, Truth loses ground steadily to the combined forces of Falsehood and human passions, prejudices, appetites. For this reason, "The Muses wove in the loom of Pallas, a loose and changeable robe, like that in which Falsehood captivated her admirers; with this they invested Truth, and named her Fiction." The highest kind of fiction is Truth in gaudy robes; it serves as an instrument of instruction. "They who profess the most zealous adherence to truth are forced to admit that she owes part of her charms to her ornaments, and loses much of her power over the soul, when she appears disgraced by a dress uncouth or ill-adjusted." [16]

Feigned narratives, in whatever form, are justified by the

16. *Works* (Yale), 7 : 82; *Rambler* 168.

flavor they impart to the "insipidity of truth." If this is an ornamental theory of fiction, we must make the best of it—as Johnson does. Fiction may be a means to an end, but so is life itself; and just as Johnson's conviction that mortality is a term of probation does not prevent him from enjoying life ardently, so the fact that he assigns to fiction a relatively humble position in the general scheme of things does not prevent him from appreciating some fictions keenly, and paying them full honors.

"Minute and Slender Criticisms"

While not a daring innovation in critical theory, Johnson's attitude toward fiction is highly individual. Its ingredients are commonplace, but the way Johnson combines them and the use he puts them to are distinctively different from analogous criticism by his contemporaries and by his predecessors. Enthusiasm for romance and for the "faery kind of writing," which had smoldered in the background throughout the Augustan age, found eloquent sponsorship around this time. Writers such as Collins, Gray, and Horace Walpole took pride in "daring to depart from sober truth," and in "muttering . . . wayward fancies" sometimes of resounding absurdity—helmets appearing out of thin air, for example. Many felt with Richard Hurd "the magic of the old romances," and courted "portentous specters of the imagination." [17]

Johnson parts company with ordinary neoclassical theories of fiction in interesting ways. Such theories start, as Johnson's do, with a sharp distinction between truth and fiction, as a major premise.[18] Most seventeenth- and eighteenth-century

17. See Arthur Johnston, *Enchanted Ground: The Study of Medieval Romance in the Eighteenth Century* (London, 1964), ch. 1; Hoyt Trowbridge, Introduction to Richard Hurd, *Letters on Chivalry and Romance* (Augustan Reprint Society Publication no. 101–02 [1963]); Sheridan Baker, "Fielding's *Amelia* and the Materials of Romance," *PQ* 41 (1962): 437–49, and "The Idea of Romance in the Eighteenth-Century Novel," *Papers of the Michigan Academy of Science, Arts, and Letters* 49 (1964): 507–22.

18. For example: "atque ita mentitur, sic veris falsa remiscet, / primo ne medium, medio ne discrepet imum" ("so skillfully does he invent, so closely does he blend facts and fiction, that the middle is not discordant

critics, again, like Johnson, apply the term *fiction* to any departure from literal truth—narrative, rhetorical, or figurative. Following Aristotle and Horace, or Renaissance interpretations of Aristotle and Horace, critics quite commonly insist that fiction present "true" pictures of life, and spurn falsehood.

But homage to truth in most Renaissance criticism was used to justify not only verisimilitude and probability, which Johnson respected, but also, and in some circumstances principally, those "beauties" that seemed to Johnson "the product of superfluous and ostentatious art"—the unities of time and space—or the "distinctions superinduced and adventitious" that decree that no senator can be a buffoon—the principles of decorum, *bienséance*. Thus Dryden: "The less change of place there is, the less time is taken up in transporting the persons of the drama, with analogy to reason; and in that analogy, or *resemblance of fiction to truth,* consists the excellency of the play." Similar arguments are advanced in support of consistency of character; Truth and Nature are used to vindicate the "minute and slender" dogmas of decorum, according to which rank or profession prescribes personality.[19] Falsehoods are frequently rejected in the seventeenth century not only because they contradict our experience but also because they fail to satisfy the criteria of art.

In one sense, the more artificial ("superinduced and adventitious") a critic's application of the rules, the nearer he comes to sanctioning, perhaps without intending to, purely aesthetic values in literature; and to the degree that Johnson dismisses a "nice observation of critical rules" as "an elaborate curiosity," he degrades formal excellence in one of its characteristic shapes. Truth, in many neoclassical critics, thanks to

with the beginning, nor the end with the middle"); "ficta voluptatis causa sint proxima veris" ("fictions meant to please should be close to the reality"): Horace, *Ars Poetica,* lines 151–52, 338 (LCL translation).

19. *Works* (Yale), 7 : 80, 7 : 65; Dryden, *Essays,* ed. W. P. Ker (1900; rpt. New York, 1961) 1 : 128 (my italics). For distrust of the "marvelous," based on similar assumptions, see René Bray, *La Formation de la Doctrine Classique en France* (Paris, 1927), pp. 231–39; Henry Fielding, *Tom Jones,* bk. 8, ch. 1.

an armful of respectable sophistries, sanctifies beauty; Truth, in Johnson, hallowed by its kinship with Goodness, transcends Beauty.[20]

Excellence in fiction, for Johnson, must satisfy the claims not only of art but also of common sense, must be "at once natural and new." "Every man who has tried knows how much labour it will cost to form such a combination of circumstances as will have at once the grace of novelty and credibility, and delight fancy without violence to reason." Milton is eulogized for "an imagination capable of painting nature and *realizing fiction.*" Everywhere in the seventeenth and eighteenth centuries, in poetry, drama, and criticism, in art, architecture, and music, we meet similar attempts to reconcile opposites that are keyed in one way or another to conflicting ideals of freedom and restraint. But Johnson's formulation of the powers and responsibilities of fiction seems less provincial than some of the drawing-room paradoxes of earlier critics (for example, "Though deep, yet clear . . ."; "Those Rules of old . . . are Nature still"). When Jean Chapelain, one of the most widely respected of mid-seventeenth-century French academicians, remarks that "c'est à la verité une haute entreprise de vouloir tirer d'une chose si commune qu'est la vraisemblance un si rare effet qu'est la merveille," he seems to have in mind an elaborate set of rules and requirements for decorum and *bienséance*[21]—Johnson's theory of fiction is larger and more generous.

20. Johnson, of course, defended *good* rules, that is, universal principles, "established" because they are "right," and though conscious of its limitations, he usually worked within the framework of neoclassical genre criticism. See Jean Hagstrum, *Samuel Johnson's Literary Criticism* (1952; rpt. Chicago, 1967), pp. 31–34, and W. R. Keast, "The Theoretical Foundations of Johnson's Criticism," *Critics and Criticism*, ed. R. S. Crane (Chicago, 1952), pp. 390–92, 400–01. We may ask, also, what Johnson meant when he said that in *Measure for Measure* "the unities of action and place are *sufficiently* preserved" (*Works* [Yale], 7 : 216; my italics).

21. "It is in truth a high enterprise to wish to draw from a thing so ordinary as the probable, an effect so rare as the marvelous" (my translation): Chapelain, *Opuscules critiques*, ed. A. C. Hunter (Paris, 1936), pp. 163–64. Other quotations in this paragraph: *Lives*, 1 : 20, 211, 170 (my italics).

"The Female Quixote"

On January 13, 1752, Samuel Richardson wrote to Mrs. Charlotte Lennox with courtly modesty recommending that she "consult Mr. Johnson" about the ending of *The Female Quixote:*

> It is my humble Opinion, that you should finish your Heroine's Cure in your present Vols. The Method you propose, tho' it might flatter my Vanity, yet will be thought a Contrivance between the Author of Arabella, and the Writer of Clarissa, to do Credit to the latter; and especially if the Contraste will take up much Room in the proposed 3d Volume. If it will not take up much, it may be done, if you *will* do it, that way (which I beg you to consider, and to consult Mr. Johnson before you resolve) at the latter End of the Second Volume.[22]

Richardson had nursed Mrs. Lennox's history of a "lovely Visionary" through more than one crisis by this time, marked places where new paragraphs could be added to swell it to two volumes, criticized the probability of book 6, and defended the sentiment of book 2. But he declined the honor of implication in Arabella's "cure." That honor was reserved for Samuel Johnson, and since the book was published in March 1752, Johnson must have made his debut as a novelist in January or February of that year.[23]

Chapter 11 of book 9 of *The Female Quixote* is a fascinating performance. It is an extended conversation between Ara-

22. For the text of this letter, with admirable notes, see Duncan Isles, "The Lennox Collection," *Harvard Library Bulletin* 18 (1970): 340–41. I am grateful to William H. Bond, Director of the Houghton Library, for permission to read the Lennox Papers before they were published.

23. *Harvard Library Bulletin* 18 (1970): 338–40. Chapter 11 of book 9 of *The Female Quixote* was first attributed to Johnson by Rev. John Mitford in *The Gentleman's Magazine,* n.s. 20 (1843): 132, aand n.s. 21 (1844): 41. Mr. Isles points out that the attribution "rests largely on internal stylistic evidence," and recommends that the chapter be regarded as "wholly Mrs. Lennox's until definite evidence to the contrary is found" (Appendix, *The Female Quixote,* ed. Margaret Dalziel [London, 1970], p. 421). To my ear the stylistic evidence is very strong. Richardson's advice to "consult Mr. Johnson" about Arabella's "cure" at least sets the stage for Johnson to intervene directly.

bella and a "pious and learned" clergyman, in which Arabella is finally convinced that the romances which she had lived by are fictitious, absurd, and "criminal," and she is thereby liberated from her delusions. It is not quite in character with the rest of the book, the dialogue of which is sprightly (except when Arabella unleashes her pack of allusions to Scudéry, La Calprenède, d'Urfé, etc.), the style merely genteel, and the pace rapid. Here, by contrast, the dialogue is formal and makes intermittent use of "the Laws of Disputation" and of Socratic third-degree; the style is unmistakably Johnsonian, always vigorous and precise, sometimes bookish; and the pace of the action has slowed nearly to zero to allow full scope for the logic and rhetoric of persuasion. Arabella is brought to her senses by rational argument, a fact which has provoked the contempt of critics, who unanimously find this chapter dry and unconvincing and wish Arabella could have been cured by experience not precept.[24]

From denigrations of this sort Johnson can be defended. Arabella's disease is defined by her immunity to experience, by the agility with which she invents romantic explanations for unromantic events. Having successfully held out against patient remonstrance and incontrovertible fact for almost two volumes, she is not likely to give in to anything less formidable than an intellectual bulldozer, which Johnson provided. *Nec deus intersit, nisi dignus vindice nodus inciderit.* As for form, the heavy dialectics of this chapter are anticipated to some extent by Arabella's disquisitions on the philosophy of Romance, and by previous attempts to reason her out of her delusions. The chapter in question is not without drama, not without comedy, and linked at several points with the principal action. Arabella embodies not only romantic folly but also romantic virtues; her high-mindedness, graciousness, innocence, and sincerity evoke chivalry from menfolk wherever she goes, and the comedy of the novel consists partly in the way she manages to impose her romantic view

24. M. R. Small, *Charlotte Ramsay Lennox* (New Haven, 1935), p. 82; G. H. Maynadier, *The First American Novelist?* (Cambridge, Mass., 1940), pp. 43–44; Mary Lascelles, *Jane Austen and her Art* (Oxford, 1939), p. 56.

of life on the sensible, often coarse-grained, always ordinary people around her. Poor Glanville, who has had the happy misfortune to fall in love with her, exasperatedly finds himself engaged in courtly debate, romantic vows, and romantic duels, almost before he knows what is happening to him.

Understanding this, Johnson has his clergyman stumble into compliment with more gallantry than befits his cloth, as Arabella gently reminds him; and the progress of her disillusion is charted by blushes and by heroic resolves, narrative emblems of her modesty and idealism. The comedy of embarrassment and misunderstanding play a role here, as earlier in the novel.

For present purposes, however, Johnson's chapter in *The Female Quixote* is important chiefly because it sums up his opinions on romance in no uncertain terms (and allies him vaguely but reliably with the narrative tradition of *Don Quixote*). Under ordinary circumstances a chapter in a novel is less valuable as an index to critical opinions than is a discourse or an essay, but in this case I think the risk is worth taking. It is a clergyman who speaks, for one thing. And the copiousness of his exposition, its abundance of detail and fertility of argument, is irresistible—if Johnson felt differently about romance at other times and on other occasions, his feelings are lost to us, or so faintly preserved as to be pretty much irrelevant. Johnson disapproved of his own fondness for romances of chivalry, and even went so far as to "attribute to these extravagant fictions that unsettled turn of mind which prevented his ever fixing in any profession" [25]—prevented him, if we can believe Dr. Percy here, from making a valid choice of life.

We should start by recognizing the severity of Johnson's indictment of seventeenth-century French romances. The mere fact that they are "Fictions" counts heavily against them, because of a natural "Love of Truth in the human Mind." Since "the great End of History, is to shew how much human Nature can endure or perform," narratives which are

25. Boswell, 1 : 49.

not true accounts of what human nature really has endured or performed are tossed away "with Contempt as a Trifle, or with Indignation as an Imposture." [26]

Having demonstrated the "falsity" of romances by easy allusion to history, the clergyman turns to their "absurdity":

> Who can forbear to throw away the Story that gives to one Man the Strength of Thousands; that puts Life or Death in a Smile or a Frown; that recounts Labours and Sufferings to which the Powers of Humanity are utterly unequal; that disfigures the whole Appearance of the World, and represents every Thing in a Form different from that which Experience has shewn? It is the Fault of the best Fictions, that they teach young Minds to expect strange Adventures and sudden Vicissitudes, and therefore encourage them often to trust to Chance. A long Life may be passed without a single Occurrence that can cause much Surprize, or produce any unexpected Consequence of great Importance; the Order of the World is so established, that all human Affairs proceed in a regular Method, and very little Opportunity is left for Sallies or Hazards, for Assault or Rescue; but the Brave and the Coward, the Sprightly and the Dull, suffer themselves to be carried alike down the Stream of Custom. [2 : 314–15]

The standards for truth assumed here, normative and realistic, are so important to Johnson that we may legitimately wonder why in his view any one reads romances at all. Their appeal, we learn elsewhere, is to immature minds: "while the judgment is yet uninformed and unable to compare the draughts of fiction with their originals, we are delighted with improbable adventures, impracticable virtues, and inimitable characters: But, in proportion as we have more oportunities of acquainting ourselves with living nature, we are sooner disgusted with copies in which there appears no resemblance. We first discard absurdity and impossibility, then exact greater and greater degrees of probability, but at last become cold and insensible to the charms of falshood, however spe-

26. *The Female Quixote,* 2d ed., "Revised and Corrected" (London, 1752), 2 : 310–11. Subsequent references to this novel will appear by volume and page.

cious, and from the imitations of truth, which are never perfect, transfer our affection to truth itself." Romances are, in other words, an inferior literary kind, childish things, to be put away when one becomes a man. They can rise to general popularity only when the common reader is comparatively unenlightened: "Nations, like individuals, have their infancy"; "the English nation in the time of Shakespeare was yet struggling to emerge from barbarity," and so the Elizabethans delighted in "adventures, giants, dragons, and enchantments"; but "maturer knowledge is offended" by the "incredibility" of romance.[27]

Any violation of the truth is "dangerous," in Johnson's mind, and the falsity and absurdity of romances necessarily imply a "criminal" potential. But romances are particularly dangerous because their "immediate Tendency" is "to give new Fire to the Passions of Revenge and Love; two Passions which, even without such powerful Auxiliaries, it is one of the severest Labours of Reason and Piety to suppress" (2:317).

I have quoted *The Female Quixote* at length to show how strongly Johnson felt about "the power of example," as he terms it in *Rambler* 4. It is fair to assume, I think, that in fact only a tiny percentage of the readers of romance have ever trusted them as a version of reality, like Arabella, or learned from them "pride and cruelty," like Imperia (of *Rambler* 115); but Johnson takes the mimetic and moral infectiousness of romance for granted—concedes to narrative fiction more potency than perhaps many of his readers would. "The power of example is so great, as to take possession of the memory by a kind of violence, and produce effects almost without the intervention of the will." Although *Rambler* 4 may have helped to intensify the moralism of fiction after 1750,[28] it is premised on real respect for narrative. Chapter 11 of book 9 of *The Female Quixote* leaves us in no doubt of the dangerousness of romance, its capacity to shape the mind and color the passions of man.

27. *Rambler* 151; *Works* (Yale), 7 : 81–82.

28. Robert D. Mayo, *The English Novel in the Magazines, 1740–1815* (Evanston, Ill., 1962), p. 100.

ANTIROMANCE

Romances had been under attack before 1752, of course. In the sixteenth and seventeenth centuries, representatives of every realm of literate authority had censured them, for offenses against truth, taste, or morality, or any combination of the three; and on this subject there were Catholics and Protestants, bishops and puritans, humanists and poets, critics of every school and persuasion, in cordial agreement. Erasmus, Ascham, Baxter, Burton, Bunyan, Boileau, Isaac Watts, Swift, William Law, and Richardson, for example, all of whom Johnson is known to have read and respected (in different ways and for different reasons), all disparage romance. Even the defenders of romance tacitly acknowledge its vulnerability to charges of *invraisemblance,* by claiming, from Scudéry to Scott, to have purged and banished the old absurdities: "incredible actions would degenerate into ridiculous Fables, and never move the mind," says Georges de Scudéry in 1641, referring to authors "who have made one man alone defeat whole Armies." Even the sponsors of romance agreed that it was more popular among women, children, and barbarians than among educated adults: in the Dark Ages, according to Huet (1670), "Historians degenerated into True Romancers." [29]

Amid all this variety of disapprobation three distinct (but not mutually exclusive) attitudes can be isolated. The first is characteristic of men whose primary allegiance is to historical or philosophic truth, and who are therefore suspicious of fables and fictions simply because they are false.[30] The second

29. Johnston, *Enchanted Ground,* pp. 32–40 (a magnificent summary); Benjamin Boyce, *Prefaces to Fiction* (Augustan Reprint Society Publication no. 32 [1952]), Introduction, and p. 6 for Scudéry; Sir Walter Scott, "Miss Austen's Novels," *Quarterly Review,* January 1821; Pierre-Daniel Huet, *The History of Romances,* trans. Stephen Lewis (London, 1715), p. 104 (see also pp. 35–44, 121).

30. For example: *Republic* 595A–608B; Strabo, *Geography* 1.2.8–9; Macrobius, *Commentary on the Dream of Scipio,* trans. W. H. Stahl (New York, 1952), pp. 84–86; Hobbes, "Answer to Davenant," *Critical Essays of the Seventeenth Century,* ed. J. E. Spingarn (Oxford, 1908), 2 : 61–62; Fielding, Author's Preface, *A Voyage to Lisbon* (London, 1755).

is common among critics, men interested primarily in literary excellence, in the purest refinements of neoclassical art. Romance from this point of view (which was more articulate in France than in England) is an insidious poison which corrupts the taste, and by gross sensationalism spoils the palate for a just relish of classical artistry, conciseness, consistency, polish.[31] These standards, diluted or full strength, produced countless allusions to "romantick absurdities," to "idle romances which are filled with monsters, the productions not of nature, but of distempered brains" (*Tom Jones,* book 4, chapter 1). Such allusions were as commonplace before 1740, before the triumphs of the "new realism," as after, and were delivered as complacently by Mrs. Heywood as by Mr. Fielding.

The third distinctive attitude toward romance is fundamentally moralistic: romances insinuate themselves into every corner of eighteenth-century culture as part of the furniture of luxury, and as emblems of moral decay. Bunyan's Mr. Badman as a child devoured "beastly Romances, and books full of Ribbauldry," and Phronissa's children, in Isaac Watts, are "bred up in a just apprehension of the danger and mischief" of romances and plays. Such reflections are no surprise in a puritan tract published in 1680, or in the saintly hymnologist Dr. Watts, but may give us pause when they appear in a "rather loose" (according to the *DNB*) novel of 1754, *The Sisters,* by William Dodd, in which the vanity, folly, and affectation of two young ladies are nurtured by "Cassandra, Cleopatra, Heywood's novels, and above all, the works of the inimitable *Fielding*"[32] (my italics).

31. For example: Boileau, *Satire* 2, lines 77–79, *Satire* 3, lines 43–44 (and see Georges May, *Le dilêmme du roman au XVIII e siècle* [New Haven and Paris, 1963], for full documentation of this attitude in France); Shaftesbury, "Advice to an Author" (1710), cited in Joseph B. Heidler, *The History, from 1700 to 1800, of English Criticism of Prose Fiction,* University of Illinois Studies in Language and Literature, vol. 13, no. 2 (Urbana, Ill., 1928), p. 28; Richard Blackmore, *Essays upon Several Subjects* (1716: rpt. New York, 1971), pp. 27–33.

32. Bunyan, *The Life and Death of Mr. Badman* (1680), ed. John Brown (Cambridge, 1905), p. 43; Isaac Watts, "A Discourse on the Educa-

The novelty of chapter 11 of book 9 of *The Female Quixote,* then, is largely a matter of emphasis and range. "Prove," says Arabella, "that the Books which I have hitherto read as Copies of Life, and Models of Conduct, are empty Fictions" —that is, perversions of historical truth—"and from this Hour I deliver them to Moths and Mould." A heroic renunciation, and it rings true in Arabella, as it would in any austere philosopher or historian, but it carries reverence for truth several steps farther than most romancers and critics of our period will go.

Two sentences in the clergyman's analysis of the "criminal" tendencies of romance deserve special attention.

> It is impossible to read these Tales without lessening part of that Humility, which by preserving in us a Sense of our Alliance with all Human Nature, keeps us awake to Tenderness and Sympathy, or without impairing that Compassion which is implanted in us as an Incentive to Acts of Kindness. If there be any preserved by natural Softness, or early Education, from learning Pride and Cruelty, they are yet in Danger of being betrayed to the Vanity of Beauty, and taught the Arts of Intrigue. [2 : 318]

Here Johnson meets the *précieuses* on their own ground. They had felt that romances stimulate tenderness and foster a generous sensibility. Johnson bases tenderness and sympathy on the "humility" which preserves in us "a sense of our alliance with all human nature." The cold stateliness of romance, he says, pretends to elevate us above common humanity. This is perhaps an innovation in antiromance, since in effect Johnson is bringing benevolist (not sentimental) morality into action. It harkens back to the *Rambler,* to "the universal league of social beings" (no. 81) which decrees that "the great end of society is mutual benevolence" (no. 56), to "that habitual sympathy and tenderness, which, in a world of so much misery, is necessary to the ready discharge of our most important duties" (no. 80), and to Johnson's suspicion

tion of Children and Youth" (1741), *Works* (London, 1753), 5 : 405; Dodd, bk. 1, ch. 1. See also "Before and After" (1736), *Hogarth's Graphic Works,* ed. Ronald Paulson (New Haven, 1965), Pl. 152; Swift, "The Progress of Love" (1719), lines 47–48.

of all forms of secular retirement, self-immolation, and disengagement from "the great republick of humanity" (no. 77).

That the clergyman of *The Female Quixote* fails to accuse romances of contaminating literary taste should not surprise us. There are passages in Johnson which suggest that he was alive to this danger (e.g., his explanation for the vogue of romance in Elizabethan England: "The mind, which has feasted on the luxurious wonders of fiction, has no taste of the insipidity of truth"). His criticism as a whole, however, lacks the self-conscious self-esteem, the sense of exclusive proprietorship to a preciously difficult aesthetic ideal, of the School of Taste—except in matters of versification. Johnson's aesthetic sensibilities exercise themselves vigorously on the harmonies and harshnesses of verse.[33] In most other areas of his criticism, however, the concensus gentium and the verdict of the man in the street speak with far greater authority than neoclassical standards of beauty. He could not worry seriously about the "vulgarity" of romance.

In the end, Johnson responds to romance, and to fiction less elaborate, less seductive, as a moralist. He convicts it on three counts: falsehood, absurdity, and immorality. In other hands the second charge could be expressed in terms of disproportion or ugliness, but Johnson chooses to emphasize instead the corrupting power of absurdity ("It is the fault of the best fictions, that they teach young minds to expect strange adventures"). These are therefore three variations on one theme, the primacy of truth and reason. There are close analogies between Johnson's theories of fiction and his theories of the imagination: both the "licentious" faculty and its luxurious product are in some degree indispensable to the human condition, but both are "dangerous," and all the more dangerous because fascinating, delightful. "To indulge the

33. It could be argued that of the three major species of literary pleasure recognized by Johnson (according to Hagstrum), two—sublimity and pathos—owe their efficacy to some kind of truthfulness, and that only in "beauty" (best exemplified in Pope) does literary pleasure emancipate itself from the claims of morality and authenticity. But see David W. Tarbet, "Lockean 'Intuition' and Johnson's Characterization of Aesthetic Response," *ECS* 5 (1971): 58–79.

power of fiction, and send imagination out upon the wing," as it is described in *Rasselas,* chapter 44, is a source both of peculiar sufferings and of peculiar enjoyments; it is also, according to chapter 2 of *Rasselas,* one of the activities that "makes the difference between man and all the rest of the animal creation."

Johnson and the Rise of the Novel

Johnson's participation, however brief and didactic, in an imitation of *Don Quixote* entitles us to generalize about his relation to traditions of the novel. All misadventures of a bookish hero in an incurably practical world are imitations of *Don Quixote,* if we are willing to use the phrase in a very general way. The number and variety of narratives which conform to this model, precisely, crudely, or by derivation, is astonishing; it includes most of the better-known seventeenth-century prose burlesques, much of the new realism in eighteenth-century England, *Northanger Abbey* and *Waverley* and *The Pickwick Papers* and *Huckleberry Finn* and *Madame Bovary,* to mention only a few.[34] The experience of disenchantment and disillusion, which *Don Quixote* both pursues and evades, evolves easily into Bildungsroman, itself an archetype for the conventional novel. The Cervantic paradigm may be modified in the other direction also, away from personality and back to concept, away from realism toward satirical fictions organized around the disparity between ideal and actual, theory and practice, art and nature—*Gulliver's Travels,* for example, or *Candide.*[35] In its own abbreviated

34. Harry Levin, "The Example of Cervantes," *Contexts of Criticism* (1957; rpt. New York, 1963), pp. 79–96; Small, *Charlotte Ramsay Lennox,* pp. 92–116 (an interesting list); Ronald Paulson, *Satire and the Novel in 18th-Century England* (New Haven, 1967), pp. 29–35; J. D. M. Ford and R. Lansing, *Cervantes: A Tentative Bibliography* (Cambridge, Mass., 1931), pp. 122–39.

35. Pope read *Gulliver* this way, as a product of "Cervantes' serious air": see *The Works of Alexander Pope,* ed. Elwin and Courthope (London, 1882), 4 : 313. *The Memoirs of Martinus Scriblerus* were considered Cervantic by Warburton; see p. 68 of C. Kerby-Miller's edition (New Haven, 1950).

and idiogrammatic way, Johnson's fiction touches all these bases; his protagonists are always mocked or educated or disillusioned, and sometimes all three at once.

Johnson as narrator is hardly more than a dilettante in realism, Cervantic or otherwise, but the aspect of *Don Quixote* which is less an imitation of life than a parable on the relation between literature and life—for humanists, a perennial concern—attracted him strongly.[36] In *Rambler* 2 he paints Quixote as a comic-pathetic victim of the vanity of human wishes:

> When the knight of La Mancha gravely recounts to his companion the adventures by which he is to signalize himself in such a manner that he shall be summoned to the support of empires, solicited to accept the heiress of the crown which he has preserved, have honours and riches to scatter about him, and an island to bestow on his worthy squire, very few readers, amidst their mirth or pity, can deny that they have admitted visions of the same kind; though they have not, perhaps, expected events equally strange, or by means equally inadequate. When we pity him, we reflect on our own disappointments; and when we laugh, our hearts inform us that he is not more ridiculous than ourselves, except that he tells what we have only thought.

On the other hand, *Don Quixote* is also a marriage (in the sense of a partnership both delightful and under tension) between romance and realism, a dialogue between the woeful knight and Sancho Panza. With this partnership Johnson's fiction has nothing to do; in fact, whereas Sancho Panza types play big parts in the early English novel (they have title roles in *Joseph Andrews* and *Humphry Clinker*), the nearest equivalent to Sancho in Johnson is, in all seriousness, Imlac.

Since Johnson esteemed *Don Quixote,* and assisted in an antiromance of 1752, we might reasonably expect him to comment on the "rise of the novel"; we might reasonably

36. See Robert P. Adams, "Bold Bawdry and Open Manslaughter: The English New Humanist Attack on Medieval Romance," *HLQ* 23 (1959–60): 33–48. Other allusions to *Don Quixote* by Johnson may be found in *Rambler* 200 and *Adventurer* 84; two copies of *Don Quixote* are listed in the Sale Catalogue of his library (ed. A. E. Newton, London, 1925), nos. 141 and 649.

expect to be able to know his detailed opinions of the four early masters of English fiction who published between 1740 (*Pamela*), when Johnson was thirty years old, and 1771 (*Humphry Clinker*), when Johnson was sixty-two. Neither expectation is fulfilled. Johnson's only full-dress written critique of what we now call the novel appeared in 1750, and it names no names; for more specific judgments we must fall back on inference and anecdote. We cannot, moreover, take it for granted that this newly hatched literary species dazzled eighteenth-century readers as, in retrospect, it does us. It was seldom altogether clear in the late eighteenth century that the novel was rising,[37] that the art of prose narrative was developing a set of techniques and attitudes at once flexible enough to allow for rich variety and limited enough to constitute a viable convention, or set of conventions, or traditions, within which future masterpieces would be written. Between 1751 and Johnson's death in 1784 only two major novels were published, and one of these was so "odd" that its popularity seemed to Johnson simply a passing fad. Novels were written during this period, of course, in increasing quantities, but their quality might have justified uncertainty as to whether the novel as a genre was rising or falling. Contrast the excitement of Fielding and Richardson over their new discoveries in the 1740s, with Jane Austen's aggressive-defensive outburst in *Northanger Abbey,* aimed at readers of the 1790s who dismissed such works as "only a novel." [38]

Nevertheless, accepting these limitations, and accepting the need of caution in interpreting Johnson's conversation, something can be said about Johnson and the novel. In fact the

37. Ian Watt, in *The Rise of the Novel* (London, 1957), treats the second half of the century only in passing.

38. "'Nothing odd will do long. "Tristram Shandy" did not last'" (Boswell, 2 : 449 [March 1776]). *Humphry Clinker* is the other novel I have in mind, but my point still stands if any reader wishes to raise the number of "major" novels, double it, or triple it. The dates of this "thin" period in English fiction, well supplied with minor masterpieces but also littered with trash, could be extended to 1811. See J. M. S. Tompkins, *The Popular Novel in England, 1700–1800* (1932; rpt. Lincoln, Nebr., 1961); R. P. Utter and G. B. Needham, *Pamela's Daughters* (New York, 1936).

early novelists were as much interested in subverting romance as Johnson was. As early as the seventeenth century the novel had taken steps toward hammering out its own identity in terms of the probable and commonplace, in a conscious attempt to be different from romance. From the beginning the novel devoted itself to "realism" in a way Johnson could have applauded—and did applaud, by implication, in *Rambler* 4, which distinguishes carefully between the "wild strain of imagination" in "heroic romance" and "works of fiction, with which the present generation seems more particularly delighted, . . . such as exhibit life in its true state, diversified only by accidents that daily happen in the world." Johnson, as we have seen, has no grudge against fiction as such, though he gives it far lower priority than truth: similar logic and a similar hierarchy of values qualifies him as an appreciator of the novel, in contradistinction to romance.

Why then did Johnson so emphatically repudiate Fielding? As it happens, the question can be narrowed down, since Johnson never read *Joseph Andrews* and actually liked *Amelia:*[39] Why was Johnson the implacable foe of *Tom Jones*? I am convinced that the most important reason is his suspicion-amounting-to-certainty of the moral principles it embodies. Boswell writes to Temple, ungracefully, "I am even almost inclined to think with you that my great oracle Johnson did allow too much credit to good principles without good practice." Johnson, in other words, was not a prude. In the *Lives of the Poets,* he deals much more harshly with Swift and Bolingbroke, who can be read as enemies of religion, than with Lord Rochester, who for all his obscenity died a holy death and was handed down to posterity by Bishop Burnet as a lost sheep recovered to the fold. *Tom Jones,* Johnson told Hannah More, is one of the most corrupt books ever written;[40] not because of Tom's unchastity, presumably; perhaps because of Tom's principles (he trusts the human heart); perhaps because of Tom's *lack* of principles and the

39. Boswell, 2 : 174, 3 : 43.

40. Boswell's letter is quoted by G. B. Hill, *Lives,* 2 : 200, n. 5; for the verdict on Tom Jones, see *Miscellanies,* 2 : 190.

absence of Christian witness, of a Dr. Harrison or Dr. Lewen or Rev. Mr. Villars, anywhere in the book. *Rambler* 4, published within a few months of *Tom Jones,* makes a point of recommending that novels exhibit "the most perfect idea of virtue; of virtue not angelical, nor above probability, for what we cannot credit we shall never imitate, but the highest and purest that humanity can reach."

All the other reasons for Johnson's disparagement of Fielding serve also—chiefly?—to boost Richardson. I may be forgiven for quoting this familiar passage since so much has been made of it; Johnson's preference for Richardson over Fielding has been questioned or rejected frequently enough, but so penetrating are his insights that generations of critics have been able to do little more than transpose his cadences and paraphrase his sentiments:

> 'Sir, (continued he,) there is all the difference in the world between characters of nature and characters of manners; and *there* is the difference between the characters of Fielding and those of Richardson. Characters of manners are very entertaining; but they are to be understood, by a more superficial observer, than characters of nature, where a man must dive into the recesses of the human heart.'
>
> . . . In comparing these two writers, he used this expression; 'that there was as great a difference between them as between a man who knew how a watch was made, and a man who could tell the hour by looking on the dial-plate.' [Boswell, 2 : 48–49]

It is true that Johnson preferred characters of nature to characters of manners, personalities of some depth and substance to mere caricatures (he promotes Polonius from one category halfway to the other with obvious satisfaction). It is also true that Johnson loved psychological complexity in literature. One of the "beauties" of Shakespeare that spurs Johnson beyond *explication de texte,* in his notes to the plays, is Shakespeare's insight into the human heart, which is one of the qualities Johnson calls "nature." But neither of these preferences debars Johnson from full enjoyment of the literary virtues here relegated to an inferior rank. He gloats over characters of manners in *Evelina.* I cannot help feeling that his prejudice against *Tom Jones* originates in a moral judgment, not an aesthetic one. The only formal compliment he pays to Richardson in an essay intended for publication is couched in moral terms: Richardson "has enlarged the knowledge of human nature, and taught the passions to move at the command of virtue." [41]

In many respects, then, Johnson's tastes coincide with those of early masters of English fiction. Not only does he share their aversion to heroic romance and their interest in psychological complexity of character; he was also, as everyone knows, bored by "histories of the downfal of kingdoms, and revolutions of empire," and strongly drawn to domestic fictions and to intimate biography. The story of Rowe's *Fair Penitent,* he wrote, "is domestick, and therefore easily received by the imagination, and assimilated to common life." Surely the admirer of *Don Quixote, Gil Blas, Robinson Crusoe, Clarissa, Amelia,* and *Evelina* may be counted as a friend of the new realism.[42]

But even in the eighteenth century, and even within Johnson's frame of reference, realism could mean many things. It could mean a rough-and-tumble picaresque comedy of discomfiture, for which Johnson showed no special enthusiasm: he virtually ignores Quixote's broken bones. Yet the applauder of Falstaff and Sir Andrew Aguecheek can have no insuperable aversion to "low" tavern scenes, to the realism of cakes and ale. Johnson's appetite for Shakespearean realism is somewhat diminished by neoclassical assumptions about language and decorum: he is happy that Shakespeare's senators are sometimes buffoons, but cannot bear that a true hero use the language of the stable; a scene which aspires to tragic dignity is spoiled for him by the admixture of undignified words, even if they are realistic. There is more than a residue of Renaissance doctrines of the separation of styles in John-

41. Boswell, 2 : 48–49; *Works* (Yale), 8 : 974; "touches of nature" in Shakespeare: *Miscellanies,* 1 : 282–83, *Works* (Yale), 7 : 362, 7 : 425, 8 : 982; *Evelina: Dr. Johnson and Fanny Burney,* ed. C. B. Tinker (New York, 1911), pp. 11–17, 22; *Rambler* 97.

42. *Rambler* 60; *Lives,* 2 : 67. LeSage: "Reply to a Paper in the Gazetteer" (1757), *Works* (1825), 6 : 32; Defoe: Boswell, 2 : 367–68, *Miscellanies,* 1 : 332.

son. He respects narratives which "exhibit life in its true state" because they are true, not because they are beautiful; and realism is for Johnson rather a mode of expression, appropriate to lower genres, than a way of looking at life itself—he sees *Roderick Random* and *Tom Jones* as versions of comedy, not as the distant ancestors of *Ulysses.*

2 The Choice of Life

> The World was all before them, where to choose
> Their place of rest . . .
>
> Milton

For most twentieth-century readers, fiction represents not merely an ornament to truth, or a pleasing method of instruction, but a separate kind of truth, in some sense autonomous, and certainly independent of anything that can be said about it. One of the commonest ways of responding to fiction is to explain what it means—to explicate it, to translate imaginative into expository prose; but the "purer" the fiction, the less satisfactory the translation. Except for *Rasselas,* most of Johnson's fiction is in this sense very impure. At its clumsiest it gives the impression of mere mechanical exemplification. What the stories in *The Rambler* say or mean seems in many cases all too obvious, and is often communicated to us by puppet characters, mere mouthpieces for their learned progenitor. How they saw it, on the other hand, is worth some attention, because the rhetoric of Johnson's fiction, its language, its ornamentation, its points of view and narrative strategies, is variously significant. What happens in the periodical-essay fiction is also interesting because it happens in highly distinctive ways. Reality *is* represented, within certain definite and peculiar limits, in three rather restricted modes, three children of one parent theme.

At its best, as in *Rasselas,* Johnson's fiction is still didactic, but wholly unmechanical, humane, potent, and splendid: didactic and imaginative (or aesthetic) forces work not at cross-purposes but in harmony. We should not allow ourselves to assume that didacticism (any more than commercialism) always poisons art—after all, no one would use an exemplum if it did not give some measure of delight, as well as instruction. Conversely, a story from which every vestige of idea has been purged is almost inconceivable: if an action has human consequences, it has a moral context; and if it has no consequences, that fact also is meaningful. Didacticism is not a discrete category, but a more or less precarious condition, contracted in terms of the degree and quality of obsequiousness with which event serves idea.

The didactic condition depends also on audience response and expectation. *Tom Jones* is a lesson in prudence and good nature to one reader; to another it is an action skillfully complicated and resolved. In 1750 the climate of literary expectation was more moralistic than it has since become. As characteristic of fiction-in-general in the seventeenth and eighteenth centuries as either romance or the novel were the miscellaneous tendentious forms: satire, dialogue, fable, philosophic voyage, Theophrastan Character, spiritual autobiography, utopia, dream vision, allegory, anecdote, apologue. The capacity to appreciate *art*ful instruction is virtually indispensable to intelligent reading in Augustan literature.

Not only are the stories in *The Rambler* didactic, they are also antiromance, as we might expect from chapter 11 of book 9 of *The Female Quixote*. In the *Dictionary* Johnson defines romance as "a tale of wild adventures in war and love." Most of the stories in *The Rambler* are commonplace epistolary biographies which have nothing to do with war or love. They start by sketching the correspondent's family background, describe his education, and conclude sooner or later in unhappiness of a very unglamorous sort. The world they inhabit is pedestrian and unfriendly. When chance operates, it takes the form of accident, not coincidence.

Fiction which answers to this description might be written as domestic realism of a Richardsonian caste, the kind of fiction Johnson most enjoyed reading. Antiromance as a literary temperament (ironic, practical, skeptical, reductive, sensible), in Chaucer, for example, or Jane Austen, engenders realism; but not in Johnson. His contempt for "visionary schemes" and his loyalty to real experience do not add up either to slices of life or to a rich God's Plenty of character and sensibility—he does not refine himself out of his own narratives in reverence to the objective data of observed reality; he does not allow himself to create individual personalities. Similarly, though Johnson's stories explore states of mind, they virtually ignore all psychological processes except one, the intense and complicated experience that convinces us of the vanity of human wishes.

In other authors, equally convinced of the vanity of human wishes, that experience has taken other forms; the grounds of disillusionment are altered. The Preacher of Ecclesiastes accuses life of injustice, folly, multiple futility, and a perpetual succession of changes that change nothing. "The wind goeth toward the south, and turneth unto the north; it whirleth about continually"; "as it happeneth to the fool, so it happeneth even to me; and why was I then more wise?" One corner of the world of Ecclesiastes overlaps with the world of Johnson's fiction,[1] but the concerns of *The Rambler* in general are more domestic, more provincial and practical. Juvenal's tenth *Satire* ridicules human wishes because their fulfillment is worse than their frustration: the antics of the courtier, the struttings of the hero, and the diseases of old age provoke in Juvenal a complex mixture of responses, an energetic contempt, a wry, hard-eyed distaste. Johnson's fiction does not stretch so far; its topics are less decadent; it addresses itself to commonplace presumptions, not to public shame but to private embarrassments. It deals with the human desires that sanction the quest for happiness, with the vanity of attempting a "choice of life" (the phrase is Imlac's)—or of choosing wrong.

For centuries before the age of Johnson a man was born into a "station," and grew up as a member of a relatively stable social class; often he inherited a trade or calling, and he had usually less opportunity to change his condition than he would have now. In the early part of the eighteenth century Jonathan Swift preached that "among Mankind, our particular Stations are appointed to each of us by God Almighty." But only twenty-five years after *The Rambler* a nation was dedicated to

1. Ecclesiastes 2 : 1–11 tells a story closely analogous to several of the quests.

the proposition that among man's inalienable rights are "liberty and the pursuit of happiness." The socioeconomic assumptions of Johnson's fiction lie somewhere between the Tory and the Whig of these two citations.[2]

Despite conflicting evidence, it seems clear that during Johnson's young manhood significantly more adult English males found themselves in a position to make a choice of life than had ever before. Not that each and any career was open to every talented youth: Johnson's own history rather painfully refutes any such presumption; and then as now, severe poverty robbed its sufferers of prospects, and buried them "in motionless despondence" (to borrow Johnson's words). But new money poured into England during the eighteenth century, new financial institutions put it to work more effectively, and the new affluence distributed itself more widely than in other countries. Travelers remarked on the multitude of *"middling people"* in England, as opposed to the Continent; social critics exclaimed more loudly than ever at the crumbling of class barriers. Class in England was an economic and social fact, not a legal one as in France. While the newly rich were buying land and status, younger sons of landed families increasingly invaded the professions (law, medicine, clergy, military), which themselves had become "a kind of hyphen" between the gentry and the middle class.[3]

2. Swift, "On Mutual Subjection," *Prose Works,* ed. H. Davis, vol. 9 (Oxford, 1948), p. 142. Jefferson's "pursuit of happiness" derives of course eventually from Locke. But as early as the 1720s Locke's ideas on property were evolving into ideas on the right to pursue happiness (i.e., in certain circumstances, the right to make a choice of life): "To live securely, happily, and independently, is the End and Effect of Liberty; and it is the Ambition of all Men to live agreeably to their own Humours and Discretion. . . . And as Happiness is the Effect of Independency, and Independency the Effect of Property; so certain Property is the Effect of Liberty alone, and can only be secured by the Laws of Liberty" (Thomas Gordon, *Cato's Letters* no. 68, March 3, 1721).

3. See J. H. Plumb, *The Origins of Political Stability: England, 1675–1725* (Boston, 1967), pp. 3–9; H. J. Habakkuk, "Marriage Settlements in the Eighteenth Century," *Transactions of the Royal Historical Society,* 4th ser. 32 (1950): 20; Dorothy Marshall, *English People in the Eighteenth Century* (New York, 1956), p. 52 and ch. 2. Johnson's words: *Works* (1825), 6 : 54.

At the same time, perceptible changes in the way people were thinking about happiness thrust the choice of life into the consciousness of literate folk in a new way. As Johnson understood it, the choice of life is a secular undertaking, different from the choice of eternity; the characters in his fiction cast about among professions and pastimes without immediate concern for the service of God or heavenly rewards. In the late sixteenth century Richard Hooker stated flatly that "they who placed their felicity in wealth or honour or pleasure or any thing here attained" "do evil"; that "no good is infinite but only God; therefore He our felicity and bliss"; that happiness is "that estate whereby we attain, so far as possibly may be attained, the full possession of that which simply for itself is to be desired . . . Of such perfection capable we are not in this life." One hundred and forty years later Alexander Pope agrees, in passing, that happiness "still so near us, yet beyond us lies," and that "where Faith, Law, Morals, all began,/All end, in Love of God," but cannot let the matter rest there, as Hooker does; the entire Epistle 4 of the *Essay on Man* is devoted to the subject of happiness, defined as "Health, Peace, and Competence," as benevolence, as a condition of virtuousness "Which who but feels can taste, but thinks can know"; and in order to come to these conclusions Pope must run through a survey of various admired "conditions," as if he too were making a choice of life. Now, although thoughtful men were still writing from Hooker's point of view in the eighteenth century, Epistle 4 of the *Essay on Man* could not have been written in the sixteenth century; it voices new attitudes and new possibilities.[4]

4. Hooker, *Of the Laws of Ecclesiastical Polity* (1593; Everyman ed., 1954), 1 : 202–3; *Essay on Man,* Ep. 4, lines 5, 339–40, 80, 353–54, 310, 328, 193–208. One stage in the transition from Hooker to Pope is displayed in Richard Lucas, *An Enquiry after Happiness* (1685; ten editions by 1764), which argues that happiness is an imitation of God's happiness, consisting of (a) perfection of being, (b) freedom from trouble, and (c) infinite pleasure, but that God designed us for the quest for happiness, "a real state, and really attainable, and that our disappointments and unsuccessfulness must be imputed to ourselves" (pp. xvi, 9, xv, in 8th ed., London, 1753). See also R. M. Wiles, *"Felix qui . . . :* standards of happiness in eighteenth-century England," *Studies on Voltaire and the Eighteenth Century* (1967): 58 : 1857–67.

Likewise, the perennial and continuing debate as to how best to use one's life had changed character by Johnson's time: in the middle of the seventeenth century men commonly asked themselves whether retirement was preferable to public service or the glitter of the court; in the early eighteenth century there are signs that this debate gained a broader scope and focused more narrowly on practical everyday possibilities. "In order to frame a right idea of human happiness, I thought it expedient to make a trial of the various manners wherein men of different pursuits were affected," writes Ulysses Cosmopolita in *Guardian* 35 (1713, by Berkeley), though his philosophical-satirical journey is limited to a man of pleasure and a free-thinker. *Guardian* 111 (Addison) offers a choice between health, money, victory, and honor; *Guardian* 31 (Budgell) pictures the happiness to be found in domesticity, wealth, pastoral dalliance, and the world of fashion. Among the qualities that make William Law's *A Serious Call to a Devout and Holy Life* (1728) different from seventeenth-century devotional works are not only its interest in the religious use of one's talents but also the variety of worldly activities it discusses, their relationship to the life of perpetual prayer; and Law's character of Flatus (chapter 12) more closely resembles Johnson's uneasy seekers of happiness than does any other character in fiction.

The choice of life looms large in Johnson's nonfictional writings. In the *Diaries, Prayers, and Annals* it takes the form of remorse for wasted time, resolutions to make better use of his gifts, and "schemes of life" ("To rise by eight, or earlier. To form a plan for the regulation of my daily life"). In the moral essays it is based on Johnson's belief in "the maxims of a commercial nation, which always suppose and promote a rotation of property, and offer every individual a chance of mending his condition by his diligence."[5] "Every one must form the general plan of his conduct by his own reflections;

5. *Works* (1825), 6 : 56–57 (*Review of a Free Enquiry*). Johnson ascribes "The Bravery of the English Common Soldiers" to economic individualism and the "dissolution of dependence" (*Works* [1825], 6 : 151). See Donald Greene, *The Politics of Samuel Johnson* (New Haven, 1960), pp. 176–78, for the conflicting claims in Johnson's mind of individualism and subordination.

he must resolve whether he will endeavour at riches or at content; whether he will exercise private or publick virtues; whether he will labour for the general benefit of mankind, or contract his beneficence to his family and dependents." *Rambler* 184, of which this is a part, goes on to argue, however, that chance decides many such questions for everyone; and the moral essays in general do not encourage us to believe that the individual can "choose" a happy life, though he can and must choose the path of virtue. It seems illogical that Johnson should be preoccupied with the choice of life when he knows perfectly well that "this world is not the place where happiness is promised to virtue, or where her votaries obtain their reward" [6] (to this paradox, if it is one, we shall return in our analysis of *Rasselas*).

Logic is not a determining factor in the invention of narrative, however, and Johnson's imagination returns again and again to the problem of the choice of life. His characters, middle-class one and all, take for granted their right to happiness and their responsibility for choosing the profession or activity or surroundings that will give them lasting (and guiltless) satisfaction; but all kinds of obstacles and hazards interfere with their freedom of choice. When obstacles are removed, the choice of life fails. Man's inescapable obligation to an impossible task becomes a basis for pessimism, a basis also for irony and pathos, and an incentive finally for the choice of eternity.

Complaint

In thousands of conventional novels, the hero or heroine is launched from poverty, insecurity, or loneliness on a trajectory terminating in wealth, achievement, or wedded bliss. Johnson endows his heroes in the beginning with every prospect of success and every chance of happiness, but leaves them in the end victims of their own folly or life's cruelty. Countless romances insist on a happy ending, implying that life can be beautiful. Johnson's fiction records the failure of such hopes and many others; its motto is the infelicity of human exis-

6. *Works* (Yale), 6 : 190, note on lines 10, 22–25 (from MS of *Irene* in British Museum, therefore probably written 1736–37).

tence. It illustrates not the triumph of innocence but, often, the triumph of evil, or, less melodramatically, the process by which life transforms innocence into experience by means of suffering. It is encapsulated antiromance, directed against romantic expectations rather than romantic literary conventions.

The commonest species of fiction in Johnson's periodical essays is the "complaint," a story of misery, told by an innocent victim. *Rambler* 75 is a good example. It is addressed to the Rambler from Melissa ("bee"), who begins her tale as follows:

> I was born to a large fortune, and bred to the knowledge of those arts which are supposed to accomplish the mind, and adorn the person of a woman. To these attainments which custom and education almost forced upon me, I added some voluntary acquisitions by the use of books, and the conversation of that species of men whom the ladies generally mention with terror and aversion under the name of scholars. . . . From my acquaintance with the bookish part of the world I derived many principles of judgment and maxims of prudence, by which I was enabled to draw upon myself the general regard in every place of concourse or pleasure.

The purpose of these sentences is to establish the special conditions under which Melissa is operating; they include first of all, and indispensably, the social and economic position to which she was born and the manner of her upbringing. What is important here is that, on the surface, every circumstance of Melissa's youth seems arranged to guarantee future happiness: she enjoys not only youth, beauty, health, and money, but also the strength and maturity of mind by which these may be most thoroughly enjoyed and dependably controlled. The situation seems almost too good to be true—"rigged," artificially constructed as an image of hopeful potentiality.

The wary reader, however, will observe faint symptoms of unsoundness. Melissa's acquaintances rush overhurriedly to pay her "universal veneration." They imitate her dress too willingly, copy her letters too facilely, and drink in her opinions with grotesque unanimity:

> My opinion was the great rule of approbation, my remarks were remembred by those who desired the second degree of fame, my

mien was studied, my dress was imitated, my letters were handed from one family to another, and read by those who copied them as sent to themselves; my visits were solicited as honours, and multitudes boasted of an intimacy with Melissa, who had only seen me by accident, and whose familiarity had never proceeded beyond the exchange of a compliment, or return of a courtesy.

And Melissa herself seems more conscious of her own good fortune than perfect humility would require: she "very easily persuaded herself" that she was valued for her "intrinsic qualities," and saw no reason not to hope for continued esteem.

The first particular event in the story, then, may not come as a complete surprise:

> The number of adorers, and the perpetual distraction of my thoughts by new schemes of pleasure, prevented me from listening to any of those who croud in multitudes to give girls advice, and kept me unmarried and unengaged to my twenty-seventh year, when, as I was towering in all the pride of uncontested excellency, with a face yet little impaired, and a mind hourly improving, the failure of a fund, in which my money was placed, reduced me to a frugal competency, which allowed little beyond neatness and independence.

As sharp-eyed readers we may or may not have expected trouble for Melissa, but when it comes it is pretty much an anticlimax. There is no attempt to build up to it, or to involve the reader's passions. The language of catastrophic incident in Johnson is notably sedate; disaster strikes without warning, without any stylistic emphasis at all. No flourishes of rhetoric adorn Melissa's fall from affluence, no exclamations of disbelief, and the essential facts are presented swiftly, concisely.[7] The opposite was true of her earlier prosperity, which occupies the largest part of four and one-half paragraphs, on which are lavished (in a characteristic example of what a rhetorician would call "amplification") balanced cadences, antitheses, Shakespearean metaphor ("*towering* in all the pride of uncontested excellency").[8]

7. Other examples of swift, underplayed catastrophe: *Ramblers* 73, 112, 120, 123, 130, 153.

8. "A falcon, towering in her pride of place, / Was by a mousing owl hawk'd at and kill'd" (*Macbeth,* act 2, scene 4, lines 12–13).

Melissa, who is, despite her overconfidence, a young lady of high principles and sound character, bears her losses "without any outrages of sorrow, or pusillanimity of dejection." Her contempt for money, however, turns out to be another form of overconfidence. She sallies forth into her circle of admirers "with less glitter, but with equal spirit."

I found myself received at every visit, with sorrow beyond what is naturally felt for calamities in which we have no part, and was entertained with condolence and consolation, so frequently repeated, that my friends plainly consulted, rather their own gratification, than my relief. Some from that time refused my acquaintance, and forbore, without any provocation, to repay my visits; some visited me, but after a longer interval than usual, and every return was still with more delay; nor did any of my female acquaintances fail to introduce the mention of my misfortunes, to compare my present and former condition, to tell me how much it must trouble me to want the splendor which I became so well, to look at pleasures, which I had formerly enjoyed, and to sink to a level with those by whom I had been considered as moving in a higher sphere, and who had hitherto approached me with reverence and submission, which I was now no longer to expect.

This is a crucial event in Melissa's history, because it directly contradicts her expectations. The failure of a fund, her tone seems to imply, is a natural phenomenon to which no blame need be attached—it is not even worth describing in detail. But the failure of friends demolishes the premises on which her choice of life had been made. Melissa lingers over the maneuvers by which they disguise their apostasy and mock her weakness. Her letter, nevertheless, is not essentially satirical. Melissa's friends, though energetic and ingenious, are as faceless and automatic when they torment her as they had been when they flattered her. They play out their parts in the drama of disillusionment and then vanish. *Rambler* 75 is divided almost equally between Melissa's pride and her humiliation: narrative emphasis falls on the contrast between these two conditions, not on wicked deeds, however crucial they may be to the complication and resolution of the plot.

The circumstances of Melissa's experience are firmly controlled. Recall the care with which her original happiness was built up; she is systematically endowed with every possible advantage. Then notice how efficiently the castle of her good fortune is demolished: from youth, health, beauty, virtue, knowledge, and affluence, affluence alone is subtracted, with what results we see. Melissa is not reduced to poverty, she has still "a frugal competency"; it is only the superfluous, ornamental wealth, the importance of which had not occurred to her, that is lost. The plot is arranged as if it were a controlled experiment in human behavior; all variables but one are kept constant, that one is manipulated, and the results charted in detail. The almost mechanical unanimity with which Melissa is first worshiped and then spurned contributes to the schematic quality of the plot.

We have dealt so far with formal idiosyncrasies in "complaint": its antiromantic insistence on unhappy endings, its thoroughness of organization, its hostility to expectation and overconfidence (implicitly, an expectation is a choice of life), its emphasis on the details first of confidence, then of discomfiture. Consider now the idiosyncrasies of the picture of life painted in Johnson's fiction, its properties as mimesis.

The scene of unpleasant and disillusioning experience in most of Johnson's stories is London. This is where Zosima, of *Rambler* 12, is initiated into "the world," as she searches in vain for employment in a series of agonizing interviews. Eubulus ("well-advised, prudent"—an ironical misnomer) of *Ramblers* 26, 27 embarks for London as the proper stage on which to display his genius, and ends up the pawn of patrons. Pertinax as a matter of course proceeds from the university to London, to put the final polish on his powers of argument; on arrival he recognizes London as "the place where every one catches the contagion of vanity" (*Rambler* 95). Passion, in London, has ample scope, success is intoxicating, failure convincing, opportunity everywhere, and every extreme of life represented.[9] In 1750 London was in historical fact the center of national existence; here Johnson's representation of reality

9. Other examples of London as the central arena of action: *Ramblers* 109, 141, 147, 163, 170–71; *Idlers* 26–27.

corresponds to social and economic actuality. But London was also a stinking slum, a citadel of luxury, a sweatshop for impoverished authors, and twenty other things unmentioned in Johnson's fiction—he writes about the educated middle class, who feel themselves entitled to a choice of life and, for the most part, can afford one.

Both Melissa and Zosima are victims of what Johnson calls "the world": public existence at its most brazenly competitive and malicious, orbiting around a ferocious pursuit of money (not, in Johnson's fiction, pleasure). When Verecundulus ("bashful") leaves his asylum at the university for a so-called "gentleman's" wedding anniversary feast, he is overwhelmed by "the mingled roar of obstreperous merriment," "clamour, insult and rusticity" (*Rambler* 157). Bad manners are the least one has to fear from the world:

> Every season brings a new flight of beauties into the world, who have hitherto heard only of their own charms, and imagine that the heart feels no passion but that of love. They are soon surrounded by admirers whom they credit, because they tell them only what is heard with delight. Whoever gazes upon them is a lover; and whoever forces a sigh, is pining in despair.
>
> He surely is an useful monitor, who inculcates to these thoughtless strangers, that the "majority are wicked"; who informs them, that the train which wealth and beauty draw after them, is lured only by the scent of prey; and that, perhaps, among all those who croud about them with professions and flatteries, there is not one who does not hope for some opportunity to devour or betray them, to glut himself by their destruction, or to share their spoils with a stronger savage. [*Rambler* 175]

These paragraphs are not intended as fiction but as fact: they are the general nature of which Johnson's stories are just representations. In other contexts Johnson can write of the world as a mixture of good and evil,[10] but the fiction portrays it as a pack of wolves "lured" by "the scent of prey," crowding

10. "The real state of sublunary nature, which partakes of good and evil, joy and sorrow, mingled with endless variety of proportion and innumerable modes of combination . . ." (*Works* [Yale], 7 : 66, the Preface to Shakespeare).

around to "devour" the latest "flight" of dovelike innocents. Within the world, that is, outside the shelter of family, cloister, or college, "every man would be rich, powerful, and famous"; all agree to pursue goals that are not only worldly in the theological sense, but relative, and therefore comparative, and therefore competitive. However eloquently Johnson may write in his expository prose of "the great republick of humanity," of "frequent reciprocations of beneficence" that "unite mankind in society and friendship" there is no sense of community in Johnson's fiction, no benevolent social framework larger than the family and smaller than the public at large: he is an early example of *homo urbanus.*[11]

In *Rambler* 191, Bellaria's mother tells her that the Rambler is "a philosopher, and will teach me to moderate my desires, and look upon the world with indifference." Bellaria's mother is apparently a sensitive reader of *The Rambler,* who has caught the strains of ascetic, stoic unworldliness characteristic of Johnson's more somber thoughts. While periodic retirement from the world is a religious duty, man is not so constituted, in general, as to be able to protect himself from the evils that prey on solitary and contemplative conditions. He has, moreover, certain obligations as a social being impossible to fulfill except in the world. "To know the world is necessary, since we were born for the help of one another," Johnson remarks; but he goes on, "and to know it early is convenient, if it be only that we may learn early to despise it" (*Idler* 80). The narrative of *Rambler* 147 builds up gradually to the climactic exposure of the villainies subsumed by that most worldly of virtues, "assurance." On the other hand, Verecundulus's embarrassment at dinner testifies to the necessity of some capacity to cope with the world on its own terms. These judgments do not cancel each other out if we think of a knowledge of the world as "necessary" for the practice of virtue, but "dangerous" as exposure to vice. Much of Johnson's fiction seems intended to teach us about the world, so that we may despise it.

11. *Rambler* 77, par. 8; *Rambler* 104, par. 1. For a different perspective, see Jeffrey Hart, "Some Thoughts on Johnson as Hero," *Johnsonian Studies,* ed. Magdi Wahba (Cairo, 1962), pp. 23–36.

Confronting the mindless malevolence of the world, Johnson's heroes and heroines are often, for all practical purposes, helpless. Zosima, for example, is a resourceful young lady, and might have contrived—or at least searched for—avenues of escape, but in Johnson's account none are mentioned: she is the pawn of her tormentors (*Rambler* 12). Many of Johnson's stories describe a protagonist who is helpless against the forces of evil. Hyperdulus ("super-slave"), and his sister, of *Rambler* 149, are utterly in the power of the wicked uncle who has taken them from impoverished parents, and like Zosima they are persecuted partly because of their gentle manners and cultivated minds. Misella ("miserable") (*Ramblers* 170, 171), like Hyperdulus, was rescued from want by a rich relation and in time reduced by him to a humiliating dependency. Cut off from all assistance, she is an easy victim of the unscrupulous designs of her protector, and ends up as a prostitute on the London streets. And everyone in Johnson's fiction, helpless or not, is alone: one or two counselors make their appearance at the end of ordeals, but no active companions or friends. Not even courtship and marriage generate affection. Most of the narratives of courtship are only successive disclosures of fraud, and when, as if to prove it can be done, Hymenaeus and Tranquilla find one another, their betrothal is pictured as an elaborate shoring-up against evil, rather than as the union of lovers (*Rambler* 167).

Zosima, however, unlike Misella, addresses the Rambler from a safe harbor. The manner in which forces for good exert themselves on her behalf is also typical of Johnson's narratives: as an exception to the rule, and seemingly by chance. Zosima had no reason to expect Euphemia ("words of good omen, praise, worship") to be in want of a maid, or to appear like an oasis in a desert of iniquity. In these stories, crowds of people are foolish, others are positively evil, and only scattered individuals are good. Thus, Euphemia crops up again in the last paragraph of *Rambler* 133, after Victoria has languished for two full essays at the mercy of her haughty associates, who pay homage only to beauty and wealth. Thus, at the end of the journey in *Adventurer* 84, when each traveler's counterfeit eminence has been exposed, "of one of the women only I could make no disadvantageous detection, because she had assumed no character, but accommodated herself to the scene before her, without any struggle for distinction or superiority." Thus, Betty Broom (*Idlers* 26 and 29) is shuttled from fool to knave all her working life—with one exception, a mistress learned and good who dies in fifteen months. Melissa, also, has two friends who do not mock her new poverty, introduced in the next-to-last paragraph as exceptions to the general rule (*Rambler* 75). It is as if Johnson were consciously trying to qualify the blackness of his picture of life, by painting in, when it occurred to him, at least one bright figure off in a corner somewhere. They are all minor characters; most are women.[12]

Confession

Can we blame Melissa for expecting loyalty from her friends? Surely not. The wickedness at work in *Rambler* 75 is so shadowy and impersonal that it can hardly serve as the focus of blame; it simply illustrates the way of the world. Goodness also is poorly represented here. We are asked to take Melissa's rectitude on faith, and in any case it is concocted rather of advantages (health, wealth, beauty, learning) than of moral virtues. What virtues are recommended seem merely prudential; but one cannot reasonably claim that the moral of this story is that young ladies should not trust their friends. It appears that *Rambler* 75 is less heavy-handedly moralistic than one might expect, from Johnson's reputation.

And yet we do blame Melissa, for not knowing what the Rambler knows, that "the rich and the powerful live in a perpetual masquerade, in which all about them wear borrowed characters." [13] We can blame her because we see her history

12. "Pity is in Johnson's view the only emotion explicitly associated with a supernatural source and thereby is given the highest possible sanction," according to Paul K. Alkon, *Samuel Johnson and Moral Discipline* (Evanston, Ill., 1967), p. 44. For a fictional universe similar to but clearly distinct from Johnson's (the victims are usually women, the villains usually aristocrats), see John J. Richetti, *Popular Fiction before Richardson* (Oxford, 1969), pp. 123–25, 130–31, 147–60.

13. Throughout Johnson's fiction, boughten friendship betrays: e.g., *Ramblers* 18, 120, 190; *Idler* 64.

not through the eyes of an accomplished young lady recently reduced from affluence to competence, but through the eyes of a grave and ironical moralist, high-minded and precise in his discriminations: the style is the man, Sam Johnson. It is as true of the characters in *The Rambler* as of *Rasselas* that they are intended to express not "the diversity of several views" but "the complexity inherent in one."[14] Few great writers are as deficient in negative capability as Johnson. This fact perhaps explains the absence of pathos in Melissa's story and in most of the other complaints; even Misella (*Ramblers* 170, 171), who suffers some of the same distresses as Richardson's Clarissa, queen of pathetic heroines in eighteenth-century fiction, is shielded from her own agony by measured stateliness of language. It also explains why among all the correspondents of *The Rambler* there is scarcely one who can be considered evil.

In a second large class of periodical-essay narratives, the protagonist admits to a serious mistake, or confesses a serious fault. These confessions would therefore seem to offer a fatter chance for fixing blame and defining guilt than do complaints. And there is a real sense in which Pertinax, Verecundulus, Dicaculus, Captator, Serotinus, and Cupidus may be justly convicted of obstinacy, bashfulness, scurrility, mercenariness, vanity, and overbreeding, respectively. They come to us plainly labeled, their sins spelled out in the Latin or Greek of their names.[15] One can almost tell a confession from a complaint by the name of the main character alone, because it translates into a moral deficiency. The names of complainers are morally neutral; sometimes they imply suffering, sometimes female vivacity—Bellaria, "dessert, including fruit, nuts, candy, sweet wine." But the scope of moralistic praise and blame in the confessions is small, and only a very few of the abundant varieties of depravity known to Johnson the moralist blossom into narrative. Four of the eleven major confessions in *The Rambler*, for example, issue from people who have misused

14. Mary Lascelles, "*Rasselas* Reconsidered," *Essays and Studies by Members of the English Association*, n.s. 4 (1951): 45.

15. See Edward A. Bloom, "Symbolic Names in Johnson's Periodical Essays," *MLQ* 13 (1952): 333–52.

their intellectual talents, three from people whose imaginations—using the word loosely to mean the faculty that invents wishes—have got out of control.

Not only is the range of Johnson's moralism in confessions narrow, its edge is blunted. There are complicating factors, which prevent us from relaxing in confidence that we know what is innocent here and what culpable.

For one thing, the early environment of the people in Johnson's fiction determines to a very large extent their moral characters, and severely limits their professional aspirations; they live out the implications of their education. Frustrating, but not damaging, is the training of a commercial apprenticeship; Misocapelus ("hater of retail trade") cannot escape the mannerisms of the shop however he tries. Similarly, Gelasimus, Liberalis, and Verecundulus, though very different people, as their names suggest, have been unfitted for the world by a scholarly education.[16] The opposite is more harmful, a childhood within the fashionable world, which develops "assurance" (*Rambler* 147) or "brass" (*Rambler* 132), the unpleasant callousness of vanity. When a child is brought up by flatterers, and deprived of effective moral authority, he will turn into someone like Squire Bluster, or Turpicula ("ugly, deformed"), chilling examples of spiteful pride (*Ramblers* 142, 189). But the most crippling education is the discipline enforced as a single-minded preparation for a particular way of life, an education which treats the pursuit of happiness almost as a technical trade. Such is Victoria's youth, a highly specialized training as a belle, such the upbringing of the young lord in *Ramblers* 194, 195, an environment so tightly controlled that its denizen can hardly avoid distorted values; such is Cupidus's education in *Rambler* 73, which concentrates all his powers on the inheritance that will eventually descend to him from his aunts. This pattern of events implies what might be called the "bent twig" theory of character development. It owes a great deal to Locke. It provides one more reason for Johnson's interest in biography, in the full life-span, since childhood and

16. *Ramblers* 116, 123, 179, 163, 157.

youth play a crucial role in the formation of mature excellence or deformity. But it also takes the sting out of whatever moral strictures we might be tempted to make in response to the confessions: it wasn't Victoria's, Captator's, Florentulus's, or Pertinax's fault that he or she was brought up as a beauty, legacy hunter, fop, or skeptic. Confessions often register valid complaints.

Precise assignment of praise and blame is also undermined by the almost hypnotic potency of expectation everywhere in Johnson's fiction. Human beings throughout *The Rambler* deceive themselves into fancying that their choice of life will eventually prove to be a good one. If, as Imlac puts it, "all power of fancy over reason is a degree of insanity," then all homo sapiens is tinctured with madness; but a weakness common to all men is less culpable than particular crimes might be. Johnson described a hasty second marriage, we recall, as "the triumph of hope over experience."

Rambler 73 is worth examining in some detail as an example of confession, since it illustrates these points and suggests some others. Cupidus ("desirous") opens his story with an account of his birth and education: his family "boasts alliances with the greatest names in English history," including Tudors and Plantagenets; he is therefore kept "untainted with a lucrative employment." But his father's inheritance has been consumed in paying the portions of three maiden aunts "neither young nor beautiful, nor very eminent for softness of behaviour," and so his immediate family is doomed to eke out the weeks and months and years in expectation, waiting for his aunts to die.

> In all the perplexities or vexations which want of money brought upon us, it was our constant practice to have recourse to futurity. If any of our neighbours surpassed us in appearance, we went home and contrived an equipage, with which the death of my aunts was to supply us. If any purse-proud upstart was deficient in respect, vengeance was referred to the time in which our estate was to be repaired. We registered every act of civility and rudeness, enquired the number of dishes at every feast, and minuted the furniture of every house, that we might, when the hour of affluence should come,

be able to eclipse all their splendor and surpass all their magnificence.

Upon plans of elegance and schemes of pleasure the day rose and set, and the year went round unregarded, while we were busied in laying out plantations on ground not yet our own, and deliberating whether the manor-house should be rebuilt or repaired. This was the amusement of our leisure, and the solace of our exigencies; we met together only to contrive how our approaching fortune should be enjoyed; for in this our conversation always ended, on whatever subject it began.

Cupidus and his family are slaves to the "hunger of imagination"; but they have plenty of company. Examples of tantalizing "disquiet and suspense" in the periodical-essay fiction are so plentiful that it would be unfair to the reader to try to list them all, since virtually every letter to the Rambler describes an expectation which has been disappointed, and Johnson's fiction is full of "innumerable projects of pleasure, which restless idleness incited me to form," "imaginary states of delight and security, perhaps unattainable by mortals," hearts which "dance" indiscriminately at the thought of pastoral pleasures or urban amusements. (Don Quixote, to Johnson, is a man who has allowed his "imagination to riot in the fruition of some possible good," in *Rambler* 2.)

Although Johnson's expository prose acknowledges that "we are in danger from whatever can get possession of our thoughts," it also recognizes the restlessness of the imagination as "a strong proof of the superior and celestial nature of the soul of man"; indeed, "the great task of him, who conducts his life by the precepts of religion, is to make the future predominate over the present." "It is, indeed, the faculty of remembrance, which may be said to place us in the class of moral agents." The imagination in all its ramifications and extensions, from memory to "schemes of merriment," must be "regulated rather than extinguished."[17] In other words, the expository essays balance distrust of the imagination with an affirmation of its value and importance. But the prose fiction of the periodical essays makes no such acknowledgment; it

17. *Rasselas,* ch. 32; *Ramblers* 7, 41; *Idler* 58; *Rambler* 49.

ignores the usefulness of man's imaginative powers. Misocapelus finds himself "deluded by projects of honour and distinction" despite the number of his previous "disappointed expectations," and the heroes of *Ramblers* 15, 16, 18, 27, 42, 95, 101, 165, and many others are similarly deluded. As Melissa's complaint shows, to anticipate good fortune by a single thought is to invite disaster. Any attempt to impose one's personal formula for the future on the natural and unpredictable course of events seems in Johnson's fiction certain to fail.

Cupidus's history is an extended dramatization of the kind of expectation most of Johnson's characters undergo. His aunts are surprisingly tough, and have a tantalizing knack for getting his hopes up, so that he waits and waits. Johnson twists the dagger in the wound, by making the last aunt a hypochondriac, who frequently summons Cupidus to hear her last will, only to recover when the weather improves, by letting this same aunt fall sick and be given up for lost by the doctors three times, by surrounding Cupidus with poor relations who, anxious for his patronage, exaggerate his aunt's ill health. After a lifetime of bondage in "the shackles of expectation," he gets his money, and for two months is "pleased with that obsequiousness and reverence which wealth instantaneously procures"; but soon enough he returns to his "old habit of wishing," to "the tyranny of every desire which fancy suggests," and is faced with a remnant of life passed "in craving solicitude."

Rambler 73 is organized so that the reader pays primary attention to an essentially subjective phenomenon. Its plot would have allowed Johnson to fiddle with any number of related actions: squabbles within the Cupidus family (Jane Austen might have enjoyed sketching discomfort of this kind—as in the first two chapters of *Sense and Sensibility* or chapter 3 of *Sanditon*); skirmishes with his creditors; intrigues against other possible heirs; a love interest. But all these avenues of incident lead away from what Johnson is most interested in, a state of mind, Cupidus's diet of hope—interested because it lies at the heart of the complicated ordeal which convinces us eventually of the vanity (futility, absurdity, self-defeating tendencies, and destructiveness) of human wishes. Between the first stirrings of hope, desire, or expectation and the final aftertaste of failure, disappointment, or disillusion, all kinds of psychological conditions are possible, a many-hued bouquet of moods, attitudes, and predicaments. Most of the lyrical moments in Johnson's prose celebrate one or more of the various shades and successive stages of this experience (or set of experiences); his powers of expressing emotion are more fully exploited in *The Rambler* than in his poem *The Vanity of Human Wishes.*

Quest

A third class of plot in Johnson's narratives is the quest: a search or survey that fails. In its purest form, the quest leads its hero through a series of promising opportunities, all of which prove merely specious, or worse, so that he is forced in the end to question the basic premises of his search. The quest is not to be rigidly distinguished from complaint or confession, since its narrator may be complaining about his failure, or confessing the foolishness that started him on the quest in the first place. But his expectations are more general than those of the typical complainer or confessor, and he tests them more deliberately, by running systematically through an inventory of the major subcategories of relevant experience. The hopeful assumptions of the heroes of complaint and confession become organizing principles of the action of the quest, explicit programs for an item-by-item investigation of life.

Rambler 123 recounts the "projects of honour and distinction" in which Misocapelus engages, his quest for status. As a younger son, he was apprenticed (in *Rambler* 116) to a shopkeeper, and flourished for four years. The one day at a tea party, to his lasting dismay, he was laughed at because of his middle-class manners, because he knew nothing but retail trade and conversed only of fashions in clothes. Fortunately, his elder brother, the heir, "died of drunken joy, for having run down a fox that had baffled all the packs in the province," and set Misocapelus free to find a genteel identity. He holes up in his room, "practising a forbidding frown, a smile of condescension, a slight salutation, and an abrupt departure," to use when his splendid new clothes are ready. "Twice the usual quantity of lace," however, fails to dazzle the middle or impress the upper class, and he decides that "a shining dress, like a weighty weapon, has no force in itself, but owes all its efficacy to him that wears it."

He then changes his lodgings, and ventures "into the publick walks," so that he may be recognized and accepted as a gentleman. These "ambulatory projects" are "blasted" by a lady who assures him that when he sets up his own shop he may expect to see her among his first customers.

> Being therefore forced to practise my adscititious character upon another stage, I betook myself to a coffee-house frequented by wits, among whom I learned in a short time the cant of criticism, and talked so loudly and volubly of nature, and manners, and sentiment, and diction, and similies, and contrasts, and action, and pronunciation, that I was often desired to lead the hiss and clap, and was feared and hated by the players and the poets. Many a sentence have I hissed, which I did not understand, and many a groan have I uttered, when the ladies were weeping in the boxes. At last a malignant author, whose performance I had persecuted through the nine nights, wrote an epigram upon Tape the critick, which drove me from the pit for ever.

Indefatigable, he pursues his ambitions at the gaming table, in the field as a hunter, and in social chatter among the ladies of the neighborhood, with the same lack of success.

This is, as Misocapelus points out in the second paragraph, "a history of disappointed expectations" like most of the other stories in the periodical essays, but since it is a quest it is constructed in distinctive ways. Its hero is easily discouraged: one satire drives him from a position of some prominence in the theater; one police raid extinguishes his ardor for gambling. Don't people in real life tend to get involved? Misocapelus conducts his survey in a frame of mind that lacks single-minded pertinacity, in some respects tentative and unappeasable. His commitments are abstract, not personal.

The episodes of *Rambler* 123 are artificially arranged and constructed. Early embarrassments are painted in more detail and at greater length than later ones, so that the pace or tempo with which things happen gradually speeds up. Misocapelus's failure as a fashionable stroller in London takes three good-sized paragraphs and comes as the climax of a variety of hopes and fears, but his failure in "domestick pleasures" is told from start to finish in fifty words, in five lines of prose. Despite the variation in quality and quantity of buildup, the actual disappointments themselves are ordinarily narrated with a swiftness almost abrupt. Failure occurs in the last sentence of each paragraph (e.g., paragraphs 7, 8, 9, 10, 12) without warning, as a sudden deflation of the hopes raised by the main text of the paragraph. This is the same technique as what we saw in *Rambler* 75 when Melissa's fund failed, here condensed and multiplied. By squeezing a whole defeat into one sentence, Johnson achieves an effect of calculated despondency: the event itself is startling because climactic, but it is described with such economy, and with such ease, that we feel we should have expected it.

Abrupt episodes and an accelerating pace contribute to a general atmosphere of exaggeration in the quests, an atmosphere common to most of the fiction in Johnson's periodical essays. Elizabeth Carter, one of the most learned ladies of her time, read *The Rambler* as it came out and appreciated it, but observed nevertheless that "people know" the author of these essays "by the sure mark of somewhat a little exaggerated in the expression. In his Screech Owl [*Rambler* 59] were *so many* merchants discouraged, *so many* ladies killed, matches broke, poets dismayed!" [18] Narrative hyperbole contributes to our overall impression that Johnson's fictions are consciously arranged as experiments in the moral sciences.

Aspects of the quest conspire to make it Johnson's favorite narrative form, a literary kind that offered him special advantages. Prose complaint is a natural vehicle for satire or pathos; it subsists on the vitality of the wickedness or pain it describes.

18. *A Series of Letters between Mrs. Elizabeth Carter and Miss Catherine Talbot,* ed. Montagu Pennington (London, 1809), 1 : 357.

Some of Johnson's complaints seem contrived, because no one is badly hurt. It is hard to feel deeply sorry for Melissa, who is well rid of her false friends, or for Tranquilla, who need only dismiss her suitors to escape their molestations. Often a story assembles the full apparatus for complaint, but concludes by emphasizing an experience or an attitude more suitable to quest. Why is Euphelia (in *Rambler* 42) so unhappy about a boring visit to the country? Half a dozen such disappointments, or rather, an anthology of important disappointments such as any quest presents, might justify her sonorous melancholy, which seems as it is, factitious.

Prose confession, in seventeenth- and eighteenth-century England, usually addresses itself either to a puritan's unregeneracy before rebirth or to a highwayman's adventures before capture. It is constructed so as to illuminate the dynamics of wickedness, its origin, development, consequences. Johnson's confessions eschew adventure and ignore most of the seven deadly sins; they treat instead the "artificial passions," ambition and vanity and their cousins, all of them venal, worldly.[19] Often, in Johnson, a confession seems unconvincing because it handles one minor passion as if it were as serious as the sum of all human wishes. The dangers of the desire to excel in wittiness, for example, are announced with a resonance more appropriate to a more universal activity—or to a survey of important inadequate activities such as many quests attempt. The frustrations of six or eight ordinary stories can be bundled into one quest, *seriatim,* for more and sharper disappointments per column inch, for greater narrative efficiency and a more plausible objective correlative, at the price of a marked increase in artificiality of construction.

The quest is also more effective at summary than are other plot forms; it answers the need to come to conclusions. A large proportion of Johnson's narratives are offered to us as conclu-

19. Examples of puritan confession include many of the recapitulatory discourses and pious conversations of Christian, Hopeful, and Faithful in *Pilgrim's Progress.* See also G. A. Starr, *Defoe and Spiritual Autobiography* (Princeton, 1965), and, for "artificial passions," Alkon, *Samuel Johnson and Moral Discipline,* pp. 14–20.

sive statements. They come from people who have reached maturity, achieved something professionally, and are asking themselves what they have made of their lives; they fall easily, therefore, into the form of a quest, an episodic summary of a history of multiple disappointments.

What I have called the lyrical moments in Johnson's fiction, too, are more nearly justified in the quest than in most of the complaints and confessions. They are tuned to restlessness, and to resignation. We have seen Cupidus delivered up "to the tyranny of every desire which fancy suggests," his mind "corrupted with an inveterate disease of wishing." This kind of insatiability seems faintly absurd in a simple confession, to the degree that it is passive, unearned. Mercator (of *Adventurer* 102), on the other hand, used his money to organize a long-term quest of satisfaction which is presented to us in some detail, and so his lyrical boredom makes more sense:

> In this gloomy inactivity, is every day begun and ended; the happiness that I have been so long procuring is now at an end, because it has been procured; I wander from room to room till I am weary of myself; I ride out to a neighbouring hill in the centre of my esate, from whence all my lands lie in prospect round me; I see nothing that I have not seen before, and return home disappointed, though I knew that I had nothing to expect.

The note of pious resignation with which Johnson ends many of his histories (and his best poem) is also more authoritative in a quest, for similar reasons.

The Choice of Life

The principal motif of Johnson's fiction is "the choice of life": selection of the activity, profession, or surroundings that will determine one's way of life and produce whatever happiness one is entitled to this side of heaven. Those who attempt the choice of life are sooner or later convinced of the vanity of human wishes.[20] The inhabitants of Johnson's imagination are preoccupied with *choice,* with old and unfortunate deci-

20. See W. J. Bate, *The Achievement of Samuel Johnson* (Oxford, 1955), chs. 2–4, for a skillful interpretation of some of the periodical-essay fiction, emphasizing the vanity of human wishes.

sions, with new and specious possibilities, with the limits of an individual's control of his destiny. Is there any role or station or career that will be permanently satisfying? Can the individual impose his will on crass casualty to a degree that sanctions hopes and expectations? What forces restrict our freedom to pursue happiness? All three of the stories that served as major examples in this chapter deal with the choice of life: the narrative structure of *Rambler* 75 emphasizes disparities between the apparent unassailability of Melissa's role as reigning toast and its actual fragility; Cupidus is the prisoner of a choice that he cannot unmake and cannot fulfill—a victim of the persistent delusion that "correct" choice is possible; Misocapelus, of course, once he breaks the articles of his apprenticeship, is publicly consumed by the problem of making a choice of life.

Obstacles to free choice play a leading role in the periodical-essay fiction. Frequently young ladies in *The Rambler* complain of domestic confinement, and plead for freedom from arbitrary rules and restrictions, freedom to choose the way they want to live: Cleora in *Rambler* 15 objects to being chained to the card table; Miss Maypole in *Rambler* 55 suffers the tyranny of a mother unwilling to admit that her daughter is ready to be treated as a woman, not a child; Rhodoclia, Myrtilla, and Properantia (in *Ramblers* 62, 84, 107) long for emancipation from the nursery and for open access to the delights of London. Often a man's choice of life is predetermined by his upbringing and education, in which case he has a right to complain (*Ramblers* 73, 109, 116, 141) or an obligation to confess (*Ramblers* 95, 181, 197, 198). The complaints include a whole tribe of authority figures who willfully obstruct choices of life: tyrannical patrons (*Ramblers* 27, 163), cruel relations (*Ramblers* 149, 170), and aged plutocrats playing cat-and-mouse with anxious heirs (*Ramblers* 73, 112, 162, 197, 198). Poverty makes it impossible to plot one's own course through life, and delivers its victims up to chance and a brutal world (*Ramblers* 12, 149, 170). There are those who are prevented from making a reasonable choice of life by simple indecisiveness (Polyphilus of *Rambler* 19 and Eumathes of *Rambler* 132, both gifted scholars), by insufficient self-knowledge (resulting in affectation—i.e., the assumption of a role for which one is not naturally suited—in *Ramblers* 16, 24, 61, 116, 123, 179), or by vanity (*Ramblers* 26, 165, 189).

The urgency of finding one's proper place in life also pushes into center stage certain topics that might otherwise be less prominent: marriage, travel, and the use or abuse of intellectual talent. (1) No one falls in love in Johnson's fiction; people select their wives or husbands with a particular kind of domestic existence in mind. Marriage represents a choice in life styles, and a selection among various secular goods, money, the pleasures of high society, or a tranquil household. The fact that Johnson's characters approach courtship as a choice of life explains perhaps why there is only one satisfactory match in all the periodical-essay narratives (*Rambler* 167); it is not marriage as an institution that is under attack but the assumption that life can be managed and controlled by means of marriage. (2) Similarly, the country-versus-city issue in Johnson's fiction does not concern itself with the priority of either, as it does in Fielding and Smollett, but with change of place in general as a remedy for chronic discontent. Euphelia reads pastorals and is seized with a passionate longing for trees and flowers and sheep; Eubulus is lured to London by accounts of "the beauty and felicity" of that brave "new world"; but in Johnson's fiction both country and city betray those who count on them to guarantee happiness. Many of the quests experiment with change of place as a possible cure for melancholy. This is the proper context for Johnson's celebrated skepticism on the value of retirement: he has nothing against the mean and sure estate per se, but laughs at it when proposed as a panacea. The fact that London offers the maximum variety in opportunities and desirables justifies its position as the principal theater of operations in *The Rambler*. (3) The large number of scholars in Johnson's fiction are best classified not by their specialties as scholars but by the use they choose to make of their intelligence. Pertinax ("tenacious, obstinate"), of *Rambler* 95, shows us how the capacity to doubt, question, and challenge ideas can evolve into nihilism. The heroes of

Ramblers 141 and 174 devote themselves to wit and humor and neglect solider excellences; both put their case histories before us as if they had made a conscious choice of the channel into which their brainpower will flow; wit is conceived here not as a pleasure, and not as a faculty, but as a career open to intellectuals.

The formal and structural peculiarities of Johnson's fiction owe something also to the choice of life. No choice is possible without a plurality of options; episodic form multiplies options; quests are episodic narratives; the act of deciding what kind of existence one wants may therefore be most variously and explicitly demonstrated by a quest. On the other hand, the history of this critical decision is displayed most clearly in a biographical framework. The reason why so many of the correspondents of the Rambler delve back into their childhood is to gather from time past facts that are relevant to present regrets over a blundered choice of life.

Contexts: The Novelists

We can discern a degree of kinship between Johnson's fiction and the writings of all the major novelists of the mid-eighteenth century except Richardson, plus one major author in France. For Fielding, Goldsmith, Voltaire, and Smollett the world is a wicked place; in London, or Paris, worldly vices are triple distilled, and the well-intentioned youth who ventures into the city expecting a humane welcome will be comically disappointed or cruelly abused; disaster will come swiftly, by the agency of any number of faceless "friends" or enemies acting with almost mechanical unanimity. In all these authors the good man is hard put to find allies. (He *may* fall in love and drop entirely out of this dangerous world into the world of romance, in which case his *ambiance* will be quite different from the one we have been discussing; he will speak and behave like a different person, as Joseph Andrews and Roderick Random do in their love scenes.) He carries on plenty of conversations but never achieves anything like the intimacy of personal communication we find in Richardson; and the odds against him—the chances of any passing acquaintance being a rogue—are often very high. In *Joseph Andrews* and *The Vicar of Wakefield,* the choice of life turns up as a digression: both Mr. Wilson's history (book 3, chapter 3) and George Primrose's adventures as a "philosophic vagabond" (chapter 22), like Johnsonian quests, are built around a series of disappointed expectations, and force their central figures into "expertise." Roderick Random's fortune-hunting in London, though a coarse-grained affair at best, goes through some of the same stages as several of the quests in the *Rambler, Adventurer, Idler.* The "representation of reality" in Johnson's fiction, which appears so peculiar at first glance, has much in common with the world of picaresque comedy in Fielding and his followers, or seems to from a distance.[21]

If we look more closely, the outlines of this general kinship fade, and essential differences between Johnson's fiction and that of his contemporaries emerge. Voltaire provides us with a concise example of eighteenth-century fiction that subsists more or less within Johnson's world but in which components to be found in *The Rambler,* slightly modified, are assembled into a much more sporty machine. When Candide indulges his curiosity in a flying visit to Paris, he has hardly unpacked before the vultures descend:

> A peine Candide fut-il dans son auberge qu'il fut attaqué d'une maladie légère causée par ses fatigues. Comme il avait au doigt un diamant énorme, et qu'on avait aperçu dans son équipage une cassette prodigieusement pesante, il eut aussitôt auprès de lui deux médecins qu'il n'avait pas mandés, quelques amis intimes qui ne le quittèrent pas, et deux dévotes qui faisaient chauffer ses bouillons.

21. Passages where expectations are disappointed in a manner that bears some family resemblance to the same events in Johnson: *Joseph Andrews,* bk. 2, chs. 13–14; *David Simple,* bk. 1, chs. 4, 8, 9, 11; *The Vicar of Wakefield,* chs. 2, 20. Sudden catastrophes: *Joseph Andrews,* bk. 1, ch. 5, par. 1 (death of Sir Thomas Booby); *Tom Jones,* bk. 2, ch. 8 (death of Capt. Blifil); *David Simple,* bk. 1, ch. 6 (death of Nanny), bk. 2, ch. 6 (death of Cynthia's father); *Roderick Random,* vol. 2, ch. 1 (deaths of captain and doctor); *Vicar,* ch. 2 (loss of money), ch. 22 (house burns down), ch. 28 (sudden appearance of George in jail). Loss of money equals loss of friends: *Joseph Andrews,* bk. 1, ch 12, bk. 2, ch. 14, bk. 3, ch. 3; *Roderick Random,* vol. 1, chs. 7–23, vol. 2, chs. 9–18; *Citizen of the World,* Letter 27.

Martin disait: "Je me souviens d'avoir été malade aussi à Paris dans mon premier voyage; j'étais fort pauvre: aussi n'eus-je ni amis, ni dévotes, ni médecins, et je guéris."

Cependant, à force de médecines et de saignées, la maladie de Candide devint sérieuse.[22]

It reads like a caricature of the world of Johnson's fiction; but Voltaire has so violently exaggerated Parisian villainy, and has set up Candide as an easy mark with such patent artificiality, that his narrative transcends didacticism, passes beyond it into comedy. A few sentences after the last one quoted, "Candide guérit"—Candide recovers, as quickly and painlessly as he fell sick; and within a paragraph or two the illness is forgotten as though it had never been. Candide, a true comic hero, bounces from one catastrophe to the next, indestructible as a hard-rubber ball. Johnson's characters may be grotesque, pseudo-comic, but they are far from invulnerable.

Other devices characteristic of Johnsonian narrative appear in this passage from *Candide,* also with a difference. The casual, swift disasters of *The Rambler* are in some sense analogous to the "relentless, unrelated torrent of mishaps [in *Candide*] pouring down from a clear sky on the heads of perfectly innocent and unprepared people whom it involves by mere chance"—Erich Auerbach's words, arguing that the "almost slapstick speed" of Voltaire's narrative, and the way it drastically oversimplifies "the reality of experience," in part by giving credence only to material and natural phenomena, ignoring the historical and spiritual, make for comedy but not for realism.[23] Johnson distorts the "reality of experience" into

22. "Scarcely was Candide in his lodgings when he was attacked by a slight illness caused by fatigue. Since he had on his finger an enormous diamond, and in his baggage had been noticed a prodigiously heavy casket, immediately he had near him two doctors whom he had not sent for, some intimate friends who did not leave his side, and two pious ladies who had his broth warmed. Martin said, 'I remember having been sick also in Paris on my first trip; I was very poor; accordingly I had neither friends nor pious ladies nor doctors, and I recovered.' However, as a result of medications and bleedings, the illness of Candide became serious" (ch. 22; my translation).

23. *Mimesis* (1946; Doubleday Anchor ed., 1957), pp. 360–61. There are of course many kinds of swift narration, not all of which are comic.

didactic tales, not comedy. He is much more interested in the self-deceptions of his heroes—who act and suffer, presume, anticipate, plan, and expect in earnest—than in the material and natural motives of his supporting cast, however laughable they may be. And where Voltaire's language, by virtue of a certain inimitable vigorous carelessness, is the perfect vehicle for satirical comedy, Johnson's equally inimitable stateliness—with certain notable exceptions—blunts the edge of his satire.

Had we used Fielding instead of Voltaire, juxtaposing, for example, Zosima and Parson Adams's encounter with Trulliber, or Misargyrus and Booth, or Misocapelus and Mr. Wilson, we should have come to similar conclusions, though a different set of adjustments and qualifications would have been necessary; but the comparison would have involved similar variables. "I know not any thing more pleasant or more instructive than to compare experience with expectation, or to register from time to time the difference between Idea and Reality," wrote Johnson in 1758. Out of discrepancies between the "idea" and "reality" the novelists constructed satirical comedy; by contrast, Johnson's emphasis on instructing his readers emerges sharply from the next sentence in this letter of 1758: "It is by this kind of observation that we grow daily less liable to be disappointed." [24]

Johnson's stories do not resemble other moral tales very closely. They are not cautionary tales, in the manner of Aesop or Hannah More,[25] nor are they lessons in princely prudence

---

Aesop's fables and other didactic fiction use extremely condensed and rapid narrative to convey a moral more efficiently. Ian Watt's principle, "that the importance of the plot is in inverse proportion to that of character" (*The Rise of the Novel* [1957; rpt. Berkeley and Los Angeles, 1959], p. 279), is relevant here, if for "character" we read "personality" or "psychological complexity."

24. *Letters,* 1 : 110. For an illuminating analysis of "the encounter of abstraction and experience" as a crucial event in comedy, see A. N. Kaul, *The Action of English Comedy* (New Haven, 1970), pp. 24–42.

25. Hannah More's *Coelebs in Search of a Wife* (1809) is a vastly extended Johnsonian quest, padded with edifying discourses, and her *Search after Happiness* (1773), a pseudo-pastoral drama, is also organized as a choice of life—but these texts are not so much examples of a narrative tradition on which Johnson was drawing, as evidence of Johnson's influence on one of his young lady friends.

like the famous *Télémaque* of Archbishop Fénelon, much less *contes moraux* like Marmontel's. They often fail to reward virtue and punish vice, as even the most salacious romances claimed to do. They pay less attention to virtues and vices than do the expository essays of *The Rambler,* which are genuinely interested in, for example, charity, good humor, and idleness. All this surely is a consequence of their overriding concern with the choice of life, a lonely enterprise only obliquely related to prudential or social ethics. Johnson's protagonists are not allowed to feel affection, lust, jealousy, hatred, and anger, so that they may make their choice of life uninterrupted and undistracted. Their aloneness is neither alienation nor exile; it is rather the isolation of men whose talents will be demanded of them someday, and who know that the night cometh in which no man can work—that the choice of a temporary life is ultimately a decision for which they are responsible to divine authority.[26]

26. John 9 : 4—"The night cometh, when no man can work." Part of this verse was inscribed on the dial of Johnson's watch, in Greek (Boswell, 2 : 57), and he quotes it in the *Prayers and Meditations* (*Works* [Yale], 1 : 118), in *Idler* 43, and in *Adventurer* 120. On the importance of the parable of the talents to Johnson, see Chester F. Chapin, *The Religious Thought of Samuel Johnson* (Ann Arbor, Mich., 1968), pp. 51, 56.

3 Satire

> You was at home all evening and grew bold by reading Johnson's satires.
>
> *Boswell in Holland*

Johnson flirted intermittently with the muse of satire. He was sensitive to the impurity of human motivation, and to the unjustness of much human suffering; he had insight and indignation in abundance, wit and aggressiveness and even—within limits—a talent for subversion. But though he "tried in his time" to be a satirist, somehow sympathy, or piety, was always breaking in. His fiction is frequently satirical. Antiromance as a general literary phenomenon is fertile ground for satirical weeds of every complexion, medicinal, noxious, bittersweet. Johnson's pessimism subsumes a highly critical view of human pretensions; and his self-consciousness expresses itself sometimes in narrative irony of considerable complexity and depth. At the same time, most of the little stories he tells in the periodical essays seem to operate, as narrative, in a region where satirical, comic, and didactic modes overlap.[1]

This chapter deals along the way with Johnson's prose style at its "lowest"—which is not very low. (Chapter 4 will inspect the highest peaks of the Johnsonian massif, which are very imposing.) We recognize a low style in Johnson by the number of particular details and technical terms it employs, and elsewhere by colloquial idiom and informality. A middle style, the "elegance of its construction" and "harmony of its cadence" (*Rambler* 208) noticeably enhanced, is Johnson's ordinary medium in *The Rambler,* but the language of the narratives

1. For the temperament of a satirist in Johnson, see W. J. Bate, "Johnson and Satire Manqué," *Eighteenth-Century Studies: in Honor of Donald F. Hyde,* ed. W. H. Bond (New York, 1970), pp. 145–60; for Johnson's "subversiveness," see Bertrand Bronson, *Johnson Agonistes* (Cambridge, 1946), pp. 1–52, and Donald Greene, *The Politics of Samuel Johnson* (New Haven, 1960), esp. pp. 232–45.

varies significantly, from majesty to pertness. Johnson never in fact escapes the gravitational field of an upper-middle style for long, either to soar or to stoop, but when he does it is for satire, at one extreme, and sublimity at the other.

Realism and Rhetoric

In the Renaissance and through the eighteenth century the art of satire figured very often as a kind of verbal karate; we hear everywhere of "strokes of wit," of wounds and smarts dealt out to the dunces, of satire as a dangerous occupation, of its objects as victims or enemies. According to this approach, excellence in satire is therefore skill in inflicting damage; and critical analyses of satire will focus on weaponry, the whip or bludgeon of Juvenal and the rapier of Horace, on undermining, reducing, stripping, and trapping. According to another approach, we can examine satirical writings as fiction, assuming satire to be in essence and in substance an imaginative literary form. All satire implies a criticism of some sort, and is based therefore on standards of some kind. But, obviously, not all criticism is satire, and it is precisely the imaginative or fictional aspects of satire that differentiate it from mere expository analysis.[2] One can also read satire as a mode of expression: it is hard not to respond to Juvenal's tumultuous indignation (in the early satires), or to Horace's playfulness (e.g., in book 2, no. 7); despite our habit of ascribing these qualities to the author as a person, they make their effect

2. For satire as a weapon, and the art of satire as dexterity in handling that weapon, see Juvenal, *Satire* 1; Persius, *Satire* 1.107–10; Boileau, *Satires* 7 (1663), 9 (1667); Swift, "To Mr. Congreve" (1693), lines 133–34; Pope, "To Mr. Fortescue" (1733). The distinction between excellences proper to Juvenalian satire and excellences proper to Horatian satire was a commonplace of perennial vigor; see Dryden, "A Discourse concerning the Original and Progress of Satire" (1693), *Essays,* ed. W. P. Ker (1900; rpt. New York, 1961), 2 : 78–98; Dennis, "To Matthew Prior, Esq; Upon the Roman Satirists," *Critical Works,* ed. E. N. Hooker (Baltimore, 1943), 2 : 218–20. For an early formulation of the relation between moral judgment and fiction in satire, see L. I. Bredvold, "A Note in Defence of Satire," *ELH* 7 (1940): 259–60; and of the relation between satire as attack (rhetoric) and as "imitation," see Maynard Mack, "The Muse of Satire," *Yale Review,* n.s. 41 (1951): 83–84.

on the reader only by appearing ("expressed") in the work of art.

In *Rambler* 61 Ruricola ("countryman, farmer") fulminates against haughty visitors from London. His example is a fellow townsman, "one Frolick," who was originally "a tall boy, with lank hair, remarkable for stealing eggs, and sucking them"—a pleasing rustic. But when he comes back from London, this same Frolick has undergone a disturbing metamorphosis: "he shewed us the deformity of our skirts and sleeves, informed us where hats of the proper size were to be sold, and recommended to us the reformation of a thousand absurdities in our cloaths, our cookery, and our conversation. When any of his phrases were unintelligible, he could not suppress the joy of confessed superiority, but frequently delayed the explanation, that he might enjoy his triumph over our barbarity."

If Frolick had "pointed out that our skirts and sleeves were out of date, recommended to us the reformation of many unfashionable styles in our clothes, and enjoyed his triumph over our ignorance," we as readers would feel informed about Frolick's vanity, but we would not feel ourselves in the presence of satire. What Johnson actually says is that Frolick showed us *deformity,* enumerated *a thousand absurdities,* and triumphed over our *barbarity;* he has turned a harmless country bumpkin into a prodigy of insolence. *Rambler* 208 pleads that "some exaggeration" be allowed to "burlesque." Ruricola, unfortunately, does not allow Frolick to stay a grotesque; he stoops to truth, and lets his satire sink to mere critical analysis. Toward the end of the essay he bad-humoredly notices that when Frolick "talks on subjects known to the rest of the company, he has no advantage over us, but by catches of interruption, briskness of interrogation, and pertness of contempt." To the extent that this is accurate it is unsatirical.[3]

Rambler 12 illustrates vividly the satirical powers of complaint. Its heroine is Zosima, who bears with some reason the name of the Greek slave whose epitaph Johnson had translated

3. Butler's Character of "A Humorist": "He knows no mean; for that is inconsistent with all Humour, which is never found but in some Extreme or other" (*Characters,* ed. A. R. Waller [Cambridge, 1908], p. 138).

in 1740.[4] The "daughter of a country gentleman" of straitened means, she has traveled to London to procure a servant's place, and tells us of the employers she has visited, each nastier than the last. Madam Bombasine, "two yards round the waist," routs her with a volley of coarse sarcasms about needy "gentlewomen," at the conclusion of which "her broad face grew broader with triumph." Zosima's next interviewer is Mrs. Standish, whose husband has recently been promoted to rank sufficient to employ a maid:

> To Mrs. Standish I went, and, after having waited six hours, was at last admitted to the top of the stairs, when she came out of her room, with two of her company. There was a smell of punch. So young woman, you want a place, whence do you come?—From the country, madam.—Yes, they all come out of the country. And what brought you to town, a bastard? Where do you lodge? At the Seven-Dials? What, you never heard of the foundling house?

To Johnson, "simple narration" was a distinct species of writing, defined in terms of its freedom from ornament, its plainness, as opposed to "copiousness" or "elegance," and its function, listing facts or events. One reason the *Lives of the Poets* are statistically less cloudy and rich than *The Rambler* is the number of pages they devote to simple narrative biography.[5] There are, nevertheless, many degrees of plainness; in most of Johnson's narratives his most famous mannerisms are muted and relatively unobtrusive, but as satirist he is capable of positive homeliness: "There was a smell of punch." Elsewhere, Leviculus ("light-minded"), hunting the fortune of Madam Prune, "sometimes presumed to mention marriage; but was always answered with a slap, a hoot, and a flounce" (*Rambler* 182).

4. Edward A. Bloom, "Symbolic Names in Johnson's Periodical Essays," *MLQ* 13 (1952): 346.

5. *Narratio* in forensic rhetoric referred to the stating of the facts of the case, a relatively straightforward process. See Quintilian, *Institutio Oratoria* 4.2. Johnson's ideas on "simple narration" are sketched in *Ramblers* 122, 188. For "copiousness" see *Lives,* 3 : 165–66, *Rambler* 122; for different kinds of ornament and the problem in general see *Rambler* 152, *Adventurer* 138.

Zosima addresses the Rambler in her first paragraph with the hope that this "species of cruelty" "may become less common when it has been once exposed in its various forms, and its full magnitude." Exposure implies demonstration, as opposed to criticism or analysis. As a satirical technique, it is a folly or crime arranged (and, therefore, often fictionalized) to give itself away, to illumine its own shortcomings. It is a kind of showing, not telling, and may be highly dramatic. Zosima feels free to comment on her persecutors, but when she is actually in their clutches she lets their conversation speak for itself. These dialogues display a surprising command of the vernacular, of urban idiom, expletive, the verbal leer and simper, vulgar innuendo, well-bred malevolence, and coarse jocularity: "Wait on me, you saucy slut! Then you are sure of coming—I could not let such a drab come near me—Here, you girl that came up with her, have you touch'd her? If you have, wash your hands before you dress me—Such trollops! Get you down. What, whimpering? Pray walk." It seems to me reasonable to think of such passages not as exceptions or anomalies, though they are relatively uncommon, but as extremes, as samples of Johnson's narrative imagination in its oldest clothes.

To dramatize folly is to give a thief enough rope so that he hangs himself, an efficient way of disposing of him. Johnson often incorporates into his narrative some of the phrases or arguments his subject would use if he were justifying himself in his own words, without calling attention to it by punctuation, sometimes without the syntactic signs of indirect quotation. Evidence for guilt is displayed still alive and warm, not dried into abstractions and packaged in moral categories. Hymenaeus of *Rambler* 113, in search of a wife, courts a number of young ladies who appear to be good matches but in reality are not, among them "the prudent, the oeconomical Sophronia," who "discoursed with great solemnity on the care and vigilance which the superintendence of a family demands; observed how many were ruined by confidence in servants; and told me, that she never expected honesty but from a strong chest, and that the best storekeeper was the mistress's eye." They adjust the settlements, and everything seems to favor the marriage, when one morning Sophronia's maid, in tears, appeals to Hymenaeus for protection because she has been turned away for breaking six teeth in one of Sophronia's combs, and fears starvation or worse in the London streets. When Hymenaeus confidently applies to his lady he is told "that if she neglected her own affairs, I might suspect her of neglecting mine; that the comb stood her in three half-crowns; that no servant should wrong her twice; and that indeed, she took the first opportunity of parting with Phyllida, because, though she was honest, her constitution was bad, and she thought her very likely to fall sick." The person who makes us aware of the disparity between appearance and reality in Sophronia's character is Sophronia herself.[6]

Her language does not smell of the fish market like Madam Bombasine's, but it has a distinctly bourgeois odor, in part because of its use of proverbs. "Expect no honesty but from a strong chest," and "the best storekeeper is the mistress's eye"—in Johnson's fiction rustic apothegms and homely saws, especially the proverbs of commerce and trade, are always a sign of specious rationalization. The mother of the hero of *Rambler* 197 tells him that "all must catch that catch can," that "many a little made a mickle," that "Brag was a good dog, but Holdfast was a better," as part of his training as a legacy hunter. Linguistic vulgarity implies in this context moral inferiority—contrast Zosima's disconcertingly heroic speech ("Sir, why should you, by supposing me a thief, insult one from whom you had received no injury?") with the coarseness of Madam Bombasine. The children of light in Johnson's fiction are usually well educated. Renaissance principles of the separation of styles are very undemocratic (and rather longer-lived than is usually supposed: even Oliver Twist expresses himself genteelly).[7]

6. A talent for the invention of self-betraying dialogue is what made Fanny Burney's readers, including Johnson and Mrs. Thrale, chortle over the "satire" in her writings, as later the same obsevations were made of Jane Austen.

7. See Erich Auerbach, *Mimesis* (1946; Doubleday Anchor ed., 1957), ch. 15. Johnson criticized Fielding for "lowness" (Boswell, 2 : 174). But all Fielding's heroes are well educated, and only his comic characters express themselves in the vulgar idiom; he too observes decorum.

The language of Johnson's satire, then, can be realistic in one of the modern senses of the word: commonplace, colloquial, low. It can also be low in the old sense and *un*realistic in the new by means of enumerated particulars and technical terms. There is lots of detail in Johnson's fiction, but it is used rhetorically, not realistically. To put it another way, the mere presence of everyday objects and particular circumstances does not of itself constitute realism, even in the eighteenth century. For example, compare the "cosmetick discipline" inflicted on Victoria (in *Rambler* 130),

> part of which was a regular lustration performed with bean-flower water and may-dews; my hair was perfumed with variety of unguents, by some of which it was to be thickened, and by others to be curled. The softness of my hands was secured by medicated gloves, and my bosom rubbed with a pomade prepared by my mother, of virtue to discuss pimples, and clear discolorations . . .

with Richardson's Pamela's self-satisfied catalog of clothes:

> Then I bought of a pedlar, two pretty enough round-eared caps, a little straw-hat, and a pair of knit mittens, turned up with white calico; and two pair of ordinary blue worsted hose, that make a smartish appearance, with white clocks, I'll assure you; and two yards of black riband for my shift sleeves, and to serve as a necklace; and when I had 'em all come home, I went and looked upon them once in two hours, for two days together. . . .

Both passages are highly specific, and both are crowded with the furniture of femininity, but details in Richardson express personality, while in Johnson they illustrate a moral extravagance.[8] We are not often interested in Johnson's characters or events as real people, or as free experience; they have been tampered with, to enhance their moral relevance. They are important to Johnson (and therefore to us) because they repre-

8. Are Victoria's cosmetics an example of what Quintilian refers to as "accumulation"? See *Institutio Oratoria* 8.4.26–27. According to Hugh Blair, amplification "may be carried on by a proper use of magnifying or extenuating terms, by a regular enumeration of particulars, or by throwing together, as into one mass, a crowd of circumstances" (*Lectures on Rhetoric* [1783; rpt. Carbondale, Ill., 1965], 1 : 360).

sent important truths about the real world; they have only limited vitality as autonomous excerpts from life.[9]

Where Johnson most copiously enumerates particulars, and rattles off technical terms, he is often trying to establish the expertise of his characters. People are constantly trying out roles in the periodical-essay fiction (often, as part of their attempts to make a choice of life). Given the didactic nature of these stories and their tendency to resort to extremes, for purposes of unmistakability, it is natural and consistent that every role be played out thoroughly, expertly. Misocapelus rose to the top of his coterie of poetasters "in a short time," and "talked so loudly and volubly of nature, and manners, and sentiment" that he was "often desired to lead the hiss and clap." Euphelia knew before she was "ten years old all the rules of paying and receiving visits, and to how much civility every one of my acquaintance was entitled" (*Rambler* 42). Hilarius (*Rambler* 101) and Dicaculus ("satirical") (*Rambler* 174) are superwits, one a specialist in imagination "heated" to a state of "ebullition," the other a virtuoso raconteur. Being experts, these people seldom hesitate to use the technical terminology of their special fields: the bean-flower water of cosmetics; the "sleeves, button-holes, and embroidery" of foppery; the rents, legacies, mortgages, and indentures of legacy hunting; the crucible, athanor, and electricity of the scientist.[10]

As experts, and for emphasis in general, they keep careful track of their own progress; indeed, they deluge us with statistics: Tranquilla discarded two lovers for tone deafness, three for drunkenness, two for simultaneous courtship of other ladies, six for concealing their debts; down the throats of his flatterers Misellus poured "two hogsheads of port, fifteen gallons of arrack, ten dozen of claret, and five and forty bottles

9. Auerbach (*Mimesis*, esp. p. 185) demonstrates how characters may be graphic and vivid but not real as individuals. In *Rambler* 107 Properantia ("hasty") is very sprightly indeed—cleverly contrived rather than clever, however, a scholar's exemplification of sauciness.

10. *Ramblers* 130, 194, 197–98, 199. For expertise as essential equipment in a mad projector, Tom Stucco, see Johnson's letter to *The Public Ledger* for December 16, 1760 (E. L. McAdam, "New Essays by Dr. Johnson," *RES* 18 [1942]: 197–207).

of champagne." Resolute and conscientious scorekeeping is intensely characteristic of Johnson's satire, and of his fiction in general: it is a species of exaggeration, and a shorthand version of the narrative hyperbole discussed in chapter 2; it is a way of reducing mere incident to tabular form, to make room for full concentration on expectation and disappointment; it is stripped-down particularity functioning as exemplification. Quest-ors—including Rasselas—are likely to fall into this mannerism, which is a numerical mini-quest in its own right.[11]

Johnson and Swift

Without repudiating the common reader, who responds very differently to the Doctor and the Dean, I would like to describe three of Johnson's satirical fictions as analogues to characteristic satires by Swift. Like the dialogues of *Rambler* 12, they are remote provinces among the regions of his imagination, thinly populated, but indisputably on the map. We do not know whether Johnson was consciously imitating Swift, but since Swift was the outstanding genius of a school of satirical arts widely patronized in the eighteenth century, we may take him as its exemplar and representative.[12] The comparison helps to define Johnson's limitations as a prose satirist.

Rambler 117 is a letter from Hypertatus ("uppermost, highest"), announcing his discovery that character and intelligence vary according to distance from the center of the earth. The higher one is, the thinner the air, the more volatile one's intel-

11. *Ramblers* 119, 16. Other examples of satirical enumeration: *Ramblers* 42, 59, 62, 142, 153, 191, 199; *Adventurer* 41. Swift is fond of this device; see *A Tale of a Tub*, sect. 5, par. 4; *Against Abolishing Christianity*, pars. 11–12; *A Modest Proposal*, pars. 6–7, 10–11, 14.

12. For some of Johnson's "close affinities with Swift" (thus the editors of the Yale *Idler*, p. 317 n. 1), see W. B. C. Watkins, "Vive la Bagatelle," *Perilous Balance* (Princeton, 1939), pp. 25–48; W. J. Bate, *The Achievement of Samuel Johnson* (Oxford, 1955), pp. 94, 112–13, 117, 125–27. The two men shared a number of basic positions, among which the most important surely was their serious and deeply rooted allegiance to the Church of England. Chester F. Chapin, *The Religious Thought of Samuel Johnson* (Ann Arbor, Mich., 1968), pp. 118–32, suggests that on the issue of church and state Johnson held the same position he (Johnson) ascribes to Swift in *Lives*, 3 : 53.

lect and imagination; hence the excellence of garrets as lodgings for philosophers and poets:

> I have discovered, by a long series of observations, that invention and elocution suffer great impediments from dense and impure vapours, and that the tenuity of a defecated air at a proper distance from the surface of the earth, accelerates the fancy, and sets at liberty those intellectual powers which were before shackled by too strong attraction, and unable to expand themselves under the pressure of a gross atmosphere. I have found dulness to quicken into sentiment in a thin ether, as water, though not very hot, boils in a receiver partly exhausted; and heads in appearance empty have teemed with notions upon rising ground, as the flaccid sides of a football would have swelled out into stiffness and extension.

The personality that presents us with this ingenious theory bears a marked family resemblance to the fatuous pedant of *A Tale of a Tub:* both are fond of the first person singular, and conscious of their own importance; both exude confidence, in themselves and in their solutions to old and knotty problems; both claim to be modest and public-spirited.

We can point also to satirical techniques in *Rambler* 117 that Johnson might have found consummately demonstrated in Swift. Before stating the scientific principles of his theory, Hypertatus runs effortlessly through selected classical precursors to enlist them in his support. This is argument by authority, a well-worn device of the Grub-Street scholar who tells *A Tale of a Tub.* Conscious violation of logic is the bread and butter of the paradoxical encomium, a favorite exercise of ironical humanists including Swift and the young Fielding; [13] thus Johnson argues that "agitation" excites the

13. Henry Knight Miller, "The Paradoxical Encomium," *MP* 53 (1956): 145–78, and *Essays on Fielding's Miscellanies* (Princeton, 1961), pp. 281–88. The traditional machinery of antiquarian learning is burlesqued in analogous ways in *Marmor Norfolciensis,* a mock-pedantic attack on Walpole similar to Swift's Bickerstaff tomfoolery, modeled in particular on "Merlin's Prophecy" (see Swift, *Prose Works,* ed. H. Davis, vol. 2 [Oxford, 1939], pp. 167–70). See Greene, *The Politics of Samuel Johnson,* pp. 96–108, for analysis of the two early satires in a "Swiftian vein" (*Marmor Norfolciensis* and *A Compleat Vindication of the Licensers of the Stage,* both 1739): Greene suggests that if the *Vindication* is "cruder than . . . some of

spirit, motion round the center of the earth is a form of agitation, therefore garret dwellers (who move around the earth faster than most people because farther from the center) excel in "gaiety and sprightliness."

Note, moreover, that Hypertatus is arguing the same general kind of theory that attracts the pedant of *A Tale of a Tub*. Section 1 of Swift's satire plays on the relation between physical altitude and philosophical eminence. The metaphysics of Aeolism (section 8) resolve all enthusiasm into wind. Both Johnson and Swift are practicing the complicated form of meiosis which attacks innovations in learning or religion by degrading the life of the spirit (by ironic fantasy) into a mere mechanical operation. Then, too, by its implication that to grow in wit and wisdom we have only to move into garrets, *Rambler* 117 is a variety of recipe, a Ready-and-Easy-Way, a Projector's Formula; these are major weapons in the war against the Dunces and in the Battle of the Books. In addition, Johnson had adopted for purposes of this essay the attitude of Swift and Pope and their friends that links authorship and poverty. Their vision of the Garrets of Grub Street, inhabited by Dunces and haunted by Duns, is part comedy, part poetry, part protest. Cackling contempt for starving scribblers was fashionable in the eighteenth century: Johnson is perfectly willing to ridicule poetasters and pedants, but this it one of the few cases on record where he laughs at poverty.[14]

Hypertatus, however, never succeeds in being as repulsive as the pedant of *A Tale of a Tub*. He does not foam at the mouth, or grovel and whine. Since the stateliness of his ex-

---

Swift's great pieces of irony, its faults arise from an excess of emotion, from the exuberance with which the scornful innuendoes come tumbling out one after another" (p. 101).

14. The Swarm-of-Scribblers hyperbole goes back to Juvenal, and had been a staple of satire in English since the seventeenth century; see Boileau, *Satire* 1 (1666); Dryden, *Essay of Dramatic Poesy* (1668), *Essays*, ed. Ker, 1 : 29–30; Halifax, *The Character of a Trimmer* (1684), *Complete Works*, ed. Walter Raleigh (Oxford, 1912), p. 47; see also Alvin Kernan, *The Cankered Muse* (New Haven, 1959), pp. 7–9. For Johnson's approval of attacks on incompetent authors, see *Lives*, 3 : 242; but his sympathy with impoverished authors is well known.

position is authentic, his jokes and sallies are a trifle stiff; the hand is not, as it is in Swift, quicker than the eye. Notice the deliberate way he parades his allusions in paragraph 6, to duns ("visitants, who talk incessantly of beer, or linen, or a coat") and to *Spectator* 412 ("some, yet more visionary, tell us that the faculties are inlarged by open prospects"). Hypertatus gets interested in his subject, and seems to enjoy the opportunity for inventiveness, with the result that we emerge from his letter amused, not jarred to the bone. The scholarly clothing in which Johnson dresses his argument is comfortable and conservative: there is, for example, more laughter than mockery in his allusion to Lucretius (fond of garrets, as we discover "in his description of the lofty towers of serene learning, and of the pleasure with which a wise man looks down upon the confused and erratic state of the world moving below him"). Swift, on the other hand, seems to attack not only the pedantry of floating an argument on footnotes, but also the authorities themselves.

"A Project for the Employment of Authors" (1756),[15] like *A Modest Proposal,* is a special form of recipe: it advertises a cure so much worse than the disease as to force the reader to reexamine his willingness to be sick; it is not parody, like *Rambler* 117, but reductio ad absurdum. Both Swift and Johnson face a problem of overpopulation—too many Irish, too many authors; both satires suggest solutions that are shocking because inhuman, and all the more shocking because plausible, because they seem to speak the language of *Realpolitik.*

Two birds can be killed with one stone, Johnson suggests; the shortage of soldiers can be supplied from the surplus of authors. Authors would make good soldiers because they are "used to suffer want of every kind," and "accustomed to obey the word of command from their patrons and booksellers,"

15. So titled in *Works* (1825), 5 : 355, though it was published originally as "Reflections on the Present State of Literature," in *The Universal Visiter,* April 1756. E. A. Bloom, *Samuel Johnson in Grub Street* (Providence, R. I., 1957), pp. 122–24, stresses the "lighter, more amusing" aspects of this satire. For comical aspects of *Rambler* 117, see W. K. Wimsatt, *Philosophic Words* (New Haven, 1948), pp. 119–21.

because "they have long made their minds familiar to danger, by descriptions of bloody battles, daring undertakings, and wonderful escapes." Some of them are, perhaps, a trifle "emaciated," and some "humbled and crushed" by patrons, but these can be fattened up or sheltered behind fife and drums. "Ladies of the pen" are harder to deal with:

> It is, indeed, common for women to follow the camp, but no prudent general will allow them in such numbers as the breed of authoresses would furnish. Authoresses are seldom famous for clean linen, therefore, they cannot make laundresses; they are rarely skilful at their needle, and cannot mend a soldier's shirt; they will make bad sutlers, being not much accustomed to eat. I must, therefore, propose, that they shall form a regiment of themselves, and garrison the town which is supposed to be in most danger of a French invasion. They will, probably, have no enemies to encounter; but, if they are once shut up together, they will soon disencumber the publick by tearing out the eyes of one another. [*Works* (1825), 5 : 362]

The quiet modulation from modesty to contempt in this passage is one of Swift's most effective gambits, as in the famous verdict of the Brobdingnagian monarch, which begins so accommodatingly and ends with "little odious vermin" crawling "upon the surface of the earth."

Johnson's vituperation, however, reaches its climax with the slaughter of lady authors. The "Project for Authors" only echoes Swift at isolated points: indeed, its most obvious weakness as satire is uncertainty of tone and attitude. The first eight paragraphs, despite sprinklings of irony, are serious and sympathetic. So long as Johnson is affirming the value of letters in general ("human life would scarcely rise, without them, above the common existence of animal nature"), he is in command of his own vehemence; but the realization in paragraph 9 that the cause of "the great misery of writers" is their "multitude," that literature is "open to every man whom idleness disposes to loiter," shakes his composure. If the suffering of authors is real, so is the suffering of "a toad under a harrow," or "a dog with a stick at his tail," in paragraph 11; and by paragraph 12, contempt has conquered sympathy. This is one of the very few of Johnson's satirical writings which end on a negative note. *Adventurer* 115, concerned like "A Project for Authors" with the swarms of scribblers in London, dips briefly into sarcasm but then addresses itself seriously to the problem and to possible solutions.

Johnson compares man to animals when he wants to describe pitiless cruelty or inexplicable suffering, a relatively infrequent objective for him. In "A Project for Authors," the scribbling tribe are tormented and hunted like beasts; in the *Review of a Free Enquiry,* man is likened to birds, fighting cocks, frogs, and kittens tortured for sport; in *The Rambler,* innocent youth is "parcelled out among the different ministers of folly, and . . . torn to pieces by taylors and jockeys, vintners and attorneys." [16] Animal imagery in Swift is far more abundant than in Johnson, and often used not merely to describe "inhumanity" but to degrade and humiliate mankind. Part 4 of *Gulliver's Travels* springs to mind, but think also of Gulliver in Brobdingnag, chased like a weasel, abducted by a monkey, and capsized by a frog, or of "The Beast's Confession." Johnson's anger, even in his most Swiftian moments, is adulterated with pity; Swift seems to despise his victims, or to want to give the impression of despising them. This difference emerges clearly from the original *Idler* 22, which was later withdrawn from the collected edition of *The Idler.*

Like Swift in "The Beast's Confession," Johnson introduces his satire as harmlessly as possible, with one or two general scientific remarks on the capacity for speech among animals. The animals of the Fourth Voyage of *Gulliver,* the Yahoos, also sneak up on us, appearing at first sight merely as peculiar fauna native to an uninhabited shore upon which Gulliver has been stranded by a highly plausible mutiny. In each case the object is to lull the reader into accepting a fiction which will not have succeeded unless it hurts.

Beast-satire is in effect a device of perspective, analogous to

16. *Rambler* 53; see also *Rambler* 175, and *Rambler* 176, par. 4. Cecil S. Emden, "Dr. Johnson and Imagery," *RES,* n.s. 1 (1950): 33, maintains that animal imagery occurs largely in Johnson's conversation, not in his writings.

the commentary of an alien but rational traveler, and related to *ingénu* satire in general. It acquires a special edge and bite by violating the assumption imbedded in Christian humanism that man is a higher form of life than other animals, set above them by rational and spiritual capacities in which they have no share. To let birds and beasts censure man is to debase him from his self-assumed eminence—apart from whatever relevance their censure may carry on its own merits. Johnson's satire in this respect has a theoretical advantage over Swift's, because his mother vulture, however wise in the ways of men, is still a vulture, and thinks in terms of pillage and prey; whereas Swift's horses are far more rational than human beings. It is from one point of view not especially disturbing that man does not measure up to the standards of Houyhnhnms, considering how high (or low? or wide of the mark? some ambiguity here) these standards are. But to be scolded for wastefulness and classified as a mobile vegetable by a being whose values are merely predatory, is, or ought to be, humiliating.

These judgments are established when the mother vulture tries to explain to her children the singular relationship between vultures and man. Man is too strong to be killed like rabbits and lambs, and would not qualify for the diet of vultures "had not nature, that devoted him to our uses, infused into him a strange ferocity," causing him to gather in "herds" which destroy one another with "fire which flashes along the ground." (The idea that man is as much the servant of beast as beast of man turns Genesis 1:26 upside-down, and in Pope and Montaigne counts against the old anthropocentric orthodoxy.) [17]

'But when men have killed their prey,' said the pupil, 'why do they not eat it? When the wolf has killed a sheep he suffers not the vulture to touch it till he has satisfied himself. Is not man another kind of wolf?' 'Man,' said the mother, 'is the only beast who kills that

17. *Essay on Man,* Ep. 3, lines 45–46; Montaigne, *Essais,* ed. M. Rat (Paris, 1958), 2 : 129–73; see *The Poems of Alexander Pope,* Twickenham ed., vol. 3, part 1 (London, 1950), pp. 95–96, notes to lines 27–46.

which he does not devour, and this quality makes him so much a benefactor to our species.'

Similar arguments may be found in Hobbes, in Rochester—"*Birds,* feed on *Birds. Beasts* on each other prey, / But Savage *Man* alone, does *Man,* betray"—and in Mandeville.[18] The young vultures find this wastefulness inexplicable, and so does their mother; she falls back on the opinion of "an old vulture who dwelt upon the Carpathian rocks," that "men had only the appearance of animal life, being really vegetables with a power of motion; and that as the boughs of an oak are dashed together by the storm, that swine may fatten upon the falling acorns, so men are by some unaccountable power driven one against another, till they lose their motion, that vultures may be fed." To this speculative vulture, it seems, human behavior appears as unreasonable and unspiritual as animal behavior did to Descartes; and the great conflicts of nations, where men are "driven one against another, till they lose their motion," are as mechanical as a collision of inert objects.[19]

The viewpoint of the family of vultures between whom this dialogue takes place, however, is less esoteric than that of the Carpathian sage: they accept the irrational savageness of man as a natural phenomenon. The young birds consider man-flesh "the natural food of a vulture," and their mother admits that "vultures would seldom feast upon his flesh, had not nature . . . devoted him to our uses." Human beings, in other words, act as though they were more interested in feeding scavengers than in their own welfare. This is bitter

18. "A Satyr against Mankind," lines 129–30. Compare Hobbes, *Leviathan,* part 2, ch. 17; Boileau, *Satire* 8; Mandeville, *The Fable of the Bees,* ed. F. B. Kaye (Oxford, 1924), 1 : 176–81, 2 : 238 ("No wild Beasts are more fatal to our Species, than often we are to one another"). But see also *Guardian* 153, *Free-Thinker* 114, and *Universal Spectator* 111, where beast-man comparisons are more whimsical than savage.

19. Johnson, *Works* (Yale), 2 : 320 n. 2. See Donald Greene, "Samuel Johnson and the Great War for Empire," *English Writers of the Eighteenth Century,* ed. John H. Middendorf (New York, 1971), pp. 55–58, for *Idler* 22 as "Johnson's response to the butchery at Ticonderoga and the conquest of Louisbourg."

enough, if we take it seriously. And yet the Houyhnhnm's indictment of European "Yahoos" is much more bitter: "Although he hated the *Yahoos* of this Country, yet he no more blamed them for their odious Qualities, than he did a *Gnnayh* (a Bird of Prey) for its Cruelty, or a sharp stone for cutting his Hoof. But when a Creature pretending to Reason, could be capable of such Enormities, he dreaded lest the Corruption of that Faculty might be worse than Brutality itself." The savagery of this passage depends on tone, because the momentum gained in the first sentence by impartiality enhances the shock value of the final period; and on content, because it postulates a degree of degeneracy below the subhuman, "worse than Brutality itself"—which is more hateful than mobile vegetation. Nevertheless, in both works satiric wit depends on the persuasiveness of the case for man's inferiority to beast.

Again, the relative innocence of Johnson's satire is a matter not only of the judgments and opinions it implies, but also of style. There is in *Idler* 22 no equivalent to the snarl of the king of Brobdingnag about "little odious vermin," or to Gulliver's crowded synopses of depravity and vice in part 4. Swift's working prose habitually employs the rhetoric of euphemism, of vulgar particulars and degrading generality tricked out in shabby-genteel idiom and cliché. The language of Johnson's vultures, by contrast, is genuinely modest and dignified—which blunts the edge of their judgment on man.

"Satyr is a sort of Glass"

Swift very seldom (if ever) intrudes as a character in his own prose satire; his irony expresses itself through a whole wardrobe of masks (not all of which are intended to hide his real feelings). Johnson has nothing of Swift's mobility in the use of mask or persona, and most of the time he takes pains to limit his irony to "a mode of speech in which the meaning is contrary to the words," as he defines it in the *Dictionary;* that is, to a figure of rhetoric which assigns blame quite unambiguously by praising, and vice versa. We are not permitted to doubt that Hypertatus is cracked-brained, or that his theories are ironically specious. The vultures of *Idler* 22 are stationed so that their criticisms make consistent sense, both literally, for vultures, and when translated into human perspectives. When Johnson's irony is directed at himself, however, its voltage rises, because simple questions of blame and praise fade away in the light cast by self-scrutiny. No man is a deep-dyed villain to himself; it is a measure both of Johnson's gifts as a writer and of his complexity as a man that when he steps into his own fiction the reign of simple moralism ends, and that he more than once succeeds in making art from introspection.

The portrait of Sober occupies paragraphs 9–12 of *Idler* 31. It is a dialogue of Johnson with himself about the quality of Sober's (Johnson's?) unhappiness or guilt: [20] its irony consists of a self-conscious multiplicity of oblique judgments, the sum of which is painful self-knowledge.

At least three distinct voices undertake the exposure and evaluation of Sober. He is introduced as a paragon among Idlers, as an expert in the art "by which life may be passed unprofitably away." He has practiced this art for many years "with wonderful success." In other words, he is introduced as an exemplum of total failure, in a voice of sarcastic hyperbole. But paragraph 9 continues: Sober's desires "can seldom stimulate him to any difficult undertaking"—for *seldom,* read *never.* His passions will not let him "lie quite at rest": this too is an understatement. The dry voice of ironic analysis in these phrases sounds to my ears quite different from the heavy sarcasm of "wonderful success." Paragraph 9 concludes by acknowledging that Sober is "weary of himself"—a third voice, faintly elegiac, the voice of Sober's unhappiness.

Paragraph 10: "Mr. Sober's chief pleasure is conversation; there is no end of his talk or his attention"—overstated sarcasm again. Sober gluts himself on conversation because "he still fancies that he is teaching or learning something"—according to the analysis of the second voice, Sober's dearest beliefs are merely "fancy," a quiet but discomfiting substitution.

Paragraph 11: "But there is one time at night when he

20. According to Mrs. Thrale (*Miscellanies,* 1 : 178), Johnson "intended" Sober "as his own portrait." Johnson's intentions need not determine how we respond to *Idler* 31, however.

must go home, that his friends may sleep"—no sleep for Sober?—"and another time in the morning, when all the world agrees to shut out interruption"—Sober alone of "all the world" thirsts to be interrupted and to interrupt. The impersonal construction here ("there is one time . . .") is a gentle parody of the portentousness with which an authentic emergency of aloneness might be described; Sober's need for conversation is so unnatural as to hurt him not once a month or so, in special circumstances, but twice in the normal cycle of a twenty-four-hour day: the mixture of compassion and derision in these sentences is very subtle, and does not seem to belong exclusively to any one of the three voices. The paragraph continues: "These are the moments of which poor Sober trembles at the thought"—*poor* Sober: condescension; but he *trembles:* sympathy? a far cry from the Sober of paragraph 9 who could not "lie *quite* at rest." "But the misery of these tiresome intervals, he has many means of alleviating"—now the moments at which Sober had shuddered with dread in the previous sentence are merely *tiresome,* a vexation, a nuisance: we have returned to the voice of crass ridicule. It carries us almost through the list of Sober's pastimes in paragraphs 11 and 12. In the last sentence of paragraph 12 the reiterated dripping of drops of "essence" from Sober's retort revives Johnson's sympathy and wakens the muse of boredom.

If any one of these three voices could express the whole truth about Sober, it would drown out the other two; but the portrait of Sober is shaped by Johnson's attitude toward him, which is a mélange of contradictory emotions—contempt, amusement, and compassion. Sober is quite different from such simple illustrative characters as Gelidus ("icy-cold"), who so obsessively personifies a moral defect as to be wholly inorganic.[21] (One other character in the periodical essays has something of the same range and intensity of atti-

21. *Rambler* 24. Other flat, illustrative characters: *Ramblers* 74, 98, 189, 206. The rhetorical or merely didactic use of characters is discussed by Quintilian in *Institutio Oratoria* 1.9.3, 9.1.31 and 44 (quoting Cicero). See Benjamin Boyce, *The Theophrastan Character in England to 1642* (Cambridge, Mass., 1947), pp. 11–52.

tudes, Dick Linger of *Idler* 21, who is, like Sober, dangerous not to the world around him but to himself.) The irony of *Idler* 31 is also distinctive, for a number of reasons: its toughness, unforgivingness, and unsentimentality; its sense of loss, of permanent damage done; the degree of responsibility it is willing to take. A useful contrast is the relatively rambunctious self-parody of *Rambler* 103, where the Rambler mocks periodical writers who compose flattering letters to themselves, and then swells with pride as he reads to himself just such a letter: [22] Johnson the man is not implicated here, cannot accuse himself of this particular kind of vanity, and so can relax.

Reflexive irony in *Idlers* 1–3 operates on a larger scale than in *Idler* 31; it seems less inhibited in tone, and less personal. As a serious comedy of morals, with something like exuberance to sustain it, and something like universality of relevance, this sequence of essays is, I think, Johnson's best prose satire.

The first paragraph of *Idler* 1 is a brief fidget on "the difficulty of finding a proper title" for a periodical essay. After that the Idler finds his feet, and embarks on a fine discussion of his own pertinence:

> It will be easily believed of the Idler, that if his title had required any search, he never would have found it. Every mode of life has its conveniencies. The Idler, who habituates himself to be satisfied with what he can most easily obtain, not only escapes labours which are often fruitless, but sometimes succeeds better than those who despise all that is within their reach, and think every thing more valuable as it is harder to be acquired.
>
> If similitude of manners be a motive to kindness, the Idler may flatter himself with universal patronage. There is no single character under which such numbers are comprised. Every man is, or hopes

22. Self-parody appears in a phrase or a line in *Ramblers* 10, 54, 109, 113, 119, 167. See also A. T. Elder, "Irony and Humour in the *Rambler*," *UTQ* 30 (1960): 57–71. Closely related are passages in the periodical essays where Johnson corrects his own positiveness: *Idlers* 16 and 18; *Ramblers* 135 and 138; *Ramblers* 147 and 157. See also an essay that complements and supplements my argument, Patrick O'Flaherty, "Johnson's *Idler:* The Equipment of a Satirist," *ELH* 37 (1970): 211–25.

to be, an Idler. Even those who seem to differ most from us are hastening to encrease our fraternity; as peace is the end of war, so to be idle is the ultimate purpose of the busy.

There is perhaps no appellation by which a writer can better denote his kindred to the human species. It has been found hard to describe man by an adequate definition. Some philosophers have called him a reasonable animal, but others have considered reason as a quality of which many creatures partake. He has been termed likewise a laughing animal; but it is said that some men have never laughed. Perhaps man may be more properly distinguished as an idle animal; for there is no man who is not sometimes idle. It is at least a definition from which none that shall find it in this paper can be excepted; for who can be more idle than the reader of the *Idler?* . . .

Scarcely any name can be imagined from which less envy or competition is to be dreaded. The Idler has no rivals or enemies. The man of business forgets him; the man of enterprize despises him; and though such as tread the same track of life fall commonly into jealousy and discord, Idlers are always found to associate in peace; and he who is most famed for doing nothing, is glad to meet another as idle as himself.

Since the purpose of *Idler* 1 is to establish the identity of the Idler, and to justify his claims to attention, it takes the form of demonstration, and makes its appeal through logic; we can feel the Idler prying at the tumblers of our minds with proofs inductive, deductive, analogical. Perhaps the Idler of this opening essay owes his attractiveness in some measure to his strong-mindedness. He is self-conscious, like the narrator of *Idler* 31, but he manipulates attitudes of attack and defense with a certain panache. His elegance, his expansiveness, help to make this "encomium" more "paradoxical": we are not intended to admire the Idler's efficiency or universality any more than we ought to respect the efficiency of a tyrant, or the universality of pride.

Nevertheless, the Idler makes some claims that we cannot brush off lightly. He has ethical standards: his tribe lives in peace, above the discord of competition and jealousy. He has literary standards: "conscious dulness has little right to be prolix." He has goals: the serenity and freedom from strife toward which, as he points out, most human effort is directed. His claim to universality, then, draws its power from the fact that it is true. "Who can be more idle than the reader of the *Idler?*" *Vous, hypocrite lecteur, mon semblable, mon frère.* An eighteenth-century Englishman, for whom essays like *The Idler* would count as light reading, might well feel that he had been maneuvered into self-indictment here.[23]

The remainder of *Idler* 1 informs us what kind of periodical essay Idleness will produce. In these paragraphs Johnson is working with what had by 1759 become a widely established convention; it was tacitly understood, or at least universally practiced, that in one of the first few numbers of a serial-essay periodical the author would declare his purposes, his biases political or aesthetic, his limitations, and his special subjects. He would often appeal to the reader for a charitable reception, as if in the prologue to a play, and protest his own inadequacy but sincerity. Johnson writes within this convention, but mocks it, again with half-serious results. He excuses himself from issuing a definite manifesto, on the basis of his antipathy to contracts (they destroy idleness). He promises "diminutive history" and "satire" because "the Idler is always inquisitive" and "naturally censorious." If any reader at this point begins to approve or applaud, Johnson gently knocks him down: "I think it necessary to give notice, that I make no contract, nor incur any obligation. If those who depend on the Idler for intelligence and entertainment, should suffer the disappointment which commonly follows ill-placed expectations, they are to lay the blame only on themselves."

23. "There is still a vast difference betwixt the slovenly butchering of a man, and the fineness of a stroke that separates the head from the body, and leaves it standing in its place. A man may be capable, as Jack Ketch's wife said of his servant, of a plain piece of work, a bare hanging; but to make a malefactor die sweetly was only belonging to her husband" (Dryden, "A Discourse concerning . . . Satire," *Essays*, ed. Ker, 2 : 93). Whether or not it can be counted among the excellences proper to Horatian satire, skill in trapping or fooling the reader played a significant and interesting part in satire of this period. Among its consequences were smoke screens concerning authorship, anonymous publication, pseudo-dedications, personae.

What Johnson does here is with fine insolence to twist a modest disclaimer, which is standard operating procedure, into an ethical reproof, which is not.

Idlers 2 and 3 continue to exploit the special privileges and insights of Idleness. Number 2 is largely a complaint that no one has written him either to praise or blame; but despite the inherent ungraciousness of the subject, the Idler manages to extort from it some uncomfortable reflections on the relation between fame and indolence. The first few paragraphs of *Idler* 3 consider the possibility that the world's supply of entertainment is running low. This idea, happily, deflects Johnson into a meditation on the plight of idlers in general, on pains which "the whole race of Idlers will feel with all the sensibility that such torpid animals can suffer"; the satire of *Idler* 3 is not so much logical as psychodramatic:

> When I consider the innumerable multitudes that, having no motive of desire, or determination of will, lie freezing in perpetual inactivity, till some external impulse puts them in motion; who awake in the morning, vacant of thought, with minds gaping for the intellectual food, which some kind essayist has been accustomed to supply; I am moved by the commiseration with which all human beings ought to behold the distresses of each other, to try some expedients for their relief, and to inquire by what methods the listless may be actuated, and the empty replenished.

This paragraph confronts us with something very like the mixture of disdain and sympathy that colored the portrait of Sober. We should recognize the duplicity of the Idler: first (in *Idler* 1) he defended indolence, then (in *Idler* 3), pretending to be worried about the "innumerable multitudes . . . freezing in perpetual inactivity," he attacks them as "torpid animals," as nestlings "gaping for intellectual food"; his solicitousness is certainly genuine, because idlers do suffer, but certainly also ironic because they deserve to suffer.

At the same time, if we remember that the architect of this duplicity was himself a prince of indolence, the irony of the Idler illuminates a doubly self-conscious irony in the author of *The Idler,* and the writing of *Idlers* 1–3, 21, and 31 becomes an act of self-knowledge more complex and revealing than any simple self-criticism because polarized around laughing, hurting, sneering personae all of whom bear a more-than-mechanical relation to their creator. A measure of the artistry required for complex self-satire like this is its rarity.[24] Horace invented it in his satires in defense of satire: (1) portraying himself as "weak-/Minded, uninventive, chary of, wary in, speech"; (2) a few lines further on picturing himself in a tight-lipped soliloquy ("'This is better . . . I'll be happier if I do that . . . my friends / Will like me for this . . . that was NOT nice'") and "once in a while toying with poetry"; (3) proclaiming himself "a fighter . . . from frontier stock," heroic defender of beleagured virtue. In book 2, no. 7 Horace dramatizes himself as the irascible object of his own slave's sermon on self-control, self-knowledge, and consistency. A producer could stage these poems as farce;[25] we can feel Horace laughing at himself—at the flat, sometimes foolish caricatures of himself that he chooses to project as voices in his satire; but this kind of laughter is only possible for someone supremely confident of himself and of the value of his own sophistication. Johnson's satire is the product of humility, not confidence, less cheerful, more personal, less uninhibited, more fundamentally divided against himself; his self-satire is tinged with remorse and darkened with melancholy.

24. Joan Webber, *The Eloquent "I": Style and Self in Seventeenth-Century Prose* (Madison, Wisc., 1968), treats self-consciousness within the conventions of Christian apology or confession, quite a different phenomenon from Johnson's. Kernan, *The Cankered Muse,* pp. 38 and 96–107, discusses Kinsayder as a spokesman for Marston whom Marston makes fun of in one or two passages; the element of self-mockery is too faint to be truly comparable to self-mockery in *The Idler*. Swift's poems include some pleasant self-satire, at the climax of "Cadenus and Vanessa," for example. For contradictory stances in Horace, see Niall Rudd, *The Satires of Horace* (Cambridge, 1966), pp. 90–92.

25. *Satires* 1.4.17–18 and 134–39, 2.1.34 (*Satires and Epistles of Horace,* trans. Smith Palmer Bovie [Chicago, 1959], pp. 52, 57, 100, except for "once in a while toying with poetry," my own paraphrase of lines 138–39, "ubi quid datur oti, / illudo chartis").

4 Oriental Tale and Allegory

> Whereas some say a Cloud is in his Head,
> That doth but shew how Wisdom's covered
> With its own mantles.
>
> Bunyan

Addison concludes *Spectator* 512 with "a Turkish tale, which I do not like the worse for that little oriental extravagance which is mixed with it." Extravagance of one sort or another is a common denominator of all varieties of oriental tale; they are intended to be exotic and surprising. This does not make them "pre-Romantic": there was never a time during the eighteenth or any other century when the bizarre and the marvelous were not appreciated, though the form of extravagance favored at any time will vary with the changing weather of literary standards and taste.

Although the *Arabian Nights* swept Europe from end to end in the first decade of the eighteenth century, it did not displace or extinguish some quite different kinds of "oriental" fictions, going back to Marlowe's *Tamburlaine* and much further, including not only heroic romance of the most conventional type but also didactic fables and clever, libertine *contes des fées*. Most of the stories in the big collections published to capitalize on the success of the *Arabian Nights* (*Turkish Tales, Chinese Tales, Mogul Tales*) were no more oriental than Louis XIV's wig: for example, large numbers were written by Thomas Simon Gueullette, who drew occasionally on oriental sources, but worked essentially in French modes of fiction, spinning out endless *galanteries* in a "clumsy and shallow" imitation of the "brilliant extravaganzas" of Count Anthony Hamilton.[1] Tales derived authentically from an Eastern manu-

1. Ernest A. Baker, *The History of the English Novel* (London, 1924–39), 5 : 57. See also Armand-Daniel Coderre, *L'Oeuvre romanesque de Thomas-Simon Gueullette* (Montpelier, 1934). The big collections: *Arabian*

script were usually mutilated on the way from Arabic or Turkish or Persic to French, and then vulgarized on the way from French to English.[2] Every so often some of the fantasy of the *Arabian Nights* survives translation, and we taste an extraordinary flavor through the grocery-store seasoning of the English versions. For the original *Arabian Nights* is uniquely fantastic, even to modern readers; no schooling in science fiction can prepare us for what we find in these three to four thousand pages, or dull the edge of our surprise at some of these episodes. I feel sorry for Byron and Coleridge, who had to make do with the sluggish and degenerate English translation of Galland's emasculated French (but not everyone would agree with me: the *Arabian Tales* "certainly abound with genius," wrote Robert Southey; "they have lost their metaphorical rubbish in passing through the filter of a French translation"). The first complete translations were published in limited, expensive editions in 1884 and 1886, limited be-

---

Nights, trans. from the French of M. Antoine Galland (1704–17); *Turkish Tales,* "Written originally in the Turkish Language, by Chec Zade," trans. from the French of Pétis de la Croix (1707; see D. F. Bond's note on *Spectator* 94); *Persian Tales,* trans. A. Philips from the French of Pétis de la Croix (1714); *The Travels and Adventures of Three Princes of Serendip,* trans. from the French of de Mailly (1722); *Chinese Tales,* trans. Thomas Stackhouse from the French of T. S. Gueullette (1725); Gueullette, *Mogul Tales* (1736); Comte de Caylus, *The Oriental Tales* (1745); Gueullette, *Tartarian Tales* (1759); James Ridley, *Tales of the Genii* (1764): and others later in the century. See Henry Weber, Introduction, *Tales of the East* (Edinburgh, 1812); Martha Conant, *The Oriental Tale in England in the Eighteenth Century* (New York, 1908); Georges Ascoli, Introduction, Voltaire's *Zadig* (Paris, 1929), pp. xlvii–lxv.

2. Galland's MSS were only one-sixth the length of the complete collection; he chopped it up arbitrarily into 1001 nights, omitting the poetry. Then he filled in gaps with stories from other sources (including the tales of Aladdin and Ali Baba), amounting in the end to more than one-third of the whole. He bowdlerizes, of course. The phrase "a son like the rising full moon" is omitted from the First Old Man's Story, Night 1—in deference to classical proprieties? See *The Book of the Thousand Nights and One Night,* trans. John Payne (London, 1884), and Payne's essay on the "History and Character" of the Arabic original, ibid. 9 : 263–392; Richard Burton, *The Book of the Thousand Nights and a Night* (London, 1886), 10 : 96–111 and Appendix 2.

cause many of the tales are truly, sometimes joyfully, erotic.

We may legitimately welcome the oriental tale in English as an exotic flower, a polychromatic splash amid the grays and browns of middle-class prose fiction before Richardson; but we are also forced to recognize that by and large these colorful plants are European species after all: after the multiple transfusions of translation, retranslation, and editing, most oriental tales in English have domestic blood types; they do not differ essentially from the kind of fable, romance, and satire we find in *The Spectator.*

Addison, for example, borrowed from the *Arabian Nights* an intriguing little story about the ingenious cure of a severe case of leprosy. The Arabic, in translations by Payne and Burton, relates this incident as a richly detailed and ceremonious negotiation between a great king and a still greater physician. Galland's version, in the English translation, follows the Arabic fairly closely, but makes the doctor subservient to the king, by adjusting his manner of address ("if you will *do me the honour to accept my service,* I will *engage* to cure you without drenches, or external applications") and by omitting certain meaningful details (the doctor's all-night deliberations and the house he rents to store books, scrolls, drugs, and aromatic roots). Addison reduces all this to a fable, a very brief anecdote with a surprising twist to it, out of which a moral is unexpectedly extracted. There was "a King who had long languished under an ill Habit of Body, and had taken abundance of Remedies to no purpose. At length, says the Fable, a Physician cured him by the following Method." He encloses drugs in a mallet, and orders the king to play polo until he sweats. "This Eastern Allegory is finely contrived to shew us how beneficial Bodily Labour is to Health, and that Exercise is the most effectual Physick." [3]

The commonest genre into which the oriental fictions trans-

3. See Payne's and Burton's *Arabian Nights,* Night 4, 1 : 45–48 and 1 : 38–39, respectively; *Tales of the East,* ed. Weber, Nights 11 and 12, 1 : 18–19 (Galland); *Spectator* 195. Other oriental tales reworked as fables: *Spectators* 289, 293, 512, 535; *Guardian* 99, 162; *Lay-Monk* 18; *Plain Dealer* 25; *Universal Spectator* 49.

late themselves is romance, stories of unquenchable passion, unexampled constancy, unbelievable generosity. The "beautiful Al-Raoulf" was sixteen, and "the graces had lavished all their charms" upon her "person." She read "many matters of gallantry" without feeling any special emotion. But Love "was offended" at her "simplicity," and "raised a revolt" in all her senses, so that she was "extremely smitten" without knowing how or why. One day she is reading aloud to a congenial company, and is "loaded with commendations." It is the praises of "a young Indian lord" that touch her most. Their "eyes met each other so frequently, and with such eager glances," that they are "soon made sensible of all the emotions of a violent passion. . . ."[4] Gueullette, whose worst is worse than this, manages to combine rituals derived from courtly love with those of a Parisian salon, in dull, threadbare prose. As a response to this kind of thing, the contempt for romance we talked about in chapter 1 makes perfectly good sense, and before *Pamela* (1740) no eighteenth-century English writer of romances did much better, not even Richard Steele.

Finally, orientalism may be fashioned into an occasion for satire. A major vehicle for this form of satire, the naive foreign traveler, is a specialty of the Enlightenment, and does not appear at all, so far as I know, in genuine oriental fiction. An example: in *Spectator* 557 an ambassador from Bantam complains that the English don't mean what they say: they put themselves at his service, but aren't; they beg him to make their house his own and then object when he knocks down a wall. Johnson works this vein in *Rasselas,* but not in the periodical essays.

Slovenly Prose in the Early Oriental Tales

Johnson uses orientalisms (a) to simplify and exaggerate experience, and thereby clarify its meaning, to escape from familiar contingencies into an environment almost hypothetically pure, and (b) to raise and ennoble his argument. The same forces that produce extravagant actions and rigged

4. See Gueullette, *Chinese Tales* (1725), cited from *The Novelists Magazine* 5 (1781): 29.

circumstances in the histories of Melissa and Cupidus work to eliminate circumstance and verisimilitude in the oriental tale. A rich man in an oriental tale is fabulously, incalculably rich, a wise man is a prophet or sage, and power exerts itself unhampered by legal or economic limitations, not to mention simple probability. Johnson's picture of oriental society is not diversified into particular customs and activities: the seeker after pleasure or amusement, for example, is not forced to hunt foxes or pay calls; he can confine himself chastely to major categories of experience.

The three oriental quests (*Ramblers* 120, 190, 204–05) show Johnson reworking his favorite narrative form to make it more universally relevant. The difference between Almamoulin's quest for happiness in *Rambler* 120 and Tim Ranger's in *Idlers* 62 and 64 is one of degree of generality: Tim starts to build a house, but leaves off when he realizes that "to build is to be robbed"; Almamoulin "built palaces, he laid out gardens, he changed the face of the land, he transplanted forests, he levelled mountains, opened prospects into distant regions, poured fountains from the tops of turrets, and rolled rivers through new chanels." It makes Tim seem pretty amateurish. Misocapelus, we recall, was easily discouraged, and abandoned some of his enterprises before he could possibly have exhausted their potential; here Johnson plugs that loophole by letting Almamoulin plunge into "domestick pleasures" on a gigantic scale. (*The Fountains*, a fairy tale Johnson wrote for Anna Williams's *Miscellanies* (1766), shows how far [illegible] willing to go to plug loopholes and to give his fiction [illegible]ity of a controlled experiment; he stoops even to mag[illegible] act of disinterested kindness, Floretta obtains from a[illegible]ry the power to acquire merely by wishing for it an[illegible] excellence at all. But of course no human excellen[illegible] wit, length of days) appeases the hunger of her im[illegible]very coin has two sides, and a cutting edge.)

Now since most oriental tales attempt at so[illegible]or-tray fabulous wealth, stunning beauty, or [illegible]er, they have at least the opportunity for the [illegible]d yet the language of oriental tales, before Jo[illegible], is on the whole flabby and pedestrian. Scheherazade's life depends on her ability to make her narrative sprint from one event to another, which leaves her little leisure for grand effects. The *Arabian Nights,* as Johnson would have read it, does not breathe hard over grandeur or power; its viziers and sultans bow on and off stage unobtrusively: "There was a king, who had a son that loved hunting mightily." Descriptions of phenomenal luxury detain the narrator a little longer, but they make their effect almost entirely by humdrum enumeration, without help from mellifluous periods or bold metaphors: "the castle, on three sides, was encompassed by a garden, with flowerpots, water-works, groves, and a thousand other fine things concurring to embellish it; and what compleated the beauty of the place, was an infinite number of birds, which filled the air with their harmonious notes, and always staid there, nets being spread over the trees, and fastened to the palace, to keep them in" (Night 21). The sentence limps to a conclusion, having spent its principal energies early, and frittered away precious syllables in windy superlatives ("and a thousand other fine things"). A prose style nearly resembling this—built on the same principles—could, I suppose, achieve a degree of luxuriousness by itemizing a sufficient number of luxurious objects (though at best the effect would be jumbled), but it could never achieve grandeur or dignity.

The *Persian Tales,* though translated by a man of some literary accomplishment (Ambrose Philips), adds little to the sum of elegance or magnificence in the language of the oriental tales. Its major appeal is to the "generous passions"; it is, as Philips claims in his preface, "very romantick"; nevertheless its attempts at hyperbole fall flat: "a hall of prodigious extent"; "the ladies washed their hands with the finest kind of paste of a most exquisite composition"; "an infinite number of tapers"; "she said a thousand diverting things."

None of these collections is free from blemishes all too common elsewhere in prose of the first half of the eighteenth century: the result clause used for emphasis, much too often; participle phrases used indiscriminately and profusely to record a fact or action regardless of how it is related to the main clause; slovenly coordination, clause joined to clause by means of loose adverbials and ill-apportioned relative pronouns, which has the effect of depriving verbs of their vitality and throwing the action or meaning of a sentence onto nouns; and a debilitated language of asseveration, vacant hyperbole. Syntactic peculiarities like the second and third items on this list are blemishes if we admire clarity and precision in narrative prose: the participle phrase is one of the least informative types of subordination, because it does not specify the logical relationship in which the dependent idea stands to the main idea. Item number 4, genteel periphrasis (as in the physician's speech to the king, above) is a weakness if the strength and vitality of language reside in its verbs.[5]

The prose style of oriental tales in *The Spectator* and later periodicals is neater but not noticeably more pretentious than the style of the *Arabian Nights.* Dream visions, some of them set in the Orient, occasionally rise above the safe mediocrity of the middle style, and when they do they anticipate in a wispy, flowery way the conscious grandeur of Johnson's oriental tales and allegories. A haggard old man in *Free-Thinker* 301 (by Zachary Pearce?), the personification of the old year just dying, turns to the dreamer "with a Countenance, as awful, as it was severe. 'Hear, O young Man, void of Understanding! Thou, who thinkest never to grow Old; and yet, growest Old, even whilest I speak. These Twelve long Months have I been with thee; these Twelve long Months have I observed Thee: and thou hast suffered my Weeks, my Days, and my Hours to perish, and pass away, as Water passeth. Behold, I likewise forsake thee, as the *Years* before me. . . ." [6] Elsewhere, oriental

5. For the importance of verbs in "strong" prose, see Donald Davie, *Articulate Energy* (London, 1955), pp. 43–52 (but see also pp. 52–55, 131–32). Of course strength is not the only virtue in prose style; but in the absence of any other virtue, lack of strength is indisputably a vice, except in very special situations where languidness is an intentional effect.

6. *Spectator* 159 (the vision of Mirza) and *Free-Thinker* 295 achieve special effects by imitating the Bible. For authorship of *Free-Thinker* 301, see Nicholas Joost, "The Authorship of the *Free-Thinker,*" *Studies in the Early English Periodical,* ed. R. P. Bond (Chapel Hill, N.C., 1957), pp. 116–17.

language is supposed to be "rich and figurative," as William Collins declares in his preface to the *Persian Eclogues* (1742); it is supposed to excel in "Elegancy and Wildness of Thought." These poems, however, do not venture much beyond the commonplaces of pastoral complaint, except for a sprinkling of allusions to "*Balsora's* Pearls" and the like. Clara Reeve in 1785 ranked the story of Sinbad with Homer, but only with respect to the wildness of its "imagination" and "machinery," not grandeur of language.[7]

The Rhetorical Sublime

The language of hyperbole in Johnson's oriental tales is more than grand, it is supercolossally splendid, though never for very long at a time. His Arabs and Indians stride onstage in a gilded shower of images and comparisons, but the fanfare dies down when the action begins. Gross inequalities in the language, which inflates and deflates at uncertain intervals, contribute to the impression of unripeness and lopsidedness that most of these stories give. Of the eight oriental tales, six (*Ramblers* 120, 190, 204–05; *Idlers* 75, 99, 101) chronicle the same kind of incidents as Johnson's non-oriental stories, a fact that sometimes makes for incongruities, as when the frustrations of British systems of higher education and patronage are transplanted intact to Persia in *Idler* 75. We are concerned at present, however, not with inequalities and absurdities in Johnson's oriental tales, but with their experiments in the rhetorical sublime. The magnificence of the language of (what boils down finally to) a small number of passages serves in effect to elevate the choice of life to heroic altitudes.[8]

7. *The Progress of Romance* (Dublin, 1785), 1 : 22–23. P.-D. Huet in 1670 traced romance back to "Egyptians, Arabs, Persians and Syrians, with their fondness for allegory, fable and metaphor" (*The History of Romances*, trans. S. Lewis [1715], pp. 13–14).

8. That Johnson significantly elevated the language of the oriental tale was first formally noticed—not, on the whole, sympathetically—by Martha Conant, *The Oriental Tale*, p. 90ff. A problem with which no one, so far as I know, has dealt is the relation of new subtleties of eighteenth-century prose style—high, low, and middle—to the language of the stage. Heroic drama, frequently set in the Orient, has its own conventions of bombastic

Johnson's biggest guns are fired in saluting his heroes and in testifying to their power (so that, as we have seen, they may approach perfect freedom in the choice of life). Several of these big guns deserve particular notice:

Hyperbole presuming the vassalage of nature. In *Rambler* 120 Nouradin is so rich that "the sea was covered with his ships; the streams of Oxus were wearied with conveyance, and every breeze of the sky wafted wealth" to him. In *Rambler* 190 "the sun grew weary of gilding the palaces of Morad." Seged, of *Ramblers* 204–05, "the distributer of the waters of the Nile," "sailed jocund over the lake, which seemed to smooth its surface" before him. Conceits like these are not uncommon in poetry—"The suns were weary'd out with looking on, / And I untir'd with loving," says Antony in *All for Love*—but rare in prose. Sidney's *Arcadia* is so far as I have been able to discover the only well-known English narrative that indulges in them freely.[9] Their proper domain is exalted praise.

Exotic (biblical) similes: "a voice gentle as the breeze that plays in the evening among the spices of Sabaea"; "fresh as the vernal rose, and strong as the cedar of the mountain"; "transitory, as the odour of incense in the fire"; "numerous as the locusts of the summer" (*Ramblers* 38, 120, 190, 204). The orientalism of such phrases is rather bland; we shall comb *The Rambler* in vain for images and descriptions calculated to evoke specific scenes, sounds, and smells from Arabia or Persia—perhaps because Near Eastern literature was most eloquently represented for Johnson not by the *Arabian Nights* or its jaded imitations but by the Bible. Cedar trees, incense, and dew appear in similes in the Psalms, roses and spices in

---

rhetoric. On the importance of sententiousness and didacticism in the oriental tales, see Arthur J. Weitzman, "The Oriental Tale in the eighteenth century: a reconsideration," *Studies on Voltaire and the Eighteenth Century* (1967) 58 : 1839–55.

9. *All for Love,* act 2, scene 1. "But when she was imbarked, did you not marke how the windes whistled & the seas daunst for joy, how the sailes did swel with pride, and all because they had *Urania?*" "and these fresh and delightful brookes how slowly they slide away, as loth to leave the company of so many things united in perfection" (Sidney, *Works,* ed. A. Feuillerat [Cambridge, 1922–23], 1 : 6, 57).

the Song of Solomon. The most elaborate simile in Johnson's oriental tales makes sense as a slightly contorted echo of the Psalms:

> Look backward a few days, thy father was great and happy, fresh as the vernal rose, and strong as the cedar of the mountain; the nations of Asia drank his dews, and art and commerce delighted in his shade. Malevolence beheld me, and sighed: His root, she cried, is fixed in the depths; it is watered by the fountains of Oxus; it sends out branches afar, and bids defiance to the blast; Prudence reclines against his trunk, and Prosperity dances on his top. Now, Almamoulin, look upon me withering and prostrate; look upon me, and attend. [*Rambler* 120]

The righteous man of the first Psalm is "like a tree planted by the rivers of water, that bringeth forth his fruit in his season; his root also shall not wither." In Psalm 92 the man of God is a palm tree, and a cedar of Lebanon; "those that be planted in the house of the Lord shall flourish in the courts of our God. They shall bring forth fruit in old age; they shall be fat and flourishing." The Vine of Jehovah (Psalm 80) has taken "deep root," and "filled the land. The hills were covered with the shadow of it, and the boughs thereof were like the goodly cedars." [10]

10. According to Boswell, Johnson "disapproved of introducing scripture phrases into secular discourse" (Boswell, 2 : 213). But some of the periodical essays do exactly that. *Adventurer* 120 quotes from the Bible eight times. W. K. Wimsatt, *The Prose Style of Samuel Johnson* (New Haven, 1941), Appendix E, discusses the influence of the Book of Common Prayer on Johnson's style. Most commonly for eighteenth-century readers biblical language meant passion (see *Spectator* 405), simplicity, and sublimity (see S. H. Monk, *The Sublime* [1935; rpt. Ann Arbor, Mich., 1960], pp. 77–82). See also C. S. Lewis, *The Literary Impact of the Authorized Version* (London, 1950), p. 20.

Robert Dodsley's *The Economy of Human Life* (1750) is an interesting example of mannered prose that purports to be oriental (Tibetan) but sounds like the Bible—much more like the Bible than Johnson's oriental tales. It was exceedingly popular, a kind of eighteenth-century Kahlil Gibran. I quote from part 1, sect. 1, "Consideration" (ed. cited London, 1806):

> The thoughtless man bridleth not his tongue; he speaketh at random, and is entangled in the foolishness of his own words.

Full-sentence parallelism. The famous Johnsonian doublets and triplets are *inlaid* into a sentence or a clause: antithesis and parallels occur most of the time within a sentence the syntax of which is different from that of the sentences preceding and following it. "The world has been long amused with the mention"—thus begins paragraph 5 of *Rambler* 79, and the antithesis that follows is part of the predicate—"of policy in publick transactions, and of art in private affairs." In the remainder of this sentence, parallelism plays a modest role: "they have been considered as . . . and as . . . : yet I have not found many performances either of art, or policy, that required . . . or might not have been effected. . . ." The next sentence is far more elaborate: its subject is a compound infinitive phrase of five members, the first two of which govern parallel noun clauses, the third a compound direct object modified by exactly parallel prepositional phrases, the fourth and fifth parallel objects accompanied by parallel adverb phrases; and its predicate comes home to roost in a trebly compounded direct object trebly modified by adjective clauses.[11] My point is that in this paragraph, as elsewhere in Johnson

---

As one that runneth in haste, and leapeth over a fence, may fall into a pit which he doth not see; so is the man that plungeth suddenly into any action, before he hath considered the consequences thereof.

Hearken therefore unto the voice of Consideration; her words are the words of Wisdom, and her path shall lead thee to safety and truth.

For an imitation of this, also very popular, see William Kenrick, *The Whole Duty of Woman* (1751).

11. "The world has been long amused with the mention of policy in publick transactions, and of art in private affairs; they have been considered as the effects of great qualities, and as unattainable by men of the common level: yet I have not found many performances either of art, or policy, that required such stupendous efforts of intellect, or might not have been effected by falsehood and impudence, without the assistance of any other powers. To profess what he does not mean, to promise what he cannot perform, to flatter ambition with prospects of promotion, and misery with hopes of relief, to soothe pride with appearances of submission, and appease enmity by blandishments and bribes, can surely imply nothing more or greater than a mind devoted wholly to its own purposes, a face that cannot blush, and a heart that cannot feel."

outside the oriental tales, parallelism, however intricate, takes place for the most part within each sentence, and not between sentences. But in purple passages from the oriental tales, full sentences mirror one another:

> Thus in the twenty-seventh year of his reign, spoke Seged, the monarch of forty nations, the distributer of the waters of the Nile. "At length, Seged, thy toils are at an end, thou hast reconciled disaffection, thou hast suppressed rebellion, thou hast pacified the jealousies of thy courtiers, thou hast chased war from thy confines, and erected fortresses in the lands of thy enemies. All who have offended thee, tremble in thy presence, and wherever thy voice is heard, it is obeyed. Thy throne is surrounded by armies, numerous as the locusts of the summer, and resistless as the blasts of pestilence. Thy magazines are stored with ammunition, thy treasuries overflow with the tribute of conquered kingdoms. Plenty waves upon thy fields, and opulence glitters in thy cities. Thy nod is as the earthquake that shakes the mountains, and thy smile as the dawn of the vernal day. In thy hand is the strength of thousands, and thy health is the health of millions. Thy palace is gladdened by the song of praise, and thy path perfumed by the breath of benediction. Thy subjects gaze upon thy greatness, and think of danger or misery no more. [*Rambler* 204]

The syntax and structure of this paragraph, which does not end here but continues with a string of parallel rhetorical questions, are far simpler than that of the many-branched and interlaced clauses of paragraph 5 of *Rambler* 79; its general effect is more majestic.

The diction of command. "Fly not from your benefactor, children of the dust"; "speak not rashly; consider . . ." (*Rambler* 38); "look upon me withering and prostrate; look upon me, and attend" (*Rambler* 120); "hear therefore the precepts of ancient experience, let not my last instructions issue forth in vain" (*Rambler* 190); "at length, Seged, reflect and be wise" (*Rambler* 204). Stephen Dedalus refers to a certain verbal mannerism as a "spiritual-heroic refrigerating apparatus"—could we call this of Johnson "a bardic-pathetic indoctrinating apparatus"? It strikes a pose prophetic and big with authority. Analogues for the diction of command and full-sentence parallelism of Johnson's oriental tales may also be found in the Bible.[12]

A busy supporting cast of moral personifications. "Competition withdrew into the cavern of envy, and discontent trembled at her own murmurs." "I said to defamation, who will hear thee? and to artifice, what canst thou perform?" (*Rambler* 190). Five personified abstractions cluster round that extraordinary cedar tree in *Rambler* 120, art and commerce in its shade, malevolence beholding it, prudence reclining against its trunk, and prosperity dancing on its top—which is of course a principal reason why this tree seems to grow in hothouse soil, not in the clear air of the Bible lands. Justice should be done not only to the dignity of these personifications (we may be sure they did not seem as stiff to eighteenth-century readers as they do to us), but also to their capacity to concentrate a great deal of matter into few words. "Competition withdrew into the cavern of envy, and discontent trembled at her own murmurs": what this means is that the people who would ordinarily be competing with Morad have had to restrict themselves to envying him, because Morad is so far ahead of everyone else that competition is hopeless, and anyone who might wish to complain about this state of affairs knows enough about Morad's power to be afraid to complain audibly. Johnson's way of saying it is at once compact, pictorial, dramatic.[13]

Pictorial elements (1): Throne-room scenes. In the beginning of *Rambler* 190 we are informed that certain "emirs and visiers . . . stand at the corners of the Indian throne." Then, in an explanatory codicil, we are told that they "assist the counsels or conduct the wars of the posterity of Timur." They are presented to us first of all visually, in a formal posture as part of a scene or spectacle, standing in their official positions

12. "Give ear, O my people, to my law: incline your ears to the words of my mouth" (Psalm 78 : 1). See also, e.g., Psalms 2 : 10–11, 3 : 7, 4 : 1, 5 : 1, 13 : 3. "Thou hast rebuked the heathen, thou hast destroyed the wicked, thou hast put out their name for ever and ever" (Psalm 9 : 5)—compare the first sentence of Seged's speech to himself quoted above.

13. See Morton W. Bloomfield, "A Grammatical Approach to Personification Allegory," *MP* 60 (1963): 161–71; Chester F. Chapin, *Personification in Eighteenth Century English Poetry* (New York, 1955), chs. 2 and 3.

as they might appear in a heroic portrait of the emperor; this image conveys information iconologically: anyone who stands at the corners of a throne is one of the king's henchmen, by virtue of the conventions that govern such spectacles.[14]

And anyone who stands "trembling" in front of a throne is a suppliant, or an inferior, or a witness to the greatness of the personage enthroned: "every eye was cast down" before Morad; Seged tells himself that "all who have offended thee, tremble in thy presence . . . Thy throne is surrounded by armies" (using the verb *surround* in its graphic, not military, sense); Almamoulin "stood trembling" before the princess of Astracan, who received him sitting on a throne, "attired in the robe of royalty, and shining with the jewels of Golconda." The pictures drawn by these locutions are faint, but there is evidence that the eighteenth century responded to them much more energetically as pictures than we do. The first lines from "A Song for St. Cecilia's Day,"

> When Jubal struck the corded shell,
> His list'ning brethren stood around,
> And, wond'ring, on their faces fell
> To worship that celestial sound

provoked in Joseph Warton an unequivocal reaction: "This is so complete and engaging a history piece, that I knew a person of taste who was resolved to have it executed on one side of his saloon: 'In which case, (said he) the painter has nothing to do, but to substitute colours for words, the design being finished to his hands.' "[15]

Pictorial elements (2): Icons and emblems. Scattered at various points among the oriental tales are "the sheaves of plenty," "the sabre of destruction," "the bowers of ease," "the

14. Jean H. Hagstrum, *The Sister Arts* (Chicago, 1958), p. 206. In *Paradise Lost,* bk. 2, lines 1, 43, 108, the first three speakers of the Council in Hell are positioned (a) "high on a throne," (b) "next him," (c) "on the other side"; note the way statues in *The Temple of Fame* (by Pope) are placed in lines 75, 93, 109, 145, 149–51, 161 (Alexander on a throne, other heroes standing, Epaminondas "High o'er the rest").

15. *An Essay on the Genius and Writings of Pope* (London, 1806), 1 : 51–52 (cited in Hagstrum, *The Sister Arts,* p. 131).

gardens of pleasure," "the keys of riches," "the sabre of command," "the clouds of sorrow," "the tempest of hatred," "the keys of trust," and "the seals of secrecy" (*Ramblers* 38, 65, 190; *Idler* 101). Such figures are not always pictorial, not always placed or disposed in a picturable way, but they have always some visual appeal, and often by their association with a person or a personification, they function as symbolic detail in an allegorical scene. Some are proper icons, of the kind that appear on coins or in allegorical painting. The lady representing Africa in a figure for Addison's *Dialogue upon Medals* (1721) holds a sheaf of corn, "to denote her wonderful fruitfulness." Shaftesbury, in formulating directions for the clothing and accouterments of Virtue in a painting of the Choice of Hercules, mentions a number of possible symbolic ornaments, rejects some because they "would be discoverable only by the learned," and in the end counsels that Virtue be pictured "as she is seen on medals, and other ancient emblematic pieces of like nature." [16] Icons in this sense, the meaningful paraphernalia of a personified vice or virtue, had been cataloged in Cesare Ripa's *Iconologia* as early as 1593, and widely exploited in masques, emblem books, sculpture, and painting throughout the seventeenth century.[17] As the eighteenth century wore on, iconic ornament fell from favor. Addison dreams a dream in *Tatler* 100 (1709), and is approached by what he thinks is an angel, until, "upon a nearer view, I saw about her, all the emblems with which the goddess of justice is usually described"; and the youthful Pope equips Envy with snakes,

16. Addison, *Works,* ed. G. W. Greene (Philadelphia, 1864), vol. 2, medal 2 in Series 3 of plates, and p. 92; Shaftesbury, *Second Characters: or the Language of Forms,* ed. Benjamin Rand (Cambridge, 1914), pp. 42–43.

17. See Émile Mâle, "La clef des allégories . . . au XVIIe et au XVIIIe siècle," *Revue des Deux Mondes,* 7th ser. 39 (1927): 106–29, 375–94; Erwin Panofsky, *Meaning in the Visual Arts* (Garden City, N.Y., 1957), pp. 146–68; Mario Praz, *Studies in Seventeenth-Century Imagery,* 2d ed. (Rome, 1964). Another repository for icons and emblems was pantheons, e.g., Samuel Boyse, *A New Pantheon: or, Fabulous History of the Heathen Gods, Heroes, Goddesses,* etc. . . . *Adorn'd with Figures depicted from ancient Paintings, Medals and Gems, for the Use of those who would understand History, Poetry, Painting, Statuary, Coins, Medals,* etc. (London, 1753).

Poetry with swans; but Collins's personifications are realized in psychological terms, and by delicate pastoral and literary allusion, not by inventories of iconic furniture.[18]

Exactly where icon ceases to be icon and begins to be emblem is hard to say (there has never been agreement on the nomenclature of symbolic objects)—the emblem books were eclectic and overlap with Ripa at many points; Ripa was eclectic too, and collected symbols from wherever he could find them, including early emblem books. But emblem was descended from *impresa,* and second cousin to the metaphysical conceit; it strove to be erudite and enigmatic. Although a taste for the old hieroglyphic emblem lingered on, in odd nooks and corners (on Clarissa's coffin, for example), the victory of clarity over obscurity and didacticism over ingenuity was virtually complete in the eighteenth century. Addison condemns pedantry among the virtuosos in much the same terms as he condemns "mixed wit." Johnson's emblems are never obscure: they never show themselves without a label, and are tightly chained to the abstractions that explain them. Commonly they assume a form that can be constructed from an attributive genitive reversed, with a concrete noun performing the symbolic function: "the commandingness of military power" becomes "the sabre of command"—a Hebraism, like "oil of gladness," "robe of righteousness." [19] We may be sure that such emblems are designed to sound a heroic note, because they fall flat if they try to use commonplace objects, "the rifle of command," "the stock-certificate of riches."

18. *Windsor Forest,* line 419; *Temple of Fame,* line 210. Not that icons and emblems disappear in the second half of the century; see *The World* (1753), nos. 24 and 25; Reynolds, *Discourse* 6 (1774), in *Works* London, (1798), 1 : 96. The frontispiece to vol. 1 of the *Encyclopédie* (1751) is full of icons out of Ripa.

19. John Eadie, *The English Bible* (London, 1876), 2 : 228–30, points out that the "sons of . . ." idiom in Hebrew is often avoided in translation because it seems foreign: sons of sheep, sons of lightning, sons of the bow. Compare Johnson, "children of the dust" (*Rambler* 38), "the sons of valour and wisdom," "sons of art" (*Rambler* 190), "the sons of swiftness" (Arabs, in *Irene,* act 2, scene 6, line 54), "sons of enterprise" (pioneers, in *Taxation No Tyranny*). For Addison on pedantic interpretations of medals, see *Works* (1864), 2 : 8–9.

Stylistic contrivances of this kind help to differentiate the language of the oriental tales from that of the usual Johnsonian narrative; all of them make for rhetorical sublimity: not the natural sublime with its mountains and chasms, but elevated verbiage fit for weighty themes and the big genres. Whatever aura of the Bible Johnson might manage to communicate would count for sublimity, since the Bible ranked near the top of almost everyone's list of sublime writings. Personification was considered the child of passion, a figure notable for its boldness and serviceable for sublimity. Since "by their bold *Metaphors,* and figurative *Style,* we find authors of Arabia and Persia were more than any other People addicted to *Sublimity* of *Expression,*" their Western imitators might be presumed to have a certain "Elegancy and Wildness of Thought" [20]—and perhaps Johnson's most florid passages deserved to be called 'wildly elegant'—except that they are too monumental to be wild.

Theories of Allegory

The perspective of the author of 1792 who ranked Johnson with Spenser and Bunyan as an allegorist is foreign to us, but the eighteenth century took its large corpus of short allegorical visions and dreams seriously. Many of them appeared in periodical essays that were trying to duplicate if not the character at least the success of *The Spectator;* others were published, like Johnson's "Vision of Theodore, Hermit of Teneriffe," as pleasing-but-wholesome intermissions to drier discourses. They were very popular, if we can believe Addison's reference to "this inundation of dreams, which daily flows in upon me" (and similar references by Swift, Fielding, and

20. Hildebrand Jacob, cited Monk, *The Sublime,* p. 61. "There is nothing like sense in the true eastern style, where nothing more is required but sublimity. Oh for an history of Aboulfaouris, the grand voyager, of genii, magicians, rocks, bags of bullets, giants, and enchanters, where all is great, obscure, magnificent, and unintelligible" (Goldsmith, *Citizen of the World,* Letter 33). For passion and personification, see Earl R. Wasserman, "The Inherent Values of 18th Century Personification," *PMLA* 65 (1950): 435–63.

Goldsmith).[21] Like other petit-genres of the Renaissance and eighteenth century, including Character and fable, allegory was frequently conceived and executed as a rhetorical exercise, "a figurative discourse, in which something other is intended, than is contained in the words literally taken; as, *wealth is the daughter of diligence, and the parent of authority.*" This sentence from the *Dictionary* (the harmless drudge is cheering himself on) is Johnson's only explicit contribution to the theory of allegory: the definition is broad enough, but the italicized example reduces allegory to a form of metaphor, an extended figure of speech.[22] So conceived, allegory is likely to make its bow and retire without loitering: "allegories drawn to great length will always break," says Johnson of an allegory that is, compared to many one might name, Lilliputian in dimensions, *Absalom and Achitophel.* Moreover, it is "always a fault in allegory to be too dark," as Hugh Blair puts it later in the century, thus repudiating, for example, *The Faerie Queene,* a "darke conceit clowdily enwrapped in Allegorical devises." [23]

21. *Spectator* 524; Swift, *Harrison's Tatler* 5, in *Prose Works,* ed. H. Davis, vol. 2 (Oxford, 1939), p. 178; Fielding, *Champion,* in *Works,* ed. L. Stephen (London, 1882), 5 : 227. The "author of 1792" is William Roberts, in *The Looker-On,* May 22, 1792. For copious evidence of the popularity of these allegories in the eighteenth century, see Edwin C. Heinle, "The Eighteenth Century Allegorical Essay," Ph.D. dissertation, Columbia University, 1957. I found Mr. Heinle's research very useful.

22. For allegory as an extended figure of speech, see Quintilian, *Institutio Oratoria,* 8.6.44ff.; *Spectator* 537; Anthony Blackwall, *An Introduction to the Classics,* 6th ed., with Additions (London, 1746), pp. 164–66—this last was included as part 5 of *The Preceptor;* see Hazen, p. 173.

23. *Lives,* 1 : 436–37 (Johnson means that a long allegory will certainly be inconsistent with itself sooner or later); *The Faerie Queene* is described as a "darke conceit" in Spenser's "Letter to Raleigh," usually reprinted with *The Faerie Queene* itself. For brevity as a virtue in allegory, see Pope's headnote to *The Temple of Fame,* in *The Poems of Alexander Pope,* Twickenham ed., vol. 2 (London, 1940), p. 243. For clarity, see John Hughes (whose essay Johnson praised, *Lives,* 2 : 162), "An Essay on Allegorical Poetry," *The Works of Spenser* (1715; ed. cited London, 1750), pp. xxxv–xxxvii; Addison, *Works* (1864), 2 : 24–26; Hugh Blair, *Lectures on Rhetoric and Belles Lettres* (1783; ed. cited Carbondale, Ill., 1965), 1 : 316–17.

Eighteenth-century writers justified the brevity, clarity, and didacticism of their allegories on strictly orthodox grounds, as imitations of the classics, since what they liked best among Greek and Roman allegories conformed to these standards. Plato wrapped up arguments in brief allegories. Both the "Choice of Hercules" and the *Tablet* of Cebes, the two best known and most widely copied classical allegories, are short and improving. According to Addison, it was by considering "what Homer, or Plato, or any other of those heroes in the learned world, would have said or thought" upon a given occasion that he "revived several antiquated ways of writing," among them "those allegories wherein virtues, vices, and human passions are introduced as real actors." Though the personification allegories he has in mind may seem to us feeble and contrived, they were supposed to sweep the reader off his feet; the consulting of "Homer, or Plato, or any other of those heroes in the learned world" is a "rule in Longinus" for "an author who would attain to the sublime, and writes for eternity." [24]

I have incorporated two of Johnson's pronouncements into this summary account of the theory and practice of eighteenth-century personification allegory because it seems to me that on this issue Johnson sticks pretty much to the party line. He is more touchy, in the *Lives of the Poets,* about logical consistency than are some critics, though Addison, Hughes, Blackwall, and Blair warn against inconsistency in general terms. *Spectator* 357 cites the same example of over-extended personification allegory (in Aeschylus, Strength and Necessity nailing down Prometheus) as does Johnson in the "Life of Milton," but whereas Addison praises the allegory of Sin and Death in book 10 of *Paradise Lost,* Johnson condemns it. Can the apparent contradiction between Johnson's principles in the *Lives*—"allegorical persons . . . may produce effects, but cannot conduct actions, . . . Discord may raise a mutiny, but Discord cannot conduct a march"—and his practice in *The Rambler,* where Truth conducts a march, and Wit erects buildings, be resolved in terms of genre?

24. *Guardian* 152; *Spectator* 183.

Again, Addison provides a clue to the way Johnson might have been thinking: "beautiful extended allegories are certainly some of the finest compositions of genius; but . . . are not agreeable to the nature of an *heroic poem*," however delightful they may be in a periodical essay like *The Spectator*.[25]

The Conditions of Choice

Five of Johnson's nine allegories fulfill in their own gilt-and-tinsel way one of the functions of myth: they are imaginary prehistories of the evolution of life as we know it. In *Ramblers* 3, 22, 33, 91, and 96, time passes, and events happen in a consecutive sequence of causes and effects, as the explanation of some aspect of things-as-they-are. *Rambler* 3 tells us why Time is the only reliable judge of excellence in art; it is because Criticism, a goddess armed with the torch of Truth, wearied "of attending . . . doubtful claims," and simply deserted mankind, taking Justice with her back to heaven. In *Rambler* 91 Patronage, "who was but half a goddess," made mistakes, "began to degenerate," cohabited with Pride, gave birth to Caprice and Flattery, and eventually exiled the Sciences to the cottage of Independence—which is why poets and scholars are not pampered nowadays. Addison has faint adumbrations of this kind of allegory (e.g., *Spectator* 183 and *Tatler* 146),[26] but nothing so interesting or fully developed as the best of this group by Johnson, *Rambler* 33.

In this "allegorical history of rest and labour" (as the table of contents names it), time passes, in a series of scenes and triumphs. One set piece succeeds another, personified abstractions make grand entrances, equipped with emblems appropriate to their office; and where there is human response, that is, where humanity is required to register the effect of the

25. *Lives*, 3 : 233; *Spectator* 357 (my italics).

26. Other examples: Thomas Parnell, "An Allegory on Man," *Poems on Several Occasions* (London, 1726), pp. 140–46 (facetious and witty, not grand); Mark Akenside, "Ambition and Content: A Fable," *Gentleman's Magazine* 7 (1737): 309. See also *The Student*, Supplement to 1 (1750): 361–64, an allegory on Wit and Beauty that postdates, by a little, *Ramblers* 22 and 33.

behavior of the abstractions who are the principal actors, it is unanimous, mechanical, and vehement (compare Melissa's friends' posturings in *Rambler* 75). As a result the action of *Rambler* 33 is tinny and ritualistic.[27] The conception of allegory as "figurative discourse" has also undoubtedly something to do with the absence of humanness and personality in Johnson's allegory, and it hampers the establishment of an encompassing fictive domain such as Spenser's Faerie-Land.

The first set piece in *Rambler* 33 is a luxurious tableau:

> In the early ages of the world, as is well known to those who are versed in antient traditions, when innocence was yet untainted, and simplicity unadulterated, mankind was happy in the enjoyment of continual pleasure, and constant plenty, under the protection of Rest; a gentle divinity, who required of her worshippers neither altars nor sacrifices, and whose rites were only performed by prostrations upon tufts of flowers in shades of jasmine and myrtle, or by dances on the banks of rivers flowing with milk and nectar.
>
> Under this easy government the first generations breathed the fragrance of perpetual spring, eat the fruits, which, without culture, fell ripe into their hands, and slept under bowers arched by nature, with the birds singing over their heads, and the beasts sporting about them.

The sources of this earthly paradise are not the meadows near Lichfield where Johnson walked and read as a boy but a tradition of ideal landscapes that extends back to the Garden of Alcinous in *The Odyssey*. We find spontaneous fruitfulness in Hesiod, rivers of milk in Ovid, eternal spring in Homer, playful beasts in Milton, and birds and carpets of flowers everywhere in descriptions of the locus amoenus from Homer to Pope: gardens, bowers, and vales designed to feed our hunger for ideal beauty and serenity but modeled after earlier descriptions and constructed, sometimes, in accordance with rules of rhetoric.[28] The dominion of Rest is more than just a

27. See Angus Fletcher, *Allegory: The Theory of a Symbolic Mode* (Ithaca, N.Y., 1964), p. 150.

28. *Works and Days,* lines 109–20; *Metamorphoses* 1.76–215; *Odyssey* 7.114ff.; *Paradise Lost,* bk. 4, line 131ff.; E. R. Curtius, *European Literature and the Latin Middle Ages,* trans. W. R. Trask (New York, 1953), pp. 183–200.

pleasant place, however; it is a vaguely classical Eden, and *Rambler* 33 describes the fall of man from "original integrity" to "corruption"; it is a Golden Age that degenerates into Iron. In each of these five allegorical histories the earliest conditions of existence are utopian: Criticism "bore an unextinguishable torch, manufactured by Labour, and lighted by Truth, of which it was the particular quality immediately to shew every thing in its true form" (*Rambler* 3); Patronage at her arrival on Parnassus "dispersed the gifts of Fortune, with the impartiality of Justice, and the discernment of Truth" (*Rambler* 91).

And in each of these allegories, after an ideal realm of indeterminate duration, a change takes place, and the perfection of the first ages decays. Criticism loses confidence, Patronage is seduced by Pride, and the campaign of Truth against Falsehood bogs down in inconclusive skirmishes (*Rambler* 96). "By degrees," in *Rambler* 33, universal contentment gives way to envy and violence; "the state of the earth was changed; the year was divided into seasons; part of the ground became barren, and the rest yielded only berries, acorns, and herbs." Famine and disease threaten to destroy the race of mankind.

> To oppose the devastations of Famine, who scattered the ground every where with carcases, Labour came down upon earth. Labour was the son of Necessity, the nurseling of Hope, and the pupil of Art; he had the strength of his mother, the spirit of his nurse, and the dexterity of his governess. His face was wrinkled with the wind, and swarthy with the sun; he had the implements of husbandry in one hand, with which he turned up the earth; in the other he had the tools of architecture, and raised walls and towers at his pleasure.

Superintended by Labour, the "inhabitants of the globe" set to work, and "the face of things was immediately transformed; . . . nothing was seen but heaps of grain, and baskets of fruit, full tables, and crouded storehouses."

The arrival of Labour is the second major scene or set piece of *Rambler* 33. In effect Labour accomplishes his purposes simply by arriving: the account of his genealogy, education, equipment, and exhortation fills three paragraphs; his actual deeds are worth only one sentence. The picture of Labour with his "implements of husbandry" and "tools of architecture" should be translated into meaning that mankind is industriously occupied, is laboring: Labour's appearance *is* action, as it would be in an allegorical painting, and the icons he carries in each hand tell us what he does as well as what he means. Their origin and ancestry are as much pictorial as literary. Ripa furnishes a plow for "Agriculture," and square, compass, and plumb line for "Perfect Work" (plus torches, scepters, and wands of various kinds sufficient to outfit major personifications in *Ramblers* 3, 91, and 96).[29] Labour is in fact less physically active than many of the small-scale personifications in Johnson's prose ("Competition withdrew into the cavern of envy").

It follows that there is very little narrative action in Johnson's allegories, but rather a series of relationships that are expressed by a limited number of conventional metaphors, flashed on the screen consecutively. The most important of these metaphors or relationships is sovereignty, the authority or power of one abstraction over others, over human beings, and over the environment. If a personification is presented to us enthroned or in triumphant progress, his authority is obvious, but mere presence as the focus of attention denotes power, as the arrival of Labour demonstrates in *Rambler* 33. For this reason psychomachia, which in Prudentius, and much more in Spenser, involves real fighting, is in Johnson a matter first of lists of allies and then of simple dispossession. In paragraph 12 of *Rambler* 33 the palace of Rest is "invaded" by Satiety: that is, she enters "with a languishing and repining look," throws herself into an "attitude" on a couch, and immediately "a general gloom spread itself on every side, the groves . . . lost their verdure, . . . the breeze sunk in sighs, and flowers contracted their leaves, and shut up their odours." Warfare in Johnson's allegories is generally a string

29. Cesare Ripa, *Iconologia: or, Moral Emblems* (London, 1709): scepters, fig. 33, Authority, and fig. 52, Heaven; torches, fig. 51, Knowledge, and fig. 188, Justice; sheaves of corn, fig. 1, Plenty, fig. 63, Preservation, and fig. 79, Tax.

of bloodless coups; its various episodes are intervals of sovereignty, and its final cause is a stable polity.[30]

All five of the allegorical histories reach equilibrium in a compromise of some kind. They animate polarities not to reconcile them, and not to dramatize (as Spenser does in books 1 and 2 of *The Faerie Queene*) the victory of good over evil, but to negotiate a working agreement between them. The picture these allegories paint of the decay of nature from its first perfection signifies neither chronological nor cultural primitivism ; [31] it is, rather, an etiological metaphor. In this imperfect world, Johnson is saying, neither rest nor labor is sufficient unto itself, the price of the quest for knowledge is obscurity, and truth itself is forced to borrow the weapons of falsehood. These are the conditions under which the choice of life must be made: in Imlac's words,

> 'nature sets her gifts on the right hand and on the left.' Those conditions, which flatter hope and attract desire, are so constituted, that, as we approach one, we recede from another. There are goods so opposed that we cannot seize both, but, by too much prudence, may pass between them at too great a distance to reach either. This is often the fate of long consideration; he does nothing who endeavours to do more than is allowed to humanity. Flatter not yourself with contrarieties of pleasure. Of the blessings set before you make your choice, and be content. [*Rasselas,* ch. 29]

The Moral Geography of Choice

There is no causal connection between one event and another in the rest of Johnson's allegories. The passage of time has no effect on these landscapes or their inhabitants. This is, at first glance, odd, because *Ramblers* 67, 102, and "Theodore" are ostensibly journeys; but no one really goes any-

30. See Fletcher, *Allegory,* pp. 40–41; C. S. Lewis, *The Allegory of Love* (1936; ed. cited New York, 1958), pp. 54–55, 58–59. The debate between Wit and Learning in *Rambler* 22 is a special case because it represents the powers of these two abstractions literally, not figuratively. *Rambler* 96 uses movement metaphorically.

31. A. O. Lovejoy, Foreword to Lois Whitney, *Primitivism and the Idea of Progress* (Baltimore, 1934), pp. xi–xv.

where.[32] The illusion of motion is produced by the fact that the eye of the narrator travels over a scene—which is not the same thing as the narration of a trip from one place to another. Here, as in the allegorical histories, particular symbols are positioned around a handful of big scenes separated in this case by intervals of space, not time. The purpose of these static journeys is to map the moral geography of the choice of life.

Unquestionably the authors whose example most powerfully affected the contours of allegorical landscapes in the eighteenth century were not Plato, Spenser, or Bunyan but Prodicus and Cebes, supposed to be contemporaries of Socrates, whose writings if genuine survive as "The Choice of Hercules" in Xenophon's *Memorabilia* 2.1.21–33, and as the *Tablet* of Cebes, from the first century A.D. In one, the youthful Hercules, meditating his future, is confronted by Virtue and Pleasure, each of whom states her case as persuasively as she can. In the other, visitors to the Temple of Saturn spy a tablet or painted plaque, on which are a confused succession of gates and enclosures and paths: within the Gate of Life, Fortune doles out wealth to one or two among the mob surrounding her, and Opinion hawks her wares with the aid of Desire and the Pleasures; the gate manned by Luxury and her sisters leads to Punishment and Penance; False Science presides over a crowd of academic types nearby. True Science holds court up a steep, rough, narrow road and points the way to happiness. There were certainly as many editions, translations, and adaptations of Prodicus and Cebes as of Aristotle and Plato in the seventeenth and eighteenth centuries; [33] they were served up to schoolboys as their first mor-

32. *Rambler* 65, the other allegorical journey, is an exception, since Obidah does go from one place to another and the passage of time is meaningful for him.

33. E. Wasserman, "The Inherent Values of 18th Century Personification," *PMLA* 65 (1950): 437–38, counts at least fourteen editions of Cebes, 1670–1771, twenty separate printings; Robert Watt, *Bibliotheca Britannica* (Edinburgh, 1824), s.v. "Cebes," lists nine translations or paraphrases 1680–1759, and six versions of the Choice of Hercules 1713–53, s.v. "Hercules." Scores of otherwise uncollected allusions to both works are scattered through Heinle, "The Eighteenth Century Allegorical Essay."

sels of Greek (Johnson recommended Cebes to Samuel Ford in 1735), warmed over for the older barbarians who read *The Tatler,* versified for Dodsley's *Collection* by a bishop, and paraphrased by an Oxford Professor of Modern History for *The Preceptor.*[34] Johnson in 1763 described "the contention between pleasure and virtue" as "a struggle which will always be continued while the present system of nature shall subsist," a subject neither "trite" nor "exhausted"; "for the truth is, that there is no other to be chosen; for by this conflict of opposite principles, modified and determined by innumerable diversities of external circumstances, are produced all the varieties of human life; nor can history or poetry exhibit more than pleasure triumphing over virtue, and virtue subjugating pleasure." [35]

Of the two, Prodicus is easier to visualize, and was frequently painted; but since the steep and rocky path to True Science in Cebes could equally well be the steep and rocky path to Virtue (sanctioned by Matthew 7 : 14) and therefore fits neatly into the background of the Choice of Hercules, the two allegories tend to merge.[36] The "choice" motif of Prodicus can easily be imposed on a landscape from Cebes by excising superfluous gates and arranging two paths symmetrically, as in *Tatler* 120, *Spectators* 514 and 524. Thus, Lien Chi's garden in Letter 31 of *The Citizen of the World* resembles the landscape in Cebes, and presents its visitors with the choice of Hercules.

Choice—the overwhelming choice between light and darkness—is the dominating theme of both these fictions. William Law, who envisioned every smallest act as a choice between

34. *Letters,* 1 : 7; *Tatler* 97; Bishop Robert Lowth, "The Choice of Hercules," in Dodsley's *Collection,* 3 : 7–18 (January 1748); Joseph Spence, *The Picture of Human Life* from Cebes, in Dodsley's *Museum* (London 1747). These last two both appeared in part 12 of *The Preceptor,* cheek by jowl with Johnson's "Theodore": see Hazen, p. 173. Spence's version of Cebes was printed as Johnson's by Arthur Murphy, *Works of Samuel Johnson* (1792), one of the most widely reprinted editions of Johnson.

35. Review of George Graham, *Telemachus. A Mask,* in *Critical Review* 15 (1763): 314–18.

36. See Erwin Panofsky, *Hercules am Scheidewege* (Leipzig and Berlin, 1930), pp. 37–196, and E. H. Gombrich, "A Classical Rake's Progress," *JWCI* 15 (1952): 254–56.

damnation and salvation, made a terrific impression on Johnson when Johnson was only nineteen. Many of Johnson's allegories are modeled after Prodicus and Cebes. *Rambler* 65 is his closest imitation of the Choice of Hercules. In the heat of the day, Obidah decides to leave the straight but dusty road for a flowery path that meanders charmingly into a dangerous forest. "Petty curiosity" and love of pleasure cause him to forsake "the ways of virtue." *Rambler* 67, "The garden of hope," resembles Cebes's *Tablet* in its vision of "an innumerable multitude" "tumultuously bustling" to grasp the "blessings of life" held out to them by the goddess on her throne, in the two gates into the garden of Hope, one kept by Reason, the other by Fancy, in the fact that a special place is assigned to pedants and cranks, in the "craggy, slippery, and winding path" upward to the "bowers of Content", and in the vale of Idleness below, from which there is a clear view of Hope but no way of reaching her. In "The Vision of Theodore" also the path to happiness is steep, and bordered by a sinister landscape of iniquity, the bowers of Intemperance, the maze of Indolence, and the caverns of Despair.

There are nevertheless notable differences between Johnson's use of Prodicus and Cebes, and orthodox performances in the same vein. Johnson loads the dice so heavily against Pleasure and her allies that the possibility of real choice-between-equals disappears. In place of Prodicus's two paths equally valid (i.e., equally feasible to begin with), "The Vision of Theodore" sketches for us a knife-edge ascent; the ground falls off steeply on either side of the path of Reason and Religion into darkness and gulfs and chasms and crags. The Choice of Hercules as a motif or theme must have appealed to so many people over so many years in part because it dramatizes the great Renaissance theme of temptation, a major preoccupation of Spenser, Milton, Dryden in *All for Love* (itself a version of the story of Hercules at the crossroads),[37] and even Johnson in *Irene*. Some of the most gorgeous passages in Spenser and Milton delineate the temptation or the temptress. But Johnson mutilates the fair face of

37. See Hagstrum, *The Sister Arts,* pp. 190–94.

pleasure, perhaps to protect his readers from temptation ("vice . . . should always disgust"), and almost certainly because sinfulness leading to damnation was for him a truly horrible thing. Those whom Ambition seduces from the Road to Reason, in "Theodore," stumble "from precipice to precipice, where many fell and were seen no more."

> There were others whose crime it was rather to neglect Reason than to disobey her; and who retreated from the heat and tumult of the way, not to the bowers of Intemperance, but to the maze of Indolence. . . . They wandered on from one double of the labyrinth to another with the chains of Habit hanging secretly upon them, till, as they advanced, the flowers grew paler, and the scents fainter; they proceeded in their dreary march without pleasure in their progress, yet without power to return; and had this aggravation above all others, that they were criminal but not delighted. The drunkard for a time laughed over his wine; the ambitious man triumphed in the miscarriage of his rival; but the captives of Indolence had neither superiority nor merriment. Discontent lowered in their looks, and sadness hovered round their shades; yet they crawled on reluctant and gloomy, till they arrived at the depth of the recess, varied only with poppies and nightshade, where the dominion of Indolence terminates, and the hopeless wanderer is delivered up to Melancholy; the chains of Habit are rivetted for ever; and Melancholy, having tortured her prisoner for a time, consigns him at last to the cruelty of Despair. [*Works* (1825), 9 : 174–75]

Understandably, the sight of this "miserable scene" wakes Theodore and ends the vision. Dream visions in *The Spectator* and *The Tatler* usually conclude less forbiddingly, and the dreamer is privileged finally to enter the Temple of Fame or the Valley of Liberty, or to ascend Mt. Parnassus.[38] But the Temple of Happiness in Johnson's "Theodore" is shrouded in mists that Reason herself cannot penetrate; it must be taken, quite literally, on faith.

A certain menacing quality in Johnson's allegories is the second trait that sets them apart from most others in the eighteenth century. Hardly anyone reaches the summit of the little mountain on which Hope sits smiling in *Rambler* 67.

38. *Tatlers* 81, 161; *Spectator* 514.

Reason, who guards one gate, is "surly and scrupulous," and so admits few, and those few are plagued with "unexpected obstacles" however carefully they plan their climb. "A thousand intricacies embarrassed them, a thousand slips threw them back, and a thousand pitfals impeded their advance. So formidable were the dangers, and so frequent the miscarriages, that many returned from the first attempt, and many fainted in the midst of the way." The "greater part" of the "very small number" among the few admitted by Reason "regretted the labour which it cost"—which leaves almost no one to enjoy the bowers of Content.

Rambler 102 is listed in the table of contents as "The voyage of life." "An expanse of waters violently agitated, and covered with so thick a mist, that the most perspicacious eye could see but a little way" appears before the dreamer. All around him are boats "courting the gale with full sails" on a sea "full of rocks and whirlpools," and the only distinct landmark is the " 'Gulph of Intemperance,' a dreadful whirlpool" dotted with flowery islands, "where Pleasure warbled the song of invitation." [39] Johnson concentrates his attention on the dangers of the voyage and on the irrational attitudes of his travelers. Drowning men "call loudly" "for that help which could not now be given," or caution others "against the folly, by which they were intercepted in the midst of their course," and the vessels of all are "visibly impaired in the course of the voyage." Most practice "the art of concealing their danger from themselves," and take care "never to look forward." Since only a handful consult Reason without yielding to the lure of Pleasure and Ease, the majority are sucked into the Gulph of Intemperance, if they do not shipwreck on a natural obstacle.

39. How can a whirlpool have islands in it? Inconsistencies in *Rambler* 102 reinforce our feeling that Johnson conceived of allegory as "figurative discourse," and invented correspondences between the literal sense and its meaning as he went along. How can this dreamer tell us so much about the seascape in paragraphs 11–14 if "the most perspicacious eye could see but a little way" (par. 4)? If Criticism, in *Rambler* 3, is a benevolent power, why does she hand over her duties to Flattery and Malevolence? Questions not to be asked.

In sum, the vision of the voyage of life does not allow for success or achievement or happiness. Clever navigation as such has no moral significance: "the only advantage, which, in the voyage of life, the cautious had above the negligent, was, that they sunk later, and more suddenly." Death is the only meaningful event in this allegory about life. Critics have tended to assume that *Rambler* 102 was influenced by *Spectator* 159, "The Vision of Mirza," and it is true that both visions interpret the life of man in a spatial metaphor based on opportunities for death. But the voyage of life is a traditional figure of speech, the bridge of life rather quaint. Johnson's vision differs dramatically from Addison's in tone and attitude: it pictures life as a series of frightful risks inevitably and finally concluded by death. In "The Vision of Mirza" death is merely a trapdoor (this is slightly ridiculous, in my opinion), and at the end of the river of eternity gleam the islands of the blessed. Addison's is a vision of hope, ushered in by music of ravishing sweetness; Johnson's is a vision of despair, introduced by "the shrieks of alarm, the whistle of winds, and the dash of waters."

Johnson's allegory, then, approaches the choice of life from the largest of perspectives: it outlines the history of some of the human imperfections that sabotage the quest for a secure sublunary refuge, and it demonstrates the superlative unwisdom of choosing any road but that of Reason and Religion. It shows us also that different aspects of a theme as pervasive as this may be voiced in different literary modes. Madam Bombasine (*Rambler* 12), whom we may count among the obstacles to Zosima's freedom of choice, is lampooned in plebeian language and vulgar idioms. But the pretensions of Nouradin and Morad and Seged to complete freedom of choice are trumpeted forth in ringing periods and sublime imagery; they act and suffer on a heroic plane. Johnson's notorious disdain for imperial tragedy and martial heroics can be misleading if it persuades us that he rejected the heroic ideal (the true hero was, more often than not, truly sublime) in all or even most of its branches. The Mountain of Existence in "Theodore" makes heroic demands on mankind. In all Johnson's allegories human nature is pitted against dread-full odds (like the gladiator in Boswell's simile); both her enemies and her allies are "powers of superior aspect," "capa-ble of presiding in senates, or governing nations." [40]

40. These two phrases describe Reason and Religion in "The Vision of Theodore," *Works* (1825), 9 : 167.

5 Three Voices: Periodical-Essay Fiction before 1750

> It is the imitation, for ever repeated, of mere modes of conveying ideas, which renders periodical papers of great merit rather distasteful.
>
> Vicesimus Knox, 1788

Periodical publication in the eighteenth century was staggeringly various and profuse. The sum total of essay sheets, newspapers, journals, monthly miscellanies, weekly diatribes, and daily medleys amounted to about 2,500 different titles by 1800; the span of some was but a day, others are still flourishing in the 1970s. And the variety within this boatload of shards of prose is daunting. Some periodicals were no more than literary bilge, such as *The Tatling Harlot, or, a Dialogue Between Bess o'Bedlam and her Brother Tom. By Mother Bawdycoat* (1709), an ephemeral rant. Some were more uniformly serious than *The Rambler,* and made no concessions at all to the reader's appetite for entertainment. *The Comedian, or Philosophical Enquirer* (nine monthly numbers, 1732–33) contains no fiction to speak of; each issue, except no. 1, plunges immediately into a grave religious-philosophical topic, then descants on literature or current events, and closes with "The History of the Times." *The Student* (1750–51), to which Johnson contributed his "Life of Cheynel," has no qualms about mixing piety ("On the Humiliation and Sufferings of our Blessed Saviour," in no. 4) with humor (in no. 7, a "party of pleasure" in *"Pembrokeshire"* is painted in a playful parade of words beginning with *p* not excluding a pewter piss-pot pitched at a parson's phizz). Some of the finest Ciceronian prose of the eighteenth century appears in a periodical essay, and some of the most uncouth adventures in language also. Rigorous formal classification of all these journalistic enterprises is impossible because they plundered from each other whatever feature seemed likely to increase circulation: newspapers printed essays, essay periodicals printed news; any combination of instruction and entertainment consistent with commercial viability was considered permissible.[1]

Unquestionably, Johnson knew more periodical publications of the first half of the eighteenth century than we can now name. At various times he haunted the coffeehouses, where newspapers and periodical essays were often deposited for general perusal, and his work for *The Gentleman's Magazine* forced him to notice many of the periodicals from which Cave printed selections and condensations in the 1730s and 1740s.[2] But when Johnson defends himself in *The Rambler* for failing to match the vivacity and variety of his "predeces-

1. A sample of *The Tatling Harlot* was reprinted by Richmond P. Bond, *Contemporaries of the Tatler and Spectator* (Augustan Reprint Society Publication no. 47 [Los Angeles, 1954]), along with other periodicals quite unlike *The Tatler* or *The Spectator*. Paragraph 2 of *Common Sense* 2 (February 12, 1737), by Chesterfield, is a splendid example of Ciceronian eloquence. Lawrence Eusden's letter from Cambridge in *Spectator* 78 is a loosely concatenated sludge of vague relative clauses and muddy reference. For an excellent summary account of the genre, see the editor's introduction to *Studies in the Early English Periodical*, ed. R. P. Bond (Chapel Hill, N.C., 1957).

2. We can assume Johnson's acquaintance with standard periodicals, *The Tatler, Spectator, Guardian, Examiner, Freeholder, Englishman,* and so on. The "Life of Addison" discusses predecessors of *The Tatler,* Mercuries, L'Estrange's *Observator,* and Leslie's *Rehearsal. The Gentleman's Magazine,* vols. 8–13 (1738–43) includes selections from *Common Sense, The Literary Courier of Grub Street, The Craftsman, Daily Gazetteer, The Universal Spectator, Old Common Sense, The Reveur, The Weekly Miscellany, The Nonsense of Common-Sense* (Lady Mary Wortley Montagu), *The Old Whig, The London Journal, White-Hall Evening Post, The Daily Advertizer, Faulkner's Dublin Journal, History of the Works of the Learned* (see also *Lives,* 3 : 168 n. 1), *The Country Oracle, The Champion, Westminster Journal, Old England Journal.* Johnson assisted in compiling the *Catalogus Bibliothecae Harleianae* (1743–45); Items 12131–12176 list fifty different titles of newspapers and periodicals of one sort or another, including thirty-four volumes of *The London Gazette* (1665–1739), and collections of *Post-Boy, True Briton, Mist's Weekly Journal, British Journal or The Censor* (1727–31), *Fog's Weekly Journal, Grub-Street Journal, Hyp-Doctor* (1730–31).

sors," as in *Ramblers* 10, 23, 34, 86, 97, 98, and 126, he has in mind not the entire corpus of periodical publications before 1750, but *The Spectator,* Addison and Steele, and perhaps their principal followers. It is no exaggeration to say that *The Spectator* took Great Britain by storm, or that the cumulative example of *The Tatler, The Spectator, The Guardian,* and their immediate offspring established a model of tyrannous importance for the eighteenth century. *The Gentleman's Magazine,* a new development in journalism which started in 1731 and was still going strong at the end of the century, owed its success in part to its practice of anthologizing interesting tidbits from journals written in imitation of *The Spectator.* Spectatorial conventions were of course stretched and modified in many directions, and there were mavericks who paid no attention to them, but no towering genius rose up to overthrow them, and no rival conventions competed for favor—the familiar essay, for example, virtually disappeared in the eighteenth century. The same is true of fiction in the periodical essays: the rise of the novel in the 1740s and 1750s made relatively little impression on characters and incidents in periodical publications, and when the author of *Tom Jones* turned journalist, he contented himself with variations—idiosyncratic and strong-minded, to be sure—on the tinkly tunes originally composed in the reign of Queen Anne.[3]

It seems to me that three voices are responsible for much of the fiction in most of the important periodical essays that Johnson would have known when he came to write *The Rambler.*[4] *Voices* is not perhaps the perfect word, but I have

3. Robert D. Mayo, *The English Novel in the Magazines 1740–1815* (Evanston, Ill., 1962), p. 12. The first hundred pages of this admirable book are a history of periodical-essay fiction before 1750. See also Roy McKeen Wiles, "Prose Fiction in English Periodical Publications before 1750" (Ph.D. dissertation, Harvard University, 1933), especially the Bibliographical Register, pp. 385–487.

4. Most of my examples of periodical-essay fiction before 1750 are drawn from *The Tatler, Spectator, Guardian, Lover* (1714), *Lay-Monk* (1713–14), *Censor* (1715, 1717), *Free-Thinker* (1718–21), *Plain Dealer* (1724–25), and *Universal Spectator* (1728–46). These nine are representative of the literary tradition of periodical essays, as opposed to the political;

not found a better; I mean the presiding personality from which a given fiction originates. The usual way of classifying periodical-essay fiction is by "kind": anecdote, allegory, evening at a club, letter, romance, mock-pedantic diatribe, etc.; but this approach does not work very well on the more amorphous species of fiction, which heavily outnumber distinct species like allegory and oriental tale. The voice that narrates minor anecdotes and the presiding personality that selects letters to itself eventually determine not only what topics arise and what issues are explored, but also to a lesser degree the kinds of fiction that will most frequently be patronized and even the incidents or episodes most frequently recorded in a given periodical. Although all three of these voices may be heard in *The Spectator,* later periodicals develop and exploit the second and third voices more effectively than *The Spectator* does.

The first is the voice of Addisonian humour: [5] not of Mr. Spectator, who is notoriously inarticulate and taciturn, but of the urbane arbiter elegantiarum who teases and scolds his way through *The Spectator* and other periodicals: flatterer of the ladies, master of whimsy, umpire of domestic problems. The second is the Catonist, a blunt old man of old-fashioned virtues, always outspoken and direct, often indignant, fond of Roman patriots. The third voice is no more detached and objective than the second, but his enthusiasm is more refined: the Man of Sentiment, an ardent romantic, unworldly, conscious of his own sensibility. There are of course other voices

---

they are of relatively high quality; and there is evidence that Johnson knew them all, except *The Censor,* though not necessarily before he started *The Rambler:* for *The Lay-Monk,* see *Lives,* 2 : 244–46; for *The Free-Thinker,* see *Lives,* 3 : 322; for *The Plain Dealer,* see *Lives,* 2 : 436, 339–40. Johnson was personally acquainted with Aaron Hill, editor of *The Plain Dealer* (see Boswell, 1 : 198 n. 4) and Henry Baker, first editor of *The Universal Spectator* (see *Journey to the Western Islands,* fifth-to-last paragraph). Later numbers of *The Universal Spectator* were more frequently plundered by *The Gentelman's Magazine* than was any other nonpolitical periodical.

5. I spell the word *humour* to indicate reference to the eighteenth-century literary quality, not to modern humor, simple risibility.

in eighteenth-century journalism; there are individual voices (Fielding's cocky irony); and there are whole categories of periodical-essay fiction that function independently of these three voices (the insolent mockery of *Pasquin,* 1722–24, or the roaring-boy vitality of *The London Spy,* 1698–1700). But the fiction of *The Rambler* was written within the tradition that these three voices speak for, a tradition of polite letters shunning controversy and dedicated to civilized and instructive entertainment. Since Johnson has himself a distinctive voice and distinctive preoccupations (among others, the choice of life), his attempts to imitate one of these three voices sometimes end in disorder.

In *Rambler* 208 Johnson claims the "privileges" customarily allowed to those who write from behind a "mask," showing his awareness at least of the usefulness of indirection in the periodical essay. These voices are not masks, however, if a mask is an identity assumed in order to hide one's real feelings, because many writers resorted to one of these three voices to express their dearest beliefs. They are not personae, in the sense of identities created purely for rhetorical or suasive ends, to manipulate or to trick the reader, because here there is seldom any manipulation or deception involved, though persuasion is an end. At least one of them (perhaps all three) has the power of a "personnage régnant," [6] a type embodying widespread ideals and speaking to the condition of the age. Their domain was not limited to the periodical press; they may be heard on the stage and in the novel, in poetry, and in private letters and journals also.

The three voices are of course an invented conceptual framework upon which the multiplicity of snips and fragments of fiction in the periodical essays may be conveniently hung. They oversimplify, necessarily, and yet usefully; periodical-essay fiction is seldom complex. Of the three, two are so closely associated with particular authors (Addison and Steele) that one could perhaps as easily define them in terms of these two

6. Hippolyte Taine, *De l'idéal dans l'art* (Paris, 1867), p. 36. See also Irvin Ehrenpreis, "Personae," *Restoration and 18th-Century Literature,* ed. C. Camden (Chicago, 1963), pp. 25–37.

writers' individual gifts and predilections as in terms of a disembodied voice. But scores of competent journalists wrote fiction similar to the most characteristic work of Addison and Steele, without a feeling of personal discipleship: these modes of fiction were not so much personal as cultural achievements. With what particular author can the Catonist be associated? (To link him with Swift is to misrepresent both Swift and the Catonist.) The Catonist is hard to delimit and circumscribe because he is an aspect of so many large, pervasive eighteenth-century modes of thought (conservatism, neoclassicism, Tory satire, Whig rhetoric; and yet one need only open one of the major literary periodicals to *hear* him speak out loud and clear—which is the chief justification for discussing him as a voice, not as the projected point of view of any single author.

The Addisonian Humourist

The Spectator had hardly been in existence more than a few months when John Gay saluted its "noble profusion of Wit and Humour." He was echoed in 1717 by Lewis Theobald ("the inimitable *Spectator,* whose excellent vein of good sense, spirit, wit, and humour, made that *Paper* the entertainment of all the gay, polite, and virtuous part of mankind"), in 1728 by Daniel Defoe ("is there no Wit or Humour left, because they [Addison and Steele] are Gone?"), in 1758 by Horace Walpole ("the delicacies of natural humour" were Addison's special talent), and by almost everyone else who interested himself in *The Spectator,* including Dick Minim, virtuoso in platitudes (*Idler* 60). "In argument he [Addison] had many equals," said Johnson, "but his humour was singular and matchless." [7] Such tributes sound as though they all meant roughly the same thing—which could be true despite incon-

7. Gay, "The Present State of Wit" (1711), Augustan Reprint Society Publication no. 7 (1947), p. 8; Theobald, Preface to collected edition of *The Censor;* Defoe, *Universal Spectator* 1; Walpole, *Royal and Noble Authors,* in *Works* (London, 1798), 1 : 431; *Lives,* 2 : 109. On one occasion Johnson uses the phrase "Wit and Humour" as a general term for the entertaining aspects of a periodical (see "Proposals for Printing . . . The PUBLISHER," 1744 (Oxford, 1930, [facsimile], par 8). Nevertheless, people seem to have agreed that Addison's humour was something special.

sistencies in the history of the word *humour* during this period.

Addison's humour was not primarily intended to excite laughter: Hobbes's theory of laughter as self-applause arising from the sudden apprehension of deformity or inferiority in someone else implied that laughter was cruel and vulgar. Wit, so frequently paired with humour in encomiums of Addison, was still in 1711 associated with the licentiousness of witty libertines, and had not succeeded in living down a reputation for irresponsibility even by 1750, as *Rambler* 22 reminds us in its allegorical contest between mischievous, fun-loving Wit and his sober half-sister, Learning. Addison registers his awareness of the destructiveness of certain kinds of wit in *Spectator* 169, pointing out that "ordinary Observers" confuse wit with ill-nature.[8] He shies away also from the satirical aspects of humour, for similar reasons: "the Talents of Humour and Ridicule in the Possession of an ill-natured Man" will produce satires "like poison'd Darts, which not only inflict a Wound, but make it incurable" (*Spectator* 23).

If it satisfies the requirements laid down by its author, Addison's humour will be cheerful, good-natured, toothless—which is not to say that it will be totally deficient in wit, satirical edge, and laughter-provoking qualities. What Addison rejected was a local incarnation of these three ranking deities, and eighteenth-century readers who were not at the time occupied by fear of such men as Hobbes and Rochester felt free to praise Addison for beauties he seems to shun. Thus, according to Johnson, Addison advances a position with "all the force of gay malevolence and humourous satire," "sometimes with argument, and sometimes with mirth"; many of his "effusions of wit" exert "powers truly comick," and "unite merriment with decency" (*Lives,* 2 : 87, 96–99). Addison was not troubled, as Swift and Pope were, by conflicting claims of urbanity and indignation; and his humour perhaps gained

8. *Leviathan,* part 1, ch. 6. Note also Rochester, "To a Lady," lines 5–8: "Let us since wit has taught us how / Raise pleasure to the Top: / You Rival Bottle must allow, / I'll suffer Rival Fop"; Pope, *Moral Essay* 2, "Flavia's a Wit, has too much sense to Pray"; see Stuart M. Tave, *The Amiable Humorist* (Chicago, 1960), pp. 47–55.

prestige from its unmistakable affinities with the grave raillery of Horace.

The voice of Addisonian humour may be defined in terms of tone, stance, and audience. The tone is self-satisfied, arch and whimsical, genteel. "I am very well versed in the Theory of an Husband, or a Father, and can discern the Errors in the Œconomy, Business, and Diversion of others, better than those who are engaged in them," remarks the Spectator as he doles out to the reader "just so much of my History and Character, as to let him see I am not altogether unqualified for the Business I have undertaken" (*Spectator* 1). He is liable to periodic seizures of "secret satisfaction," and can therefore afford to be coy about the frailties of the fair sex, and jocular about unreasonable behavior in his fellowmen. "Compassion for the Gentleman who writes the following Letter," says Steele in *Spectator* 41, "should not prevail upon me to fall upon the Fair Sex, if it were not that I find they are frequently Fairer than they ought to be." Naughty ladies! [9]

An indispensable basis for self-confident archness in *The Spectator* is a certain degree of objectivity and detachment, the ability to examine manners and morals *as* a spectator. To an apprehensive nation of hard-breathing politicians and hard-driven minorities (thirty-two religions and only one sauce), Addison's coolness was very appealing. Although a careful reader will detect political bias in some papers, one of the reasons for ending *The Tatler* and beginning *The Spectator* was to uproot weeds of faction that had sprung up in the earlier periodical. Not every contributor to *The Spectator* adapted easily to the urbanity of Addisonian humour; hence the variety of voices in the periodical as a whole. Richard

9. The Spectator is notably pleased with himself in nos. 10, 69, 106ff. (Sir Roger's estate), 135, 177. Calhoun Winton, *Captain Steele: the Early Career of Richard Steele* (Baltimore, 1964), pp. 105 and 132, notes the importance of tone in assessing *The Tatler* and *The Spectator*. Treacly, condescending playfulness of tone was certainly not the exclusive prerogative of Addison; some of the earliest examples of what I call the voice of Addisonian humour occur in Steele's portion of *The Tatler*, and some of the most characteristic examples in *The Spectator* are by Budgell (nos. 277, 365, 395).

Steele, in particular, reined in his enthusiasm only with difficulty (as Johnson put it, "some unlucky sparkle from a Tory paper" was apt to "set Steele's politicks on fire"), and Addison himself has other voices, notably that of the "parson in a tie-wig," reserved for Saturday sermons and serious cases of distress or wickedness. Nevertheless, Addison's smug irony is the presiding tone of *The Spectator,* one that caught on with correspondents and contributors, and its disengaged, objective stance sufficiently distinguishes it from other voices in the periodical essays.[10]

The arch complacency of the voice of Addisonian humour was sustained by a very special relationship between author and audience, a special degree and quality of intimacy. Simple popularity is only one facet of this, though it demonstrates how clearly this voice spoke to the condition of Great Britain in 1711. After only ten numbers Addison could preen himself on 60,000 readers. Three thousand *Spectators* were distributed every day, up to *Spectator* 446 when the stamp tax took effect. No other periodical essay of the eighteenth century was so widely endorsed. And yet, however impressive the readership of *The Spectator,* a better index of the peculiar intimacy it established between editors and audience is the way it succeeded in engaging readers in direct participation in Spectatorial activities. A surprising proportion of *The Spectator* was quite literally *written* by its readers. The opening paragraph of *Spectator*

10. *Lives,* 2 : 105. *The Spectator,* said Hazlitt, "plays the whole game of human life over before us, and by making us enlightened spectators of its many-coloured scenes, enables us (if possible) to become tolerably reasonable agents in the one in which we have to perform a part" ("On the Periodical Essayists" [1819], *Works,* ed. P. P. Howe [London, 1931], 6 : 91). C. S. Lewis, "Addison," *Essays on the Eighteenth Century Presented to D. N. Smith* (Oxford, 1945), pp. 2–3, Ronald Paulson, *Satire and the Novel* (New Haven 1967), pp. 58–64, and Peter Smithers, *Life of Addison,* 2d ed. (Oxford, 1968), pp. 214–16, 240, call our attention to Whig assumptions of *The Spectator,* Whig at least in comparison with the point of view of Tory satirists. Compared to party organs like *The Examiner, The Englishman, The Whig Examiner, The Gazetteer, The Craftsman,* and many others, *The Spectator* is nonpolitical. See *Spectators* 1, 16, 126, and 445 for declarations of neutrality.

184 shows how thoroughly they entered into the spirit of Addisonian humour:

> When a Man has discovered a new Vein of Humour, it often carries him much further than he expected from it. My Correspondents take the Hint I give them, and pursue it into Speculations which I never thought of at my first starting it. This has been the Fate of my Paper on the Match of Grinning, which has already produced a second Paper on parallel Subjects, and brought me the following Letter. . . .

Letters from readers make up a substantial part of the total bulk of *The Spectator,* and there were enough interesting letters for which space could not be found to fill up two volumes published in 1725. Addison, who relied on readers to do his work for him far less frequently than did Steele, was at least as sensitive to their responses and demands. Because author and audience were so perfectly tuned to each other, it is impossible in many cases to tell which letters were written by the editors and which by the correspondents.[11]

A large number of essayists after *The Spectator* do their best to imitate the voice of Addisonian humour. Its archness and coy, teasing tone could be reproduced without too much difficulty, though often enough not without incongruity if the character of the periodical as a whole does not justify archness. Richard Blackmore organizes *The Lay-Monk* (1713–14) around the "occasional Meetings" of six "Gentlemen of liberal Education," who converse "on Subjects of Philosophy and polite Learning." Since these relatively bookish persons have formed "a *Monastick* Society," in order to be "separated from the Crowd, and deliver'd from the Noise and Strife of the Busy," their papers achieve objectivity but not intimacy, and the

11. See Donald F. Bond, Introduction, *The Spectator* (Oxford, 1965), 1 : xx–xxix, for the popularity of *The Spectator,* and 1 : xxxvii–xlii for audience participation. Examples of audience participation: refer *Spectator* 179 back to no. 173, nos. 211 and 217 back to no. 209, no. 323 back to no. 317. Many of the species and clubs were invented by readers. See R. M. Wiles, "The Contemporary Distribution of Johnson's *Rambler,*" *ECS* 2 (1968): 155–71, for facts about the popularity of *The Rambler,* different in quality and quantity from that of *The Spectator.*

officious jocularity of no. 17 seems forced. *The Plain Dealer* (1724–25) is dominated by Aaron Hill's exuberance and sentimentality, which express themselves in playful archness of a romantic kind; but Hill is usually too bouncy to be urbane. *The Free-Thinker* (1718–21) prides itself first of all on being reasonable: it feels that a writer of periodicals "should take the Advantage of some Eminence, from which he may command an open View, and have (as it were) a large, extensive Horizon of Thought." Its fair-sexing is apt to be labored and unconvincing. After *The Spectator* "English magazines tended increasingly to separate into definite types and species," because of the general "fragmentation of the reading audience" taking place in the seventeenth and eighteenth centuries. What this means for the voice of Addisonian humour is that different periodicals specialize in different aspects of that voice, but only in individual essays do these various aspects recombine harmoniously.[12]

A handful of *Ramblers* intrude tentatively into the domain of Addisonian archness (nos. 20, 124, 126); one (no. 199) tramples through it heavily. In *Rambler* 10, what begins as banter very soon turns defensive, a little later changes into reproof, and after interesting hesitations concludes as heavy-handed irony. Having acknowledged his correspondence in paragraph 1, the Rambler declares himself unshaken by

> the anger of Flirtilla, who quarrels with me for being old and ugly, and for wanting both activity of body, and sprightliness of mind; feeds her monkey with my lucubrations, and refuses any reconciliation, till I have appeared in vindication of masquerades. That she may not however imagine me without support, and left to rest wholly upon my own fortitude, I shall now publish some letters, which I have received from men as well dressed, and as handsome, as her favourite; and others from ladies, whom I sincerely believe as young, as rich, as gay, as pretty, as fashionable, and as often toasted and treated as herself.

Then follow "four billets" written by Hester Mulso, a member of Richardson's harem, each designed in its own way to force

12. *Lay-Monk* 1; *Free-Thinker* 2; Mayo, *The English Novel in the Magazines*, p. 3.

Johnson "now and then" to "throw in, like his predecessor, some papers of a gay and *humourous* turn" (my italics). He postpones an answer to the first; to the second, who wants to know who he is, he throws a sop he might have borrowed from *Spectator* 221. The third is an invitation to a Sunday game of cards from Lady Racket, who "longs to see the torch of truth produced at an assembly, and to admire the charming lustre it will throw on the jewels, complexions, and behaviour of every dear creature there."

The Rambler's answer to this provocative little missive is surprisingly gentle, considering Johnson's "habitual reverence for the Sabbath" (Boswell, 1 : 303), gentle and courteous, *not* arch and coy: he does not tease Lady Racket, or turn her vanities to jest. His imagination catches fire from "the torch of truth," however, and produces a fantasy that is forbidding rather than playful:

> Yet I cannot but value myself upon this token of regard from a lady, who is not afraid to stand before the torch of truth. Let her not however consult her curiosity, more than her prudence; but reflect a moment on the fate of Semele, who might have lived the favourite of Jupiter, if she could have been content without his thunder. It is dangerous for mortal beauty, or terrestrial virtue, to be examined by too strong a light. The torch of truth shows much that we cannot, and all that we would not see. In a face dimpled with smiles, it has often discovered malevolence and envy, and detected, under jewels and brocade, the frightful forms of poverty and distress.

In the last paragraph of *Rambler* 10 the Rambler returns to Flirtilla, of paragraph 2 (who may or may not be a real correspondent):

> Thus have I dispatched some of my correspondents, in the usual manner, with fair words, and general civility. But to Flirtilla, the gay Flirtilla, what shall I reply? Unable as I am to fly, at her command, over land and seas, or to supply her, from week to week, with the fashions of Paris, or the intrigues of Madrid, I am yet not willing to incur her further displeasure, and would save my papers from her monkey on any reasonable terms.

The way Johnson expresses his uncertainty here closely resembles the way he is brought to a stand by a far better-known comic character in 1765: "But Falstaff unimitated, unimitable Falstaff, how shall I describe thee?" Both Falstaff and Flirtilla are attractive specimens of humanity, which somehow must be herded into the moralist's fold with other sheep and goats; and so Falstaff is dissected into discrete quantities of gluttony, cowardice, and wit, and Flirtilla's passion for pleasure is defended, ironically, by Nigrinus, "a man grown grey in the study of those noble arts, by which right and wrong may be confounded." To such lengths is Johnson forced in attempts to speak with the voice of Addisonian humour.

Subsequent ventures into archness and whimsy in *The Rambler* are perhaps less successful than *Rambler* 10 because Johnson makes a nearer approximation of true Spectatorial condescension to the ladies, which is for him quite unnatural (e.g. *Ramblers* 85, 124, and 126 except for the second letter). *The Idler,* designed to be more popular than *The Rambler,* works this vein of humour more frequently, but still, in my opinion, without conviction. "Many a tender maiden," says the Idler, British troops having set sail, "considers her lover as already lost, because he cannot reach the camp but by crossing the sea." [13] One feels that Addison enjoys the silliness of the British female (as he conceives it to be), but Johnson's fair-sexing has an edge to it, and in three cases out of four (*Idlers,* 5, 39, 87), it modulates directly into innuendo on the effeminacy of the British male, supposed at this time to be winning battles against the French.

Johnson's detachment is of a different order from Addison's, magisterial rather than avuncular, and the relationship he establishes with his readers is much more formal than that of *The Spectator.* Even if it had been possible for the Rambler to brag of "the many Letters" he received, he would never, like the Spectator, have guaranteed that they came from "Persons of the best Sense in both Sexes, (for I may pronounce their Characters from their Way of Writing)," or admitted that these letters "do not a little encourage me in the Prosecution of this my Undertaking" (*Spectator* 124). After he has made in *Rambler* 10 a heroic effort to accommodate himself to the

13. For a different judgment of *Idler* 5, see Clarence Tracy, "Democritus, Arise! A Study of Dr. Johnson's Humor," *Yale Review,* n.s. 39 (1950): 302.

demands of his readers, all of whom seem to want him to be another Spectator, Johnson confronts his correspondents again in *Rambler* 15, on the subject of cards and dice. He parodies their complaints in paragraph 1, and in paragraph 2 loftily dismisses them:

> I have found, by long experience, that there are few enterprises so hopeless as contests with the fashion, in which the opponents are not only made confident by their numbers, and strong by their union, but are hardened by contempt of their antagonist. . . .

(This essay includes, however, by way of "obviating" "censure" from his readers, a prissy little letter by Garrick, perhaps the least Johnsonian item in *The Rambler*.) In *Rambler* 23 Johnson simply decides "to place some confidence in his own skill, and to satisfy himself in the knowledge that he has not deviated from the established law of composition, without submiting his works to frequent examinations before he gives them to the publick, or endeavouring to secure success by a solicitous conformity to advice and criticism." In effect he resolves to go his own way regardless of what his readers expect from him. But at intervals throughout *The Rambler* the claims of his audience reassert themselves: not only does the Rambler apologize for the severity of his tone, for his judicial stance, and for his lack of complaisance to his readers; [14] he also experiments in varieties of fiction derived from

14. My summary does not perhaps do justice to the complexity of relations between the Rambler and his audience. To quote Professor Mayo, these "somber and magisterial disquisitions in anything but the Spectatorial manner" must have seemed to most readers "ponderous, proud, and perverse" (*The English Novel in the Magazines*, p. 94). Nevertheless, *The Rambler* was quickly recognized as something special among periodical essays, and its circulation was large enough to make it worth continuing for almost two years. The reference to a "letter from one of the universities" in *Rambler* 121 is a clue to the nature of Johnson's readership. *Rambler* 56 apologizes in detail for neglecting "a pile of papers" from correspondents, and encourages readers to send in their compositions, but warns them to wait to see themselves actually in print before claiming the rewards of authorship. This implies that Johnson might have shared *The Rambler* with anonymous contributors, had suitable articles been submitted; in fact he never did. A few friends were permitted to con-

his more popular predecessors. We turn now from the voice of Addisonian humour to the fictions that the voice most commonly sponsored.

To make fun of something is often to make fantasy out of it. Rococo *jeux d'esprit* come naturally to the Addisonian humourist. No one takes them seriously, and in this sense they are not true metaphors, as Donne's fantasies often are; they do have a function, a tepid moral purpose—they aim at the improvement as well as the entertainment of polite readers:

> There is not so variable a thing in Nature as a Lady's Headdress: Within my own Memory, I have known it rise and fall above thirty Degrees. About ten Years ago it shot up to a very great Height, insomuch that the Female Part of our Species were much taller than the Men. The Women were of such an enormous Stature, that *we appeared as Grass-hoppers before them:* At present the whole Sex is in a Manner dwarfed and shrunk into a Race of Beauties that seems almost another Species. I remember several Ladies, who were once very near seven Foot high, that at present want some Inches of five: How they came to be thus curtailed I cannot learn; whether the whole Sex be at present under any Pennance which we know nothing of, or whether they have cast their Head-dresses in order to surprize us with something in that Kind which shall be entirely new; or whether some of the tallest of the Sex, being too cunning for the rest, have contrived this Method to make themselves appear sizeable, is still a Secret; tho' I find most are of Opinion, they are at present like Trees new lopped and pruned, that will certainly sprout up and flourish with greater Heads than before [*Spectator* 98]

For all its demureness, this passage is highly inventive, with its references to thermometers or stars ("Degrees"), giants and dwarfs, snakes or horses ("cast"), and garden shrubbery. Fantasy like this, though not restricted to the foibles of the

---

tribute (for an account of them, see Curtis B. Bradford, "Samuel Johnson's 'Rambler,'" [Ph.D. dissertation, Yale University, 1937], pp. 71–89). In effect, then, Johnson ran his own show, though he did pay lip service to the special intimacy so carefully cultivated by Addison and Steele, in *Ramblers* 10, 15, 23, 34, 56, 98, 107, 109, and elsewhere less explicitly. *Rambler* 56 is characteristic, placating readers with one hand, keeping them at a distance with the other.

fair sex, thrives and prospers within a relatively narrow range of moral issues. Budgell feels he must apologize for treating atheists in a "ludicrous" manner (*Spectator* 389).

The principal strategy of fantasy in Addisonian humour is to inflate minor foibles to absurd dimensions, as Pope in *The Rape of the Lock* shows "what mighty Contests rise from trivial Things." Such fantasies as the opening paragraph of *Spectator* 98, quoted above, are only one species, perhaps the least interesting, of the large and heterogeneous class of satirical fictions based on a disparity between manner and matter. The "humour" of fantasy, moreover, cannot subsist without a prepared audience, one that shares the writer's sense of decorum, his idea of how manner and matter should be related. Perhaps it is Addison's role as mentor to an age that explains why fantasy in *The Spectator* is so frequently mock-pedantic. The rudeness of London audiences at the theater is reproved in a learned "Dissertation upon the Cat-call" (*Spectator* 361); the affectations of the beau monde are parodied in a pedagogue's treatise on "the Exercise of the Fan" (*Spectator* 102); a beau's head is dissected by virtuosos and a coquette's heart (*Spectators* 275, 281). The most popular form of mock-pedantic humour here, easily outranking recipes, projects, puffs, academies, and treatises, is the *species*, as if readers never tired of inventing flippant categories to deposit their acquaintances in: Starers, Picts, Idols, Demurrers, Inquisitives, Fribblers, and many more. All these seem to be attacking the world of high fashion; and yet one of the distinguishing qualities of fantasy produced by the Addisonian humourist is its fundamental sympathy with activities and interests that would make the society page of a modern newspaper; he chastises the beau monde because he loves it.

Few essayists writing between 1712 and 1750 spin fantasy with the dexterity of Addison and Steele, though Chesterfield and Fielding excelled in a heavier, more tendentious mode. Nevertheless, imaginative raillery in the Addisonian manner is as characteristic of the period as wigs and fans. Pope's *The Rape of the Lock* is of course a masterpiece of fantasy, whatever else it is. A combination of archness and fantasy is still a recognized kind of "humour" in the late 1740s, when Anna Howe spices her letters to Clarissa with "humourous" conceits, such as her sketch of what Hickman, Solmes, and Lovelace must have been like as schoolboys; the descriptive table of contents that Richardson added to each volume of the 1751 edition of *Clarissa* takes special note of such passages.[15]

So many varieties of mock pedantry were available to authors of this period, so many different models of satirical fantasy exploiting so many kinds of disparity between manner and matter, that each writer tends to go on his own way in this respect. Lewis Theobald, for example, embroiders cleverly on Horace's scorn of the poetry of water drinkers, and concocts a mock-pedantic formula for the effect of wine on wit—not bad at all, rather too masculine for Addison (*Censor* 14). In *Plain Dealer* 69 the author's favorite she-romp, Betty Amble, gushes over "a Project, that is newly come into our Heads," for a Parliament of Women, sure to equal all existing convocations, conventions, divans, diets, and "Prattlements" in "the *Art* of *Quarrelling*": though it follows conventions established by *The Spectator,* this essay, like others in *The Plain Dealer,* is more vivacious than corresponding essays by Addison. At the other extreme is Scriblerian satire, where mock-pedantic fantasy is biting and corrosive, as in two of Pope's contributions to *The Guardian* (11 and 78), or *Universal Spectator* 4, a recipe for the cure of "a Party Fever" by pasting a Whig newspaper back to back with a Tory gazette, cutting them into three-inch squares, smoking them in tobacco fumes, and using them "at every sitting." Other authors develop their own versions of the irony that plays a high style, heroic, courtly, or

15. *Clarissa* (Oxford, 1930), vol. 2, Letters 1, 20; vol. 3, Letters 32, 40. Elizabeth Carter, in her letters to Catherine Talbot, indulges in mild fantasy, whimsical make-believe or verbal play: see *A Series of Letters between Mrs. Elizabeth Carter and Miss Catherine Talbot,* ed. M. Pennington (London, 1809), 1 : 96, 103–04, 111, 149, 178. These passages are recognized as a distinct kind of writing (1 : 154) and compared to Anna Howe's humour (1 : 244). Fantasy and playful irony are of course essential ingredients in Elizabethan wit (e.g., in speeches by Rosalind, Portia, and Mercutio); but the Elizabethan stance is different, it lacks the didactic primness of Addisonian humour.

scholarly, against a low subject—Fielding has, for example, his own assortment of mock gallantries, mock pedantries, and mock heroics, each a blend of fantasy, archness, and learning.

There is hardly any Spectatorial fantasy in *The Rambler.* The early *Idlers* include a set of ironical proposals for public celebrations for a lady who rode a thousand miles in a thousand hours (compare *Examiner* 16) and three harmless political fantasies.[16] The humourous analogy between punch and conversation of *Idler* 34 brings out Johnson's talent at "the unexpected copulation of ideas" (his own witty definition of wit), though extended metaphors like this are perhaps more characteristic of seventeenth-century wit than of Addisonian humour. The only occasion on which Johnson attempts to be ironically facetious over women's clothing is *Idler* 39, on bracelets, which is not a successful essay. Spectatorial fantasy, in other words, is as unsuitable to Johnson's individual genius as coyness and complacence are, not because he lacked imagination, but because his imagination found more effective expression in other ways: in the miniature biographies discussed in chapter 2, for example, the proportion of which in *The Rambler* is much higher than in *The Spectator.*

Johnson's mock pedantry is that of a scholar, Addison's that of a gentleman. This is why the flowery gallantries of *Idlers* 6, 39, and 87 fall flat. Where mock gallantry is called for, Johnson's humour is as awkward as his own Verecundulus at tea table (with at least one exception—*Rambler* 126, third letter); but when it is a question of recipes, projects, treatises, expertise, statistical summary, technical terms, or philosophic words, Johnson achieves a variety and subtlety of wit that is quite beyond the reach of *The Spectator.* Mr. Spectator can scold beaux and belles charmingly because he is at home in their world; the Rambler's antipathy to the world of high fashion is authentic. By the same token, Johnson shows a gift for the humour of pomposity, though sometimes his efforts in this line are pompous without being humourous (e.g., *Idlers* 6 and 12). The triumph of Dick Minim (*Idlers* 60 and 61) is

16. *Idlers* 6, 7, 8, 20. For the political context of these essays, see Donald Greene, *The Politics of Samuel Johnson* (New Haven, 1960), pp. 174–77.

delightfully decorous burlesque, of very high quality indeed, the more admirable because it exposes not just literary cant (some of Minim's ideas were perfectly acceptable to Johnson), but also the comic speciousness of a superlatively superficial mind. Johnson does not take easily to *The Spectator*'s favorite pedantry, the species, perhaps because it is such an amateurish maneuver, almost a parlor game, or perhaps because like the doctrine of the Ruling Passion, it limits personal freedom. In general, Johnson's irony in the periodical essays is professorial. Impersonal constructions, delicate understatement, and grand generalizations are turned slightly askew or applied to an unworthy subject. For example, *Idlers* 1–3 are written from the point of view of the scholar: contrast mock encomiums of dullness in *The Dunciad,* which use the language of heroic eulogy; contrast also the point of view of the rhetorician who delivers Erasmus's *Praise of Folly*.[17]

The special intimacy between Addison and his audience produces a second large class of fictions, of more importance to periodicals than to other branches of literature: letters addressed to the editor in one of his presiding roles as arbiter elegantiarum or as public uncle. Complaints of this kind are meant to elicit answers in the voice of Addisonian humour, sympathetic, paternalistic, whimsical but not sarcastic, so confident in its own correctness that it can afford to be indulgent. And so Mr. Spectator hears stories of bad manners in church (*Spectators* 20, 158, 236, 380), in the playhouse (nos. 240, 268), in a coffeehouse (no. 155), in servants (no. 88), and in suitors (no. 145). His willingness to listen to the troubles of husbands and wives (nos. 194, 236, 252, 278, 295, 299, 326) earns a compliment in no. 278 for "having done considerable Services in this great City by rectifying the Disorders of Families." Lovers

17. *Rambler* 59 contains a species ("the human screech-owl") more or less in the Spectatorial mode, but *Rambler* 121 rebukes a correspondent for his satire on "Echoes." There are three species of detractors in *Rambler* 144. The "Idlers" of the early essays in the publication named after them are not an Addisonian species. Johnson as a moralist isolates and defines human types (e.g., "passionate men" in *Rambler* 11, "wits" in *Rambler* 128); from a literary point of view these have very little in common with the bantering mock pedantry of Addison's species.

young and old consult the Spectator about problems and procedures in courtship (nos. 79, 89, 140, 272, 280, 326). It is clearly to the Spectator that such letters are written (not to Will Honeycomb or another member of the club)—to a spokesman for good breeding and the domestic proprieties. Later periodicals printed a large number of similar letters.[18]

It is almost unnecessary to record the Rambler's forays into this corner of the world of the Spectator. Aside from *Rambler* 126, where Misocolax complains of ladies who force him to applaud the same dear gewgaws at every visit, impolite behavior hardly interests the Rambler, except as the symptom of a deeper moral sickness. Courtship and marriage in *The Rambler* dramatize those vices, virtues, and passions that determine the quality of a person's daily existence: they are crucial episodes in the choice of life, a problem that receives only passing mention in *The Spectator*. *The Idler,* on the other hand, restores marriage to its Spectatorial condition as a problem in personal and financial relations (*Idlers* 13, 28, 35, 47, 53, 86). Two of the letters written to the Idler by Johnson's friends appeal for counsel in courtship difficulties (*Idlers* 42, 54). One senses that such letters in Johnson's periodical essays have been put together according to a formula now showing signs of wear.[19]

The last of the three major kinds of fiction for which the voice of Addisonian humour is responsible consists of narratives and descriptions devoted to eccentricity of character for its own sake. "Odd and uncommon Characters are the Game that I look for, and most delight in," says the Spectator after his encounter with Will Wimble (no. 108). In London, with the same metaphor on his mind, he finds "such a Variety of odd Creatures in both Sexes that they foil the Scent of one

18. For a few of hundreds of possible examples, see *Plain Dealers* 6, 39, 40, 41, 47, 58, 62; *Universal Spectators* 3, 9, 10, 20, 21, 23, 31, 92, 112, 593 (this last excerpted in *Gentleman's Magazine* 10 [1740]: 69). For another context for similar fiction, see James Hodges, "The *Female Spectator,* a Courtesy Periodical," *Studies in the Early English Periodical,* ed. R. Bond, pp. 151–82.

19. Impolite behavior in *The Rambler:* nos. 34, 61?, 74, 98, 200. The choice of life in *The Spectator:* no. 162; see also *Guardian* 31 (Budgell).

another, and puzzle the Chace" (no. 131). This brand of humour may be traced at least as far back as Ben Jonson, who trafficked in misfits of every description, eccentric as well as obsessive and affected; but eccentrics in *The Spectator* are more harmless and more amiable than their ancestors in seventeenth-century comedy. Sir Roger de Coverley, of course, wins all the prizes for harmless, lovable eccentricity, but he is only the best known among a swarm of "amiable humourists" in *The Spectator*. The voice of Addisonian humour is exactly suited to introduce and negotiate with such characters because of its unctuousness—its hypersensitivity to the public-relations aspects of civilizing the reading public of Great Britain. The condescending affection this voice displays toward "odd and uncommon Characters" helps to establish intimacy with readers (some of whom are odd, or write as though they were), and at the same time invites readers to imitate the Spectatorial sophistication that makes such condescension possible.

Mr. Spectator himself, solemn, taciturn, and short-faced, is a notable eccentric, forced by the peculiarity of his living habits to move two or three times before he finds a landlady who "complies with my Humour in every thing" (*Spectator* 12). He has some pretensions to learning, has visited Egypt to measure a pyramid, and "collects" the conversation of all sorts and conditions of men, "Highest and Lowest" alike. Yet "the working of my own Mind, is the general Entertainment of my Life" (*Spectators* 1 and 4). These attributes qualify him as forerunner of a comic archetype of considerable importance for eighteenth-century literature, the bumbling philosopher, learned, eccentric, innocuous, and not quite part of the real world: with generous allowances for individual variation, this category includes Parson Adams, the Vicar of Wakefield, and Johnson himself in certain scenes of Boswell's *Life*.[20]

20. The dinner with Wilkes plays on Johnson's eccentricities, pictures him muttering "Too, too, too" at a crucial juncture (Boswell, 3 : 64–79). Most of the time Johnson is too alert and formidably articulate to be cast as the Bumbling Philosopher. But it is ironic that Johnson, the patron of Cervantic comedy, should himself be remembered partly as a Cervantic hero. Some of the more harmless virtuosos in eighteenth-century fiction

Mr. Spectator of course pretends that *The Spectator* is his periodical, that it is he, the short-faced, speechless recluse, who writes all these essays. This fiction is capable of striking effects, in the visit to Sir Roger's estate, for example (*Spectators* 106–32). More commonly, the Spectator makes his daily life—including a due measure of quirks and eccentric habits—the excuse for reflections on this topic or that: "upon my walking behind the Scenes last Winter . . ."; "I remember I was once in a mixt Assembly . . ."; "when I was in France I used to . . ." The amount of genuine action he performs in the periodical as a whole is small, but the intimacy established by these very slight intrusions of the "author" in his own person is bolstered by repeated use of the first person singular and a familiar style. Followers of *The Spectator* pounced on this fiction. Some developed it with more ingenuity than had Addison and Steele (e.g., *Plain Dealers* 1, 11, 13, 14, 17, 29, 32–34); others found themselves hampered by it, having chosen as editor-author a character of limited scope and inflexible character (the Censor, the Free-Thinker).

Boswell felt that Johnson was "not very happy in the choice of his title, 'The Rambler,' which certainly is not suited to a series of grave and moral discourses"; he describes how Johnson, "at a loss" for a name, fixed on "The Rambler" as "the best that occurred" to him.[21] It seems likely, however, that Johnson decided to be the Rambler so as to avoid the constraint of an editorial identity committed to a particular point of view. "Nullius addictus jurare in verba magistri, / Quo me cunque rapit tempestas, deferor hospes," is the motto of collected editions. The first sentence of *Spectator* 3 uses the word *ramble* as an equivalent for easygoing investigations into *quicquid agunt homines:* "In one of my late Rambles, or rather Speculations, I looked into the great Hall. . . ." Lewis Theobald picked up this cue in *Censor* 25: "As in the sedate

---

may be included in this category (e.g., *Tatler* 216). Scriblerian pedants are of course not amiable or harmless, but noxious and nasty. Matt Bramble and Walter Shandy are also, each in his own way, sage buffoons.

21. Boswell, 1 : 202. Mayo, *The English Novel in the Magazines,* points out that this title was used before and after 1750 as a promise of "raffishness": see pp. 93, 384 n. 22, 395 n. 28.

Moments of my Life, I take frequent Rambles of Speculation, so I never fail of having my Mind as well as Eye delighted with the Variety of Objects which occur to my Observation."

The Rambler is not intended to be a dominating personality or an active participant in the fiction of his periodical essay. Somewhat to our surprise, he comes to life in no. 109: a correspondent announces that although the Rambler seems "to have taken a view sufficiently extensive of the miseries of life," there is at least one species of wretchedness he the reader can add to the list:

> I cannot but imagine the start of attention awakened by this welcome hint; and at this instant see the Rambler snuffing his candle, rubbing his spectacles, stirring his fire, locking out interruption, and settling himself in his easy chair, that he may enjoy a new calamity without disturbance. For, whether it be, that continued sickness or misfortune has acquainted you only with the bitterness of being; or that you imagine none but yourself able to discover what I suppose has been seen and felt by all the inhabitants of the world: whether you intend your writings as antidotal to the levity and merriment with which your rivals endeavour to attract the favour of the publick; or fancy that you have some particular powers of dolorous declamation, and "warble out your groans" with uncommon elegance or energy; it is certain, that whatever be your subject, melancholy for the most part bursts in upon your speculation, your gaiety is quickly overcast, and though your readers may be flattered with hopes of pleasantry, they are seldom dismissed but with heavy hearts.

Exaggerated gloom could have been worked up as the Rambler's controlling eccentricity, and could have served as the occasion for interesting incidents. But apart from these paragraphs and a phrase or two elsewhere (nos. 59, 167, 199), the Rambler's pessimism is not a fiction but a fact, and he acts hardly at all.

The "odd and uncommon characters" he meets are more old-fashioned than those in *The Spectator:* there are no "amiable humourists" in *The Rambler,* and eccentricity takes grotesque forms. The Rambler seems to lose patience with some of the characters he describes, and despite the "union of charity and sadness" (thus the Yale editors, *Works,* 2 : xx) that we sense underneath everything, he speaks sometimes from simple exasperation. The behavior of many of the Rambler's acquaintances seems calculated to make them repulsive, not amiable. *Rambler* 138 (again, as if in emulation of *The Spectator*) sets out in quest of "original characters" and finds Mrs. Busy, a fanatical housewife; but by the end of the essay she has turned into a paradigm of culpably "absurd prudence" who lets her children grow up illiterate because of her contempt for "the nicety of a boarding school."

Mrs. Busy is one of a handful of characters in *The Rambler* with English names (Lady Bustle, Miss Maypole, Squire Bluster, Frolick, Madam Prune, and Zosima's tormentors). The switch from a Latin (or Greek) nomenclature to names like these, which seem modeled after the names of minor personages in stage comedy, is a signal that Johnson is consciously attempting to lighten his tone, reaching after humour again. In practice, as we have seen, these characters are no more amiable or amusing than the characters who wear Latin labels. Nevertheless, some of the traditional comic modes, the unfunny ones, do provide a relevant framework for Johnson's periodical-essay fiction. The embodiment of a moral defect may be quite a proper target for what Ben Jonson calls "the rage or spleen of comic writers"—satirical, not "laughing" or sentimental comedy. A crucial experience of complaints in *The Rambler* is frustration, frustration doubled, redoubled, and multiplied into (again it is Ben Jonson's phrase) "the comedy of affliction." By a slight adjustment of perspective, the trials of Cupidus in *Rambler* 73 or of Misocapelus in *Rambler* 116 appear not as gloomy tales of woe (this was how they looked to us in chapter 2), but as the comedy of repeated failure, like Charlie Brown's misfortunes on the baseball diamond. A happy ending of some sort, however, is essential to comedy, conversion or union or reconciliation, and since the nearest Johnson's heroes and heroines come to so desirable a state of affairs is resignation, their narratives make better sense as satire than as comedy.[22]

22. Jonson, *The Alchemist* (1612), Prologue: "No country's mirth is better than our own; / No clime breeds better matter for your whore, /

The Idler makes more concessions to reigning modes in the periodical essay than *The Rambler* does. Its dramatis personae all have English names, their eccentricities are relatively harmless, and sometimes even lovable (e.g., Druggett, in nos. 16 and 18).[23] The more Addisonian they are, however, the less Johnsonian; few readers find Peter Plenty's wife memorable or significant. Nor is *The Idler* entirely free from the prickliness we noticed in *The Rambler*. Its correspondents sometimes feel themselves injured by trivial discomforts, amusing foibles are transformed under our eyes into something dangerous or malicious, and the *vis comica* expires, as it had in *Ramblers* 61 and 138 (e.g., *Idlers* 46 and 86).

This is not to imply that fiction in *The Idler* is ineffectual. The familiar melancholy reasserts itself in Sober *(Idler* 31) and in the story of Dick Linger, whose idleness reduces him to "rage and despair" (*Idler* 21). When light humour in *The Idler* succeeds, it is antiromantic and literary, however, not a version of the Addisonian comedy of manners. Will Marvel's inflated account of the perils of a journey into the country lacks no species of "romantic danger but a giant and a dragon," and amusingly translates an ordinary expedition into "sounding words and hyperbolical images" (*Idler* 49). *Idler* 71 is a miniature Cervantic farce. Its hero, Dick Shifter, has erected a towering idealization of country life on foundations pieced together out of books, and "talked for several years"

Bawd, squire, imposter, many persons more, / Whose manners, now called humours, feed the stage, / And which have still been subject for the rage / Or spleen of comic writers." *Epicoene, or The Silent Woman,* act 2, scene 6: "For God's sake, let's effect it; it will be an excellent comedy of affliction, so many several noises." Compare Juvenal, *Satire* 5. 156–60, "hoc agit ut doleas; nam quae comoedia, mimus quis melior plorante gula?" ("He does it to give you pain; for what comedy, what mime, is better than a complaining belly?"). See also Northrop Frye, *Anatomy of Criticism* (Princeton, 1957), pp. 163–71.

23. Sophron (*Idler* 57) is the only person in *The Idler* whose name means something in a classical language, unless we count Dick Minim. Among the fullest discussions of the differences between characters in *The Rambler* and in *The Idler* is Boylston Green, "Samuel Johnson's Idler: a Critical Study" (Ph.D. dissertation, Yale University, 1941), pp. 58–76.

"about homely quiet and blameless simplicity, pastoral delights and rural innocence." He rents a "solitary house" thirty miles from London, and promises himself "many a happy day when he should hide himself among the trees." After writing a letter celebrating his arrival in "the regions of calm content and placid meditation," he sallies forth to meet "the true Arcadians," and is twice "decoyed . . . into a ditch," once looking for an imaginary bird's nest and once on a blind horse. The plot we have met before: Euphelia of *Ramblers* 42 and 46 was also disappointed by her country visit, but her complaints changed into acrimonious accusations, whereas Shifter's discomfiture is pleasingly frivolous.

The voice of Addisonian humour imposes a certain irregular unity on *The Spectator*. Journalists attempting to duplicate the success of Mr. Spectator—and that includes Addison and Steele—found it exceedingly difficult to hit upon an editorial personality as versatile as his; as a result, by working consciously within Spectatorial conventions they forfeited *The Spectator*'s most valuable asset, its flexibility. And so Johnson criticizes the character of the Guardian for being

> too narrow and too serious: it might properly enough admit both the duties and the decencies of life, but seemed not to include literary speculations, and was in some degree violated by merriment and burlesque. What had the Guardian of the Lizards to do with clubs of tall or of little men, with nests of ants, or with Strada's prolusions? [*Lives*, 2 : 104–5]

The Idler makes a clever compromise between narrowness and simple heterogeneity. The irony of the first three essays prepares us to accept an expansive conception of idleness: "Every man is, or hopes to be, an Idler"; "It is naturally indifferent to this race of men what entertainment they receive, so they are but entertained." The dramatis personae of *The Idler* include a few genuine loafers (Tom Tranquil, Dick Linger) and a larger number of hard-working malingerers whose idleness "dignifies itself by the appearance of business": Tom Restless, Jack Whirler, Dick Minim (*Idlers* 48, 19, 60, and 61), and the wives or husbands in *Idlers* 13, 35, 47, 53. The Idler discourses of much that appears to be busy-ness as one of the "Disguises of idleness": the virtuoso's enterprise (nos. 17, 31, 55, 56), the don's projects (no. 67), newspapers (nos. 7, 30, 40, 85), politics (no. 10). The idea of idleness in its broadest interpretation encompasses recreation (nos. 25, 34, 58), light reading (nos. 77, 84, 97), luxury (nos. 37, 39, 63, 80), various forms of intellectual indolence (nos. 78, 83, 91, 92, 94), and, as a corollary, directions for the proper use of time (nos. 24, 43, 44, 72, 74, 88, 101). Johnson manages to crowd a good deal of variety into the domain of idleness. Of course, many essays in *The Rambler* may be herded into the same corral. Thematic unity in *The Idler* is as much a result of Johnson's concern with the proper use of human resources, especially the resources of the mind, as of Spectatorial conventions.

The Catonist

"I will not meddle with the Spectator, let him fair-sex it to the world's end," Swift wrote Stella. There is one family of voices in the periodical essay that makes no pretensions to sophistication, and scorns to flatter the ladies; let us call them Catonists. Their principal claim to attention is blunt, old-fashioned virtue; they are well along in years, robust, outspoken; their irony is biting, not whimsical. They are proud to occupy a middle station between the titled aristocracy, which is liable, in their view, to corruption by foreign luxury, and the inarticulate mob of workingmen and petty bourgeois. They are intensely patriotic and intensely political. Wycherley's Plain Dealer (1676) was a surly malcontent, and Aphra Behn's Ned Blunt (1677) differed from his friends, the other banished cavaliers, by his rural gullibility ("Oh, I'm a cursed Puppy, 'tis plain, Fool was writ upon my Forehead, she perceiv'd it,—saw the Essex Calf there") rather than by his virtue: both these types persist into the eighteenth century, in the Censor ("Being lineally descended from *Benjamin Johnson* of surly Memory . . . sworn and avow'd [Foe] to Nonsense, bad Poets, illiterate Fops, affected Coxcombs, and all the Spawn of Follies and impertinence, that make up and incumber the present Generation"), and in Arbuthnot's John Bull (1712), who though "an honest, plain-dealing fellow," is too careless, intemperate, and scatterbrained to be responsible for a periodical essay. The true eighteenth-century Catonist growls but does not slaver; though more nearly allied to Juvenal than to Horace, and though he subscribes to Juvenal's nostalgic moralism, he repudiates Juvenal's cynicism.

Nestor Ironsides, the Guardian (1713), is an early model of the Catonist. Seventy-one years old, he has "nothing to manage with any person or party, but to deliver myself as becomes an old man" (no. 1), a tough and crusty old man, inured to cold (no. 102). A passionate moralist, he indulges himself in confident sarcasms at the expense of modern flimsiness, and like later Catonists he is preoccupied with the problem of the use of riches: with estate management (nos. 2, 5, 6, 9), marriage as a financial transaction (nos. 5, 57, 73, 97), the national wealth (nos. 6, 9, 52, 76). Ironsides, however, is too prissy, too much a nursemaid, and not blunt enough for a genuine Catonist. He is also given to spasms of sentiment; he palpitates over the ennobling power of love (e.g., in no. 7). So does the author-editor of *The Plain Dealer,* "a talkative *Old Batchelor*" in his "grand Climacterick." The fiction in this periodical is a mixed lot, but except for a letter in no. 26 beginning "I am a most *Catonick* Adherent to the Old, *English,* Simplicity; the Vertue, the Bluntness, and the Liberty, which were the Ornaments of our Ancestors," Catonists of the type we are concerned with do not assert themselves in Hill's pages.

One of the voices in *The Free-Thinker* (1718–21) is a Catonist, and though his interests run to morals and politics rather than fiction, his tone and stance are sufficiently uncompromising to bear quotation. No. 24, in a thumbnail history of politeness, describes how luxury spread like dry rot from the despotic East to Greece, Rome, and up into Europe, unmanning "even the stout hardy Tempers of the *North.*"

> It is by no means my Design to encourage a surly and brutal Intercourse of Life; but to bring back my Countrey-men to the Homespun Good Breeding of their Ancestours; and to banish the pernicious Refinements, which have been imported from those Forreign Countries, where Tyranny and Absolute Government prevail. Those, who dis-

dain to Fawn, will never Insult: and the Civilities proper for a Free People, are such as teach them to be neither Arrogant, nor Abject: such as an honest Man may pay with Honour, and a Man of Sense may receive without a Blush. Therefore when the Courtier happens to invite a Farmer to his Table, and gives his Service to him in a Bumper, I am pleased to hear the Elegant Plowman reprimand him by saying, *His Love is sufficient.*

Note the abruptness here, an impatience reflected in energetic apothegms ("Those, who disdain to Fawn, will never Insult") and in concise colorful anecdotes: the Catonist adopts a curt style, deliberately eschewing the refined and soothing periphrases of Addisonian humour. Catonists scoff at most aristocratic refinements, social, cultural, or economic. A correspondent calling himself Harry English confesses to *The Craftsman* that he is "one of those, whom our *Anti-Patriots* contemptuously treat as the *Mob, Mechanicks, sturdy Beggars,* and *Slaves;* One, who hath the Insolence to make Use of his five Senses, and thinks himself capable of feeling a sharp Injury, or smelling a rank Villain, as sensibly as the highest of his *Betters.*" Indignation (righteous, rather than savage), sturdy but often class-conscious independence, and deliberately roughhewn language are characteristic of the Catonist.[24]

This tone, stance, and style are precisely suited to the message they carry: the Catonist, though various in his incarnations, is a coherent personality, sustained and held together by contempt for modern times: a critical contempt based on a definite view of history, with affiliations to what has been

24. *Craftsman,* May 3, 1740, text as quoted in *Gentleman's Magazine,* 10 (1740): 235–36. The roughhewn indignation of Catonists may be sampled in many of the essays in *The Universal Spectator* signed "K" (e.g., nos. 38, 40, 44). "K," according to Henry Baker's annotated copy of *The Universal Spectator,* now in the Hope Collection at the Bodleian Library, was John Kelly (?1680–1751), playwright, journalist, translator (see *DNB;* I am indebted to Mr. D. G. Neill of the Bodleian for answers to my questions on contributors to *The Universal Spectator*). It is because Kelly writes (ordinarily) as a Catonist that his essays (nos. 24–44, even numbers, and scattered essays thereafter) make such a refreshing addition to the periodical, by the contrast they furnish with most of Henry Baker's work.

called Spartanism in economics and to various forms of conservatism in politics and ethics. Civilization, according to Catonists, is like a fruit: it evolves from harsh vigor to ripeness and then to decay—Catonists are convinced that their country is sinking into the pulpy-rotten stage. The history of classical Rome, seen as a continuous development from barbaric simplicity to decadent luxury, served countless writers as a model for the history of English civilization, and to a very large number of Englishmen—many of whom, of course, had no occasion to borrow the voice of the Catonist—the new prosperity and the new politics of the first half of the eighteenth century appeared as dangerous symptoms of a terminal disease. To quote *Free-Thinker* 24 again,

> *Rome,* which was a Medley of Nations, for a long time was but very Rude and Unpolish'd; while their Labours were wholly employed upon War and Husbandry. As they began to be civilized by Laws, to apply themselves a little to the Arts of Peace, and to multiply; Necessity brought the Inferiour People to be Humble and Respectful; and Ambition made the Great Men Affable. At last, Plenty and Luxury, joined to their Intercourse with the *Greeks* (whose ancient Vertue was degenerated into Politeness) carried Urbanity to its Perfection, towards the End of the Common wealth. After which, it languished by Degrees; and in the Decline of the Empire sunk into an insipid, effeminate and dishonourable, Way of Behaviour. From hence the sordid Politenesses spread themselves first into the *Southern* Parts of *Europe,* and in the End corrupted even the stout hardy Tempers of the *North.* . . .

If Roman backgrounds are a ubiquitous "reservoir of attitudes" for eighteenth-century Englishmen, we may chart the territory occupied by the Catonist as one substantial arm of that reservoir, merging into other large allusions to Rome at many points, but distinct in substance and tendency.[25]

25. Maynard Mack, "'Wit and Poetry and Pope,'" *Pope and his Contemporaries,* ed. J. L. Clifford and L. Landa (Oxford, 1949), p. 34, citing J. C. Maxwell, "Demigods and Pickpockets: The Augustan Myth in Swift and Rousseau," *Scrutiny* 11 (1942–43): 34–39, who cites in his turn Christopher Dawson, "Edward Gibbon," *Proceedings of the British Academy* (1934), pp. 162–64. Also useful: Addison Ward, "The Tory View of Roman History," *SEL* 4 (1964): 413–56.

One must distinguish between the Catonist's ideas or concepts and the Catonist's voice as a vehicle for fiction. Most of his ideas were common coin, and circulated far beyond the narrow pale of the periodical essay. One of the richest legacies of imperial Rome was literary and political nostalgia, for lost simplicities, for a nation of free and honest patriots living all the old pieties. Authorities as diverse as Plato and Machiavelli diagnosed the sickness of a state in terms of luxury, and some of the enemies of Mandeville trafficked in a brand of moralistic economics ("luxury corrupts") similar to the Catonist's.[26] When Pope reworks the story of Job for eighteenth-century readers, he substitutes prosperity (i.e., luxury) for affliction: "Satan now is wiser than of yore, / And tempts by making rich, not making poor." The hero of this pregnant parable (in *Moral Essay* 3), Sir Balaam, once a "plain good man," "Religious, punctual, frugal, and so forth," falls easy victim to luxury, takes a bribe from France, is impeached, curses God, and dies. Swift indicted Marlborough in 1710 on charges framed in terms of Roman integrity and simplicity (*Examiner* 16). Gulliver summons from the past a typical British yeoman, and the contrast between his stalwart virtue and modern decadence is almost comic, as if Swift were exploiting the Catonist's view of history and laughing at it at the same time (part 3, chapter 8). Within this view of history, so splendidly imprecise in its definitions, many different kinds of political discontent found refuge, Whig as well as Tory: *Cato* (1713) was written by a Whig to warn against the Pretender as a threat to the old British (Roman) liberties; and, of course, the

26. *Republic* bk. 8 (547B, 548B, 556C–E, 558D–561D); Machiavelli, *Discourses,* ed. and trans. L. J. Walker (New Haven, 1950), 1 : 213, 516. See J. W. Johnson, *The Formation of English Neo-Classical Thought* (Princeton, 1967), pp. 48–50, 56–57, for luxury as a major destructive force in history, theories of ripeness and decay, and the body-state analogy on which such theories are based; E. A. J. Johnson, *Predecessors of Adam Smith* (New York, 1937), pp. 74, 141–57, 289–93, for the economists on luxury and imports. I am grateful to Simeon M. Wade for permission to read his Ph.D. dissertation, "The Idea of Luxury in Eighteenth-Century England" (Harvard University, 1968), which supplies hundreds more such references.

Tories applauded the same play as an attack on Marlborough, considering him a similar threat to the same liberties. The opposition to Walpole on the left *and* on the right (*Cato's Letters* on the one hand, Bolingbroke on the other) based its fulminations against corruption, tyranny, and luxury on something like the Catonist's values and historical perspective.[27]

Johnson himself exploited some of these values and subsumed this view of history in 1738–39, in his inflammatory contributions to the assault by opposition "patriots" against Walpole (e.g., *London,* and the *Vindication of the Licensers*), but during the 1740s he seems to have reexamined the Catonist's creed, with the result that his mature opinions on each of the key terms of that creed—liberty, luxury, patriotism, and the good old days—are wholly free from cant. The political rhetoric of *Cato,* for example, leaves him cold: "The time however was now come, when those, who affected to think liberty in danger, affected likewise to think that a stage-play might preserve it." The stance or attitude of the Catonist (irrespective of his ideas or of the fiction associated with his voice) is indispensable in one Augustan petit-genre to which Johnson's contribution is memorable, the Letter to a Noble Lord. No matter how lofty the language of such letters—and Johnson's letter to Chesterfield strikes heroic tones—the writer cannot avoid assuming an air of sturdy independence in his appeal to standards more abiding than rank.[28]

Fiction associated with the voice of the Catonist owes its peculiar character not so much to politics as to the Catonist's

27. See J. G. A. Pocock, "Machiavelli, Harrington, and English Political Ideologies in the 18th Century," *William and Mary Quarterly,* 3d ser. 22 (1965): 549–83; Isaac Kramnick, "Augustan Politics and English Historiography: the Debate on the English Past, 1730–35," *History and Theory* 6 (1967): 33–56. Throughout the century a substantial minority of Parliament considered itself *above* party, as Catonists do: see Sir Lewis Namier, "Country Gentlemen in Parliament, 1750–84," *Crossroads of Power* (New York, 1962), pp. 30–45 (Enid Muir Lecture, 1954).

28. *Lives,* 2 : 99. Other Letters to Noble Lords: *Guardian* 123 (Addison); Pope to Lord Carteret, February 16, 1722/3 (*Correspondence,* ed. G. Sherburn [Oxford, 1956], 2 : 159–60); Pamela to Mr. B. (Everyman ed., pp. 120–21); Junius, no. 35.

violent contempt for hypocrisy, venality, and fashionable vice. Certain episodes lend themselves more readily than others to the expression of this contempt; among them I have chosen three that seem to me characteristic and comparatively easy to handle: the visit to a masquerade; a Rake's Progress (the education of a fop); and the visit to a domestic utopia (the mean and sure estate). Each of these deals directly or by implication with the use of riches, with discrepancies between meretricious appearances and sordid reality, and with the corruption of contemporary values. When any other voice than that of the Catonist narrates these episodes, different themes receive emphasis: a masquerade, for example, is the scene of a thrilling abduction in *Grandison;* and in tender-minded authors, visits to domestic utopias are the occasion for tenderness, not statistics. In general, there are fewer of the Catonist's standard fictions in Johnson's periodical essays than in any other major essay journal of the period.

To Catonists, a masquerade is a festival of hypocrisy, an emblem of the depravity of modern man.

> It has very often administer'd Matter of Wonder to me, that your grave Citizens, and some other such superstitious People, should take such Pains to display their Indignations against the modern Gaiety of *Masquerades;* since, if they would seriously consider and survey the World, they would be forc'd to confess it nothing but a mere Groupe of Maskers human Nature round; and that all the Busines of the two-leg'd rational Inhabitants, is nothing more nor less than to amuse or impose upon the rest of their Fellow-sojourners under a Vizor.[29]

Addison ridicules the Tory Fox-hunter's amazement at the sight of harlequins and dominoes early one morning in London (*Freeholder* 44). Henry Stonecastle takes a guided tour of a masquerade (in *Universal Spectator* 26) in which each masker dresses as his opposite, parading in the costume of the folly he is least suited for. "See but one Masquerade," says Miss Forward in 1740—in an essay excerpted for *The Gentleman's Magazine* during Johnson's tenure at St. John's Gate—"and

29. Preface, *The World Turn'd Inside-Out; or, Humankind Unmask'd* (London, 1737).

you will never blush again, my Life on't." Since no contemporary institution more satisfyingly exemplifies the Catonist's conviction that public values are upside down and inside out, none supplies better fuel for indignation or riper material for satire.[30]

Endowed with a satirical cast of mind, and tuned to decadence as he is, the Catonist relishes chronicles of corruption; it seems to him quite natural that flowers fester, he does not yearn for happy endings but finds the triumph of evil (quite a different thing from tragedy) aesthetically satisfying. Among the various forms in which evil triumphs in eighteenth-century art, one particularly interests the Catonist, a Rake's Progress, or the story of a promising youth's initiation into luxury, his education in the vices of the beau monde, his rapid physical and spiritual decay, and (if the episode continues so far) his eventual destruction. This episode is by no means the exclusive property of Catonists. Where it appears in picaresque fiction (e.g., *The English Rogue* [1665], chapter 10; *Gil Blas* [trans. T. Smollett, 1749] bk. 3, chs. 4 and 5; *Fanny Hill,* early chapters), the hero is permitted to enjoy his initiation into vice and wallow briefly in delicious luxury. When it appears in the Tory satirists (Swift, "To Mr. Congreve" [1693], lines 109–46; *Intelligencer* 9 [1729]; Pope, *Dunciad,* bk. 4, lines 275–336), they seem to have adopted some of the premises of the Catonist, though not his pretensions to unpretentiousness and simplicity. The Catonist is likely to draw a vivid contrast between the subject's robust usefulness before his matriculation in the school of luxury and his debilitated condition afterward: his physical and financial health receive more attention than do his profligacy or wickedness, and his role is a relatively passive one (e.g., *Spectator* 154; *Guardian* 151; *Universal Spectators* 45, 58).

A Catonist has little interest in complex human responses or moral ambiguity. This is why the domestic utopias he

30. *Universal Spectator,* January 19, in *Gentleman's Magazine* 10 (1740): 25–26. See also *Tatler* 237, *Spectator* 8, *Guardians* 142, 154, *Plain Dealer* 2, *Female Spectator* 1 (1744), *Student* 5 (1750), and *Hogarth's Graphic Works,* ed. Ronald Paulson (New Haven, 1965), 1 : 26.

sometimes visits read as if they had been constructed out of papier-maché: most of their authors' energies are channeled into moralistic economics, not the drama of human relations. We are presented in these episodes not with a group of individuals, but with a socioeconomic unit: the sobriety of the parents is balanced by industry and obedience in the children and servants; tenants and neighbors receive charity gratefully and work no less dutifully in their appointed stations. The family subsists on its own produce; it imports neither foreign luxuries nor urban amusements. This is an episode of some importance in the eighteenth-century novel.[31]

Johnson shares the Catonist's ardent contempt for hypocrisy, venality, and fashionable vice; he subscribes to most of the Catonist's negative judgments of the contemporary world. But there is no suggestion in Johnson's fiction that British society used to be better than it now is, no matter how many absurd pastimes have been invented in the past hundred years. The modernity of masquerades offends Catonists; Johnson objects to their immorality ("an entertainment . . . where bashfulness may survive virtue, and no wish is crushed under the frown of modesty" [*Rambler* 10]). Johnson agrees that "the rich and the powerful live in a perpetual masquerade, in which all about them wear borrowed characters" (*Rambler* 75), but the fact—if fact it be—that, as one Catonist puts it, "it was not in diversions, such as our modern *masquerades* in winter, and *ridottoes al fresco* in summer, that our ancestors passed their evenings" seems to him irrelevant, or merely false.[32]

31. See *Guardians* 2, 5, 6, 7, 13, 26, 31, 37, 43 (the Lizard family); *Universal Spectators* 15, 60, 95; *Praters* 3, 19 (1756) (this periodical not only follows *The Rambler* but also shows its influence; I cite it because these two essays are uncommonly fine examples of the Catonist mentality). Hogarth, "Beer Street and Gin Lane" (*Graphic Works*, Pls. 197–200), draws on some of the same political and economic values. Mr. Wilson and Matt Bramble at home inhabit domestic utopias, each after his own kind, and the Vicar of Wakefield tries to hold one together in the face of astonishing odds.

32. *Female Spectator* (1744), no. 1 (vol. 1, p. 25 of 2d ed. of collected edition [1748]). Eliza Haywood adopts a Catonist's stance only in her

Catonists make a fuss over the abuse of riches involved in a Rake's Progress: so many acres of rich bottom-land sold to support a mistress, a moderate competence squandered for the sake of luxuries. Money is an important fact in Johnson's fiction; venality is abruptly exposed in a number of the stories, where false friends steal away as soon as their friendship ceases to be profitable (*Ramblers* 75, 133, 153, 192, *Adventurer* 41). He does not often, however, in his fiction or out of it, evaluate people in economic terms.

In *Rambler* 109, listed in the table of contents as "The education of a fop," Florentulus describes his training as a ladies' man. His tone is truculent enough; not because he has wasted his substance or abandoned the paths of virtue, rather because, for all his expertise, he has made the wrong choice of life. After a few short years in which he is "universally caressed and applauded," he finds himself abandoned "to dream out [his] last years in stupidity and contempt." *Ramblers* 132, 194, and 195 are a history of Eumathes's fruitless efforts to instill a little learning into a young nobleman whose parents would rather see him a gentleman than a scholar. One finishes a reading of these three *Ramblers* with the feeling that the young man in question has not been ruined, just spoiled; Eumathes has had to compete not only with "the perpetual tumult of pleasure" by which his pupil's "imagination was filled" in London, but also and more fundamentally with parental indulgence. There is nothing very vicious in—to quote the table of contents—"A young nobleman's introduction to the knowledge of the town" (*Rambler* 195); and there is a great deal that is simply frivolous in his "progress in politeness" (*Rambler* 194). The expertise he develops as a man of fashion (*Rambler* 194) and his fledgling escapades as a rake (*Rambler* 195) seem more like comic catalogs than like the early stages of a fatal addiction to vice. Johnson does not want to talk about the degeneracy of British youth, but about the options open to British parents.

An overriding interest in positive choice is what transforms

sterner moments, in her role as governess of the ladies of Great Britain. Masquerades turn up occasionally in Johnson's writings as an emblem of fashionable bustle: *Ramblers* 39, 194, 195, *Adventurer* 34.

the story of Misargyrus (*Adventurers* 34, 41, 53, 62) from a Rake's Progress into a comedy of affliction followed by a descriptive list of Misargyrus's prison mates and what they made of their opportunities. In *Moll Flanders* and *Roderick Random,* prison is the vestibule of Hell; for Tom Jones it is a brief purgatory and the scene of serious thoughts.[33] Johnson, by quoting from book 6 of the *Aeneid* in *Adventurers* 34, 41, and 53, dabbles perhaps a little pompously in the same mythology; nevertheless, remorse and penitential suffering play minor roles indeed in this series; once Misargyrus has strutted into prison, he turns his attention to the life stories of the other inmates, for "Each has his lot," as the motto of *Adventurer* 53 tells us, "and bears the fate he drew."

The Man of Sentiment

A third important voice in periodical-essay fiction belongs to the Man of Sentiment. Like the Catonist, he is committed and passionate, but since he cares a great deal about nobility of sentiment, his style is elevated, not plain; he does not bark, he throbs. This voice speaks with full resonance in the periodical essays of Richard Steele. Presently we shall sample the narrative repertoire of this voice in *The Spectator* and its cousins, but the most colorful and carefully delineated Man of Sentiment (as an eidolon) presides over a less well-known periodical essay, *The Lover.*

This was a triweekly essay journal, forty numbers long, concocted by Steele during the spring of 1714 to "trace the Passion or Affection of Love, through all its Joys and Inquietudes, through all the Stages and Circumstances of Life, in both Sexes" (no. 1)—that is, to develop one of the many themes embraced in Steele's earlier periodicals, *The Tatler, Spectator,* and *Guardian,* in more detail than had been possible when he was responsible for manners and morals in general. The

33. *Moll Flanders* (1722; Signet ed. New York, 1964, p. 242); "This reflection sunk so deep into my soul, that I was for some days deprived of my reason, and actually believed myself in hell, tormented by fiends" (*Roderick Random,* vol. 1, ch. 23); *Tom Jones,* bk. 8, ch. 11, and bk. 18, ch. 10.

author-editor of *The Lover,* Marmaduke Myrtle by name, is a specialist in "the softer Affections of the Mind, which being properly raised and awakened, make way for the Operation of all good Arts" (no. 1). Struck down in his youth by the bright eyes of "Mrs. Ann Page," who subsequently married "a Gentleman of much greater Worth and Fortune," he has ever since been "cold to the Pursuits of Riches, Wealth and Power," and has passed the years, when not playing on the "Base-Viol," "in Observation upon the Force and Influence this Passion [love] has had upon other Men": "it is from the Experience of a Patient, I am become a Physician in Love" (no. 2). The "Simplicity" of his "Distress" and the "innocence" of his character disqualify him for more sophisticated sorts of discourse, irony or wit: having veered all unawares into whimsical mock pedantry on dancing in no. 4, he recalls himself, "But I forget that this is too elaborate for my Character." Simplicity, innocence, and deep feelings prompt him also to renounce "Names significant of the Person's Character of whom I talk; a Trick used by Playwrights" (no. 1); that is, his role as Man of Sentiment prompts him to shun a comic mode. In practice he forgets both these restrictions. Addisonian irony, with its bagful of familiar tricks (puffs, recipes, mock pedantry, whimsy, odd characters, species) gains a foothold in no. 4 and plays a not unimportant role in the periodical thereafter. Myrtle's voice, however, is intended to express romantic sentiment, and something very like his voice can be heard in numerous periodical essays in the first half of the eighteenth century.[34]

Miniature romances constitute a distinct species of periodical-essay fiction superintended, often at a distance, by a Man of Sentiment. They are easy enough to identify. Often, names give them away: Amaranthus, Bellamira, Calista, Daria,

34. For example: *Spectators* 2, 11, 26, 30, 56, 71, 84, 113; *Guardians* 7, 17, 19, 34, 37, 45, 79; *Lay-Monks* 13, 21, 27; *Free-Thinkers* 15, 33; *Plain Dealers* 12, 20, 28, 34, 40, 52. This last deserves quotation: "Poor! so deplorably poor, that his distress'd Widow, and Two or Three young lovely Children, at least *some* of 'em, are likely, e'er long, (— —O pity! pity!) even to——I *cannot* speak it!——What shall I say?——My Heart bleeds when I think of it."

Erminia, Florio, and so on through the alphabet. Equipped with such a name, protagonists need not flinch from ecstatic or desperate love, heroic or tragic generosity. "Inkle and Yarico" (*Spectator* 11) is a typical example, as is the story of Constantia and Theodosius (*Spectator* 164), which resembles in general outline the story of Eloisa and Abelard. Near kin to romance is the romantic tale that celebrates not only sublime passion but also sublime generosity or "greatness of soul." As Aaron Hill (or one of his collaborators) observes, romances frequently exhibit "some Heroick Examples of Vertue" (*Plain Dealer* 62); and in the words of the Idler, "There is no passion more heroick than love" (no. 39). Again, it is Richard Steele who polished this subspecies of narrative to a definitive brilliance, but many others worked effectively in the same medium. In a characteristic specimen, the son of an African prince, educated as a Christian at the court of Louis XIV, is insulted by one of his fellow guardsmen, and ignores it. Warned that he will be branded a coward, he challenges his insulter, disarms him, accepts his apology, and resigns his commission, declaring that "In my Countrey, we think it no Dishonour to act according to the Principles of our Religion." [35]

The Man of Sentiment is consulted and communed with by his readers, just as the Addisonian humourist was, but in a different fictional mode. *"Oh! Mr. Myrtle,"* writes Cinthio Languissante with towering obtuseness, "Had you seen her for whom my Breast pants this Moment, your *Ann Page* had been as utterly no more as *Cleopatra* who ruined *Anthony,* or *Statira* who captivated *Alexander!* heedless Man that I was—But what could Wisdom have availed me after seeing her! As she is fair, she is also inexorable. Alas! that what moves Passion should also be a check to our Desires . . ." (*Lover* 19). The Court of Love over which the Addisonian humourist presides handles simple misdemeanors, imprudence, frivolity, and

35. *Free-Thinker* 15. For other examples, see *Tatlers* 5, 60, 72, 94, 172, 185, 213; *Spectators* 292, 368; *Guardian* 17; *Lovers* 6, 30; *Plain Dealers* 5, 9, 35. On the authorship of different numbers of *The Plain Dealer,* see Dorothy Brewster, *Aaron Hill: Poet, Dramatist, Projector* (New York, 1913), pp. 157–60.

naïveté; more serious amorous predicaments are addressed to the Man of Sentiment, since pathos is his special province.

He, too, then, has his favorite episodes, stories suited to his voice, and pitched to a romantic audience. Among the most characteristic of these are tales of unhappy seduction. Like all fiction that belongs to the Man of Sentiment, these episodes of betrayal (microscopic versions of *Clarissa,* utterly unlike it in this respect) lack psychological depth and sacrifice complexity of characterization to mere pathos. They also exemplify the triumph of evil.[36]

In the most widely distributed of the Man of Sentiment's favorite episodes, a beloved person dies. The eighteenth century was fascinated with deathbed scenes—in real life as well as in fiction: we know what capital Bishop Burnet made of Rochester's death; and whether it is true or not, the story of Addison's summons to a free-thinking acquaintance to "see how a Christian can die" so neatly typifies a certain brand of Augustan piety that we cannot wish it stricken from the record. Pope versified the words of a dying Christian to his soul "in imitation of the famous sonnet of Hadrian," to show "how much superior in sense and sublimity . . . the *Christian* Religion is to the *Pagan.*" Chapter 19 of Hannah More's *Practical Piety, or The Influence of the Religion of the Heart on the Conduct of Life* (1811) is called "Happy Deaths": "Few circumstances contribute more fatally to confirm in worldly men that insensibility to eternal things which was considered in the preceding chapter, than the boastful accounts we sometimes hear of the firm and heroic deathbeds of popular but irreligious characters." Johnson refused to believe that Hume had died peacefully. Allworthy's bathetic farewell to life and Clarissa's endlessly moribund condition illustrate comic and tragic versions of the same episode; and one of the triumphs of

36. For example: *Tatlers* 33, 198 (Hazlitt: "Several of the incidents related there by Steele have never been surpassed in the heart-rending pathos of private distress"—*Works,* ed. Howe, 6 : 99); *Spectator* 190; *Guardian* 123; *Lay-Monk* 25; *Free-Thinker* 13; *Universal Spectators* 59, 67; *Female Spectator* 1 (but Eliza Haywood manages to reduce the most romantic material into cautionary tales); *Students* 6, 7, 8.

Boswell's art is "The Death of Johnson," the crisis of which portrays a virtuous man, as in Donne's poem, who passes mildly away, while some say the breath goes now, and some say no. In the periodical essays, deathbed scenes are more likely to be pathetic than pious, perhaps because of Richard Steele's influence.[37]

Given Johnson's well-known contempt for "the distresses of sentiment," for those who "*pay* you by feeling," given the majesty and solemnity, overall, of his writings between 1749 and 1759, it seems unlikely that the voice of the Man of Sentiment would be audible in *The Rambler*. The Rambler for the most part neglects the romantic passions, and omits anecdotes of heroic generosity. We may distinguish between sentimentality as an ethical, and as a literary, phenomenon; between cultivating sentiment for its own sake and "that habitual sympathy and tenderness, which, in a world of so much misery, is necessary to the ready discharge of our most important duties" (*Rambler* 80). Johnson, a man of his time, responded feelingly to literary pathos when it was not pretentious; Hannah More teased him about weeping over the tragedy of Jane Shore.

Johnson attempted two, perhaps two and one-half, of the favorite fictions of the Man of Sentiment. (The extra "half" is paragraph 13 of *Rambler* 161, where a quiet lady, attended by her sister, quietly expires. "The sister followed her to the grave, paid the few debts which they had contracted, wiped away the tears of *useless* sorrow" [my italics], and resumed the ordinary course of her life.) In *Ramblers* 186 and 187 Johnson tries his hand at romance, probably with Addison's "Story of Hilpa" (*Spectators* 584 and 585) in mind as a model. Both Johnson and Addison narrate a courtship between idealized lovers, whose union is delayed by the lady's vanity and a mercenary rival; both stories are set in a distant land among "primitive" people, and maneuver aspects of their exotic settings for some degree of comic surprise; both record love

37. *Tatlers* 82, 95 and 114, 181; *Guardian* 132; *Spectators* 84, 133, 204, 349; *Lover* 8; *Lay-Monk* 13; *Plain Dealers* 12, 28, 48, 79; *Universal Spectators* 5, 46–47; *Students* 5, 7, 8.

letters full of a "noble simplicity of sentiments"; and both are aware of the passage of the years as a threat to lovers. Johnson combines these elements in different proportions, however, according to what he can take seriously and what amuses him.

The story of Ajut and Anningait is much more noticeably "high burlesque" than is the story of Hilpa. Johnson's ritual of courtship, presented to the reader with a fine grandiloquent flourish, substitutes local artifacts for conventional gifts more self-consciously than does Addison's. Anningait announces his affections to Ajut at a feast by serving her "the tail of a whale." Eskimo similes, some of them delightfully particular,[38] are used to parody fashionable primitivisms and to poke fun at the "heroick and tender sentiments" of conventional romance. Anningait tells Ajut that "her fingers were white as the teeth of the morse" (a morse is a walrus). One of Anningait's soliloquies reminds me faintly of Swift's "Meditation on a Broomstick"—or of Johnson's own parody of ballad inanities ("I put my hat upon my head . . ."): "Oh life, frail and uncertain! where shall wretched man find thy resemblance but in ice floating on the ocean? It towers on high, it sparkles from afar, while the storms drive and the waters beat it, the sun melts it above, and the rocks shatter it below."

The parody in these two *Ramblers* is not exclusively literary, however; as in so many eighteenth-century accounts of non-Western lands, or of non-Western visitors in Europe, the joke is at the expense of readers' insularity. From a larger perspective, Johnson implies, the tail of a whale has as much absolute value as a whipped syllabub, or as little; diamonds are children's toys in the Eldorado of *Candide,* and mushroom broth prized, even at second hand, by Goldsmith's Tartars.[39]

38. For the source of these particulars, see Arthur Sherbo, "The Making of *Ramblers* 186 and 187," *PMLA* 67 (1952): 575–80. "High burlesque": David Worcester, *The Art of Satire* (Cambridge, Mass., 1932), p. 49.

39. *Citizen of the World,* Letter 32. The same effect is achieved in *Spectators* 584–85 by antediluvian chronology: Hilpa was "but a Girl of threescore and ten Years" when her first admirers came to court her; "Remember, O thou Daughter of *Zilpah,*" says Shalum, "that the Age of Man is but a thousand Years."

In this way exotic material is adopted to enlightened, not romantic, ends.

Selective quotation can give a quite different impression of Johnson's intentions here, however, because *Ramblers* 186 and 187 are a curious blend of quaintness and lyric grace. The phrase that compares Ajut's fingers to the teeth of a walrus—which really is grotesque, when one stops to think about it—is immediately preceded by a finer specimen of "noble simplicity" than any in Addison: "She was beautiful as the vernal willow, and fragrant as thyme upon the mountains." Perhaps thyme meant kitchens and pots to Johnson—not to me; and delicate rhythms here contrast sharply with the rattling anapests that follow.[40] When Ajut refuses to marry him until after the summer's harvest of fish is in, Anningait protests, and his appeal to a coy mistress—like Marvell's, part plea, part threat—is serious and beautiful. It would be more serious and more beautiful if it did not have a long, dull enlightenment joke spread out in the middle of it:

> "O virgin, beautiful as the sun shining on the water, consider," said Anningait, "what thou has required. How easily may my return be precluded by a sudden frost or unexpected fogs; then must the night be past without my Ajut. We live not, my fair, in those fabled countries, which lying strangers so wantonly describe; where the whole year is divided into short days and nights; where the same habitation serves for summer and winter; where they raise houses in rows above the ground; dwell together from year to year, with flocks of tame animals grazing in the fields about them; can travel at any time from one place to another, through ways enclosed with trees, or over walls raised upon the inland waters; and direct their course through wide countries by the sight of green hills or scattered buildings. Even in summer, we have no means of crossing the mountains, whose snows are never dissolved; nor can remove to any distant residence, but in our boats coasting the bays. Consider, Ajut; a few summer days, and a few winter nights, and the life of man is at an end. Night is the time of ease and festivity, of revels and gaiety; but

40. ◡◡′◡ ◡◡◡′ ◡′◡ ◡′ ◡◡′◡ ◡◡◡′◡; ◡◡′ ◡◡′ ◡◡′◡◡′. See Cecil Emden, "Rhythmical Features in Dr. Johnson's Prose," *RES* 25 (1949): 48–49.

what will be the flaming lamp, the delicious seal, or the soft oil, without the smile of Ajut?"

The mottled inconsistency of the story of Ajut and Anningait is a result of Johnson's dividedness. He plays the game of exotic romance with tongue in cheek, but capitalizes on the opportunities it offers for simple sublimities of metaphor, rather like the biblical sublimities in his oriental tales. The idea of the brevity of life touches a responsive chord in Johnson; it is of course a motive and a condition of the choice of life; on this theme he is urgent almost in spite of himself.

Though *Ramblers* 186 and 187 appear to fall within the province of the Man of Sentiment, as fiction they answer to the needs and demands of Johnson's personal literary consciousness, which was far less romantic than Steele's. *Ramblers* 170 and 171, our final example of Johnson's experiments with episodes much patronized by the Man of Sentiment, are pathetic rather than romantic. Their pathos, however, is curiously muffled, not weepy at all—and this in spite of Johnson's having bridled his instinct for poetic justice, for arranging things so that those who suffer, in one way or another deserve to.

Misella tells her own story. When she is ten years old, a wealthy relation offers to bring her up with his own children, in order to spare her father the expense of her maintenance. Within a few years his forgetfulness or neglect (she being wholly dependent on his patronage) reduces her to the status of an upper servant; and then suddenly he notices her again, gives her rich presents, and promises her more. He takes advantage of her gratitude and innocence to seduce her, moves her to London to give birth to his child, and finally gives up trying to convert her into his whore and abandons her. Her money is gradually spent. Bad luck and the wickedness of a neighbor prevent her from supporting herself by her needle; hunger forces her into the streets.

A simple tale, a sorry plight—but not, as Johnson tells it, truly pathetic, for a number of reasons. (1) Its circumstantiality. Misella informs us exactly how her troubles came to pass.

Her own personal responses enter into the story only as they influence what happens to her: Johnson seems to be trying to prove that she really was innocent, so that no reader can feel immune to her catastrophic affliction simply because he or she considers him or herself virtuous; Johnson is concentrating on the apparent naturalness and inevitability of the events that destroy his heroine, not on her feelings. This is especially true of *Rambler* 170, paragraphs 2–11, where the machinery of circumstances and conditions that ruin her is assembled: poverty, dependence, naïveté, lust. (2) Some of the most important particular events in this history are almost smothered by indirection: pregnancy—"Our crime had its usual consequence"; lying-in—"I was removed to lodgings in a distant part of the town, under one of the characters commonly assumed upon such occasions"; childbirth—"He provided all that was necessary, and in a few weeks, congratulated me upon my escape from the danger which we had both expected with so much anxiety." From one point of view these are circumlocutions; Johnson's reticence prevents him from entering into the details of exclusively female crises. From another, these are abbreviations; they exclude emotions. (3) When particulars do put in an appearance, it is as comic or satiric accessories, as food for indignation, and Misella for a few paragraphs reminds us of Zosima, the stalwart observer of her persecutors' meanness. For example, the first man who takes her for a prostitute recoils at the sight of her paleness and tears, "and bad me cant and whine in some other place; he for his part would take care of his pockets." [41] (4) Some of the darkest chambers of Misella's unhappiness are peopled not with childish laments but with stately personifications. "Chance had discovered my secret, and malice divulged it; and . . . nothing now remained, but to seek a retreat more private, where curiosity or hatred could never find us." "In this abject state I have now passed four years, the drudge of extortion and the sport of drunkenness." (5) The fundamental improbability

41. This not-too-obvious change of literary mode also occurs in *Rambler* 171, at the end of par. 6 and in par. 9. (Zosima is the heroine of *Rambler* 12.)

of Misella's narrative is the way she tells it: not the prose style so much as the intellectual resources behind the prose style, or within it—the powers of mind that make possible so effortless and masterful a summary of her case. A prostitute could plaster up her autobiography in a shell of pseudo-Johnsonian pomposities, but no prostitute would think the way Misella does.

The "History of Misella" may be read as a characteristic Johnsonian variation on several conventional themes. Seduction, a common motif in eighteenth-century fiction, does not commonly end in prostitution; in most cases the genteel victim is rehabilitated or mercifully exterminated well above those vulgar depths. Johnson, by contrast, does not flinch from the probabilities of the case, and describes Misella's half-accidental initiation into professional vice in frighteningly plausible detail (without a grain of erotic sensationalism). Prostitutes crop up occasionally in the major periodical essays as pathetic or disreputable objects, but very seldom as human beings.[42] Misella's degraded position, on the other hand, does not prevent her from speaking with dignity and frankness—too much dignity to be credible, perhaps, but she certainly comes across as more than a mere object of charity. Johnson's compassion and understanding and unwillingness to imagine how demoralizing four years of prostitution would almost certainly be, steer him clear of sentimentality on the one hand, grotesque comedy on the other, and lead him into a narrative realm that is at once complicated, absurd, and wise.

42. *Tatler* 33 (Jenny Distaff's encounter with a noble rake); *Tatler* 198 (a man with two wives); *Spectator* 266 (a beautiful, hungry whore); *Guardian* 123 (a letter from the mother of a seduced unfortunate to her noble seducer); *Lay-Monk* 25 (Clarissa's plight); *Free-Thinker* 13 (a well-born beauty abandoned by her seducer); *Universal Spectator* 59 (seduction and suicide); *Students* 6, 7, 8 (clergymen's daughters exploited and starving). In *Spectator* 190, Rebecca Nettletop tells her own story, but the exception proves the rule, in that she is a hard-bitten comic type, an excuse for anti-Catholic innuendo.

6 *Rasselas*

I will not print my name, but expect it to be known.
Johnson to Strahan, January 20, 1759,
writing of *Rasselas* just before publication

Rasselas is by all odds the most interesting and important of Johnson's narrative works; it is also the most problematic. Readers have disagreed as to whether it is a good book or a bad one, tragic or comic, well planned or sloppy. They have disagreed as to what kind of book it is in the first place; its generic affiliations are obscure; it has been explicated as comedy, as oriental tale, as novel, as apologue, and as the prose redaction of a poem. Critics have damned it for wooden characterization, inert plot, slipshod structure, unhealthy moral, and ponderous style; style, moral, structure, plot, and characterization have by other readers been fervently praised.[1]

Some responsibility for the heterogeneity of this haystack of commentary must devolve upon the work itself. There really is no way of knowing whether the four travelers return to the Happy Valley in the end, or simply to Abyssinia; [2] nor can we be sure what they have learned about the choice of life, since the evidence, scattered through the last seventeen chapters of the book, is scanty and contradictory. Our knowledge of the sources of *Rasselas* tells us less than one might have expected about its literary vitality. If to some degree and in certain ways it exploits the privileges of the Eastern Tale, the narrative conventions it observes are wholly occidental—acci-

1. The particular disagreements I find most revealing will be analyzed below. For various critical reactions to *Rasselas,* see William Kenney, "Johnson's *Rasselas* after two Centuries," *Boston University Studies in English* 3 (1957): 88–96; also, *Book-Lore* 1 (1884): 5–11.

2. George Sherburn, "Rasselas Returns—To What?" *PQ* 38 (1959): 383–84; Gwin J. Kolb, "Textual Cruxes in *Rasselas,*" *Johnsonian Studies,* ed. Magdi Wahba (Cairo, 1962), pp. 257–62.

dental, according to some readers, but certainly not oriental. The pace of the narrative is highly irregular, swift and slow by turns, obstructed not only by digressions on poetry and other topics but also by a disarming inconsistency of tone; for example (one to which we shall return), embedded in the philosophic nonsense of chapter 22 is a speech of deeply pathetic import by an unnamed sage, as if Hamlet at his unhappiest had interrupted a lecture by Herr Dr. Pangloss.

"Inconsistencies cannot both be right," says Imlac, "but, imputed to man they may both be true. Yet diversity is not inconsistency." We shall encounter both diversity and inconsistency in *Rasselas,* and shall impute them to Samuel Johnson. *Rasselas* tells us as much about its author as about the outside world, whether British or Egyptian. It belongs to a class of fiction the resources of which are more largely devoted to describing, expressing, and recording the author's attitudes and opinions and feelings than to the animation of characters different from him and events outside his own personal experience. We have no satisfactory name for this large class of fiction, perhaps because it is not a discrete class but rather one end of the jagged and multidimensional spectrum running between almost pure expression—propaganda, in some cases—and almost pure mimesis. At the other end of this spectrum are *tranches de vie* cut out of the fabric of the not-myself by authors interested in creating characters, painting scenes, or unfolding actions. Henry James remembers of the writing of *The Awkward Age* that "half the attraction was in the current actuality of the thing: repeatedly, right and left, . . . one had *seen* such a drama constituted." [3] *Rasselas,* of course, belongs at the didactic or expressive end of the spectrum; its kinship is with utopias, apologues, satires, and allegories more or less tightly organized around a point of view (not necessarily the point of view intended by the author). Expression versus mimesis: the dichotomy is crude

3. *The Art of the Novel,* ed. R. P. Blackmur (1934; rpt. New York, 1937), p. 102 (my italics). Whether or not mimesis as pure "creation" really exists, the term suggests a useful way of talking about many kinds of fiction.

but useful, like a large-scale map. It is true that the most dedicated realist or naturalist never succeeds in refining himself completely out of his writings, but he tries to make himself inconspicuous; he aspires to negative capability, and his work may legitimately be praised for verisimilitude, authenticity, and for the "richness" of the imaginative world he has "created." True also that even the most didactic fiction cannot avoid imitating some part of nature, however mechanically, and that the faintest trace of "represented action" is enough to catapult us into the realm of living untruth, if only for a paragraph or two. Neither end of the spectrum is perfectly clean. Most novels and romances fall somewhere between these two extremes, and manage to express an author's ideas and feelings by creating a believable realm of make-believe.[4]

Though it is convenient, and reasonable, to postulate an author behind every narrative, what is being expressed can make itself felt independently of the person or personality that did the writing: expression in this sense is part of the work, not the author; it figures among the various elements that contribute to overall aesthetic impact.[5] Critics of fiction have paid relatively little attention to works that concentrate on expression when expression is achieved, however artfully, at the expense of plot, character, authenticity, and other virtues proper to a well-wrought action. My approach differs from standard classroom thematics ("Discuss Fielding's ideas on prudence as expressed in *Tom Jones*") by the degree of its self-consciousness about fiction as art; and it differs from a

4. "It is not what a great writer has shown us he believes that matters, it is what he *is* and how his work reflects his being that counts" (Sheldon Sacks, *Fiction and the Shape of Belief* [Berkeley and Los Angeles, 1964], p. 253). I have profited greatly from insights on genre in this book, though I have not adopted the definitions in chapter 1.

The modern critical term "vision," as applied to novelists, permits emphasis on either expression or mimesis, which is one reason for its usefulness.

5. Aristotle, of course, includes "theme" as one of six constituent parts of tragedy (*dianoia:* see *Poetics* 6.8–9 and 6.22), but I am taking "expression" in a larger sense, to include emotions and attitudes as well as ideas.

common reaction *against* standard classroom thematics ("Fielding's ideas on prudence are one thing; *Tom Jones* as an aesthetic whole is quite another") by its recognition that ideas and attitudes and feelings that are sometimes hard, even impossible, to distinguish from the author's may function as the organizing principle of a work of art.

At the same time, it would be a mistake to identify expression, in the enlarged sense I intend, with Romantic self-expression. Expressive fiction, as I have defined it, may be totally unrecognizable as the spontaneous overflow of powerful feelings, may be abstract and didactic, may work entirely through literary conventions, without any reference whatsoever to personal experience or the dark recesses of a sensitive heart. Nor does what is expressed by a fiction correspond necessarily or exclusively to the aesthetic impact of a work, if aesthetics is restricted to the study of form. Perhaps we can see expression at work when a relatively inexperienced reader decides that she *loves* Jane Austen, or when a sophisticated reader decides that he does *not* like a writer whom he recognizes and appreciates as a consummate artist. One of the most interesting modern essays on *Rasselas* presents new evidence that the narrative was put together carelessly, or at any rate hurriedly,[6] and it seems to me possible for a fiction to do everything good to a reader that a work of art can do—delight, instruct, revive, console, transfigure—despite serious aesthetic shortcomings and flaws.

Didactic fictions ordinarily express more than just a concept or set of concepts. Even a relatively uncomplicated story, one of Aesop's fables, for example, is larger than its moral; the various translations or adaptations of "The Fox and the Raven" by Caxton (1483), L'Estrange (1692), and Croxall (1722) *exemplify* similar apothegms, but *embody* very different ways of looking at life.[7] No attentive reader of the Socratic dialogues will deny that Plato expresses something

6. W. K. Wimsatt, "In Praise of *Rasselas:* Four Notes (Converging)," *Imagined Worlds,* ed. M. Mack (London 1968), pp. 111–36.

7. In Caxton, the raven "wexed heuy and sorowfull And repented hym of that he had byleued the foxe"; in L'Estrange, the raven "drops his breakfast, which the fox presently chopt up and then bad him remember,

more complex and alluring than any conceivable set of philosophic statements that can be drawn from them. This chapter will investigate attitudes embodied in *Rasselas,* a composite of ideas and images, strong feelings and careful judgments, as interesting and elusive, on a smaller scale, as the man who put them together.

All the resources of the imagination may be drawn upon for expressive purposes, including some that have at one time or another been considered illegitimate in the novel—improbabilities, inconsistencies, impossibilities. A writer may communicate his point of view *more* sharply by eschewing qualities that have been highly prized in conventional fiction; he may insist upon his own mendacity, and flaunt the unreality of his inventions; he may deliberately narrow his sympathies, or tune his style to an uncomfortable pitch of refinement. His fiction may stand in all sorts of different relations to the ideas and feelings it expresses: it may be exemplary or symbolic; its ideas may be embedded in myth or organized around allusion—or translated into visual design on the printed page.

Modes of fiction in *Rasselas,* many of them familiar from our reading in *The Rambler,* range from the sublime to the ridiculous, touching base in symbolism and satire, irony and pathos, comic adventure and serious digression. Though *Rasselas* is frank and open about some of the things it means to say, the attitudes it embodies are comprised in, and veiled by, a puzzling set of narrative uncertainties and inconsistencies. The various disagreements among critics are quite understandable. Ready access to our deliberations is provided by the most striking of these disagreements, the debate over how sad or happy a story it is.

Wholesome, Debilitating, and Exquisitely Comic

John Hawkins found *Rasselas* a very sad book indeed, and linked pessimism there with the personal unhappiness of its author, his old friend: Johnson, according to him, "poured

---

that whatever he had said of his beauty, he had spoken nothing yet of his brains"; in Croxall, the fox is the hero; he "trotted away, laughing to himself at the easy Credulity of the Crow."

out his sorrow in gloomy reflection, and being destitute of comfort himself, described the world as nearly without it." Not only sad but excessively sad, so sad as to be both untrue to life and faintly blasphemous, that is, less than perfectly in harmony with what Hawkins took to be orthodox Christian views on "the dispensations of Providence." To Hazlitt, the pessimism of *Rasselas* seemed "debilitating." Such judgments as these are representative of a school of readers who attack the morality of *Rasselas,* believing that its general effect is to "extinguish hope, and consequently industry." [8]

A second party of readers agree about the gloominess of *Rasselas* but disagree completely about its moral effect, which seems to them wholesome and good. Three distinguished modern scholars recommend it as "one of the most bracing tonics in all literature," and Boswell prescribed it for himself annually.[9] But even the gloominess of *Rasselas* is denied by another, smaller group of critics, who concentrate on the quality of its humor or irony or comedy, variously described as "sympathetic," "gentle," "dark," "sardonic," and "homely." They point out that the action of *Rasselas* is repetitive and "exquisitely anticlimactic." [10]

I assume that distinct parts or aspects of *Rasselas* as a whole gave rise to some of these conflicts. We find something like the same variety of opinion in chapter 43 of *Rasselas* itself, following Imlac's description of the madness of the astronomer: the prince listened "with very serious regard, but the princess smiled, and Pekuah convulsed herself with laughter." One reader is saddened and discouraged by the long string of disappointments inflicted on the prince; another is

8. See Hawkins, *The Life of Samuel Johnson Ll.D.,* 2d ed. (London, 1787), pp. 371–72; Hazlitt, *Works,* ed. P. P. Howe (London, 1931), 6 : 102; *The Works of Mrs. Chapone* (London, 1807), 1 : 109. Patrick O'Flaherty, "Dr. Johnson as Equivocator: The Meaning of *Rasselas,*" *MLQ* 31 (1970): 195–208, stresses the "prevailing darkness" of *Rasselas,* and its "absurdist view of human life."

9. L. I. Bredvold, A. D. McKillop, L. Whitney, *Eighteenth-Century Poetry and Prose* (New York, 1939), p. 38; Boswell, 1 : 342.

10. Clarence R. Tracy, "Democritus, Arise! A Study of Dr. Johnson's Humor," *Yale Review,* n.s. 39 (1950): 303, 309–10; Alvin Whitley, "The Comedy of *Rasselas,*" *ELH* 23 (1956): 54, 66.

wryly amused by the same sequence of events: he notices, for example, that the prince bounces back after each disappointment, apparently unhurt. Both these responses seem to me legitimate, though they are not equally legitimate at every point in the story—it is the shape of the narrative, differences between the beginning, middle, and end of *Rasselas,* that permits us to decide tentatively between these interpretations of the work as a whole. I shall emphasize what develops in the last twenty chapters, and argue that the general effect of *Rasselas* is affirmative not negative, committed not defeated. Here a great deal depends on how much weight is allowed to particular passages and on the nature of the cultural context brought to bear. For my purposes the nearest analogue of *Rasselas,* its closest kin among all families and tribes of didactic fiction, is the *conte philosophique* of Voltaire; within the general context of enlightened ideas and ideals the wanderings of Imlac, the round trip of the prince, and the drifting of the two older men at the end of the story do not seem such a waste of time.

"The deep moans round with many voices"

The various passages of *Rasselas* that seem to express pessimism are not all alike. It is possible to distinguish at least four different pessimistic voices speaking at different points in the narrative.

1. The sublime and majestic gloom of the pseudo-oriental sage. This is the voice of the opening paragraphs of *Rasselas:*

> Ye who listen with credulity to the whispers of fancy, and persue with eagerness the phantoms of hope; who expect that age will perform the promises of youth, and that the deficiencies of the present day will be supplied by the morrow; attend to the history of Rasselas prince of Abissinia.
>
> Rasselas was the fourth son of the mighty emperour, in whose dominions the Father of waters begins his course; whose bounty pours down the streams of plenty, and scatters over half the world the harvests of Egypt.

Now orientalism in eighteenth-century narrative takes such exceedingly diversified forms, and ranges so widely between extremes of frivolity and didacticism, that it may be considered not as a genre but as a generic convenience, or convention, whose principal function is to free narrative from restrictions imposed by custom or tradition or by loyalty to the rules of verisimilitude and coherence. An author might take advantage of this literary freedom in many ways: the oriental tale presented him not with obligations but with opportunities from which to choose according to his purposes. After chapter 1 Johnson is not concerned with "romantick absurdities or incredible fictions"; his travelers circumambulate Egypt without meeting anything more wonderful than a hippopotamus. As for local color, "river-horses," crocodiles, and Arabian tents spread with fine or "finer" carpets make only the briefest of appearances in chapters 38 and 39. Johnson's narrative muse visits Ethiopia and Egypt not for colorful exoticism or magic or romantic love but for the grandeur of generality. His four major characters, almost denuded of idiosyncrasy, are citizens of the world, and they travel through a symbolic landscape. Among other sources of the popularity of travel literature in the eighteenth century was hunger for large perspectives; the Enlightenment urgently desired, like Imlac's poet, to "disregard present laws and opinions, and rise to general and transcendental truths, which will always be the same."

It is appropriate, therefore, that *Rasselas* announces itself as an oriental tale in periods perhaps as magnificently sententious as anything Johnson wrote. The sublime style is used here to give dignity and weight to universal truths, and yet its sublimity consists as much in the homage it pays to the Nile and its environs as in its weight and authority as moral sentiment—perhaps this first voice comes into its own only when gloomy generalizations are connected with major Egyptian landmarks:

> "Answer, great father of waters, thou that rollest thy floods through eighty nations, to the invocations of the daughter of thy native king. Tell me if thou waterest, through all thy course, a single habitation from which thou dost not hear the murmurs of complaint?"

> "Of the blessings set before you make your choice, and be content. No man can taste the fruits of autumn while he is delighting his

scent with the flowers of the spring: no man can, at the same time, fill his cup from the source and from the mouth of the Nile." [11]

Hester Lynch Thrale Piozzi reread *Rasselas* some time after 1818, and jotted down a few marginal comments, among them this, on the last page, following the printed words "The End," "—of a Book unrivalled in Excellency of Intention, in Elegance of Diction: in minute knowledge of human life—and sublime Expression of Oriental Imagery" [12]—by which she breathlessly conveys as the principal effect of what has been expressed to her, a sense of exaltation. I do not think her reaction is eccentric; for most readers it is the majesty of the pseudo-oriental sage that comes across most vividly, not his gloom. There is something heroic about the way this first voice confronts evil and faces up to human limitations. Look on my works, ye mighty, and *admire*. Like Rasselas himself, we "receive some solace of the miseries of life, from consciousness of . . . the eloquence" with which this voice expresses them, the power of this large utterance.

2. *The confident voice of the teacher of true pessimism.* From him issue summary statements that are as definite and musical as the closing of a limousine door:

Pride is seldom delicate, it will please itself with very mean advantages; and envy feels not its own happiness, but when it may be compared with the misery of others.

Human life is every where a state in which much is to be endured, and little to be enjoyed.

The life of a solitary man will be certainly miserable, but not certainly devout.[13]

11. Ch. 25, par. 4, and ch. 29, par. 14—hereafter, such citations will appear as 25.4 and 29.15. Other passages in the grand style: 18.5, 30.2–3, 32, 38.7, 41.1 and 3.

12. Quoted by Hilaire Belloc, *Short Talks with the Dead and Others* (1926; rpt. Freeport, N.Y., 1967), p. 182, from Mrs. Thrale's notations in an 1818 edition (Sharpe).

13. *Rasselas,* 9.5, 11.14, 21.9. Other examples: 8.5, 12.11, 16.9. Some resonantly didactic statements in *Rasselas* are not pessimistic (e.g., 11.9, 12.16).

It is Imlac and the Hermit who pronounce these sentences; Rasselas and Nekayah and the Arab chief and the astronomer produce similar statements later on. Note that they are all declarative, whereas the pseudo-oriental sage, whom I conceive stationed in some rocky pulpit reaching for sublimity, speaks in vocative and imperative modes ("Ye who," "thou that"; "attend," "answer," "confess"). By contrast, I conceive of the teacher of true pessimism in an armchair, or behind an improvised lectern; although his voice is more resonant and measured than the voice of common conversation or narration, it belongs nevertheless to the world of rational discourse, not to invocation or prophecy. His maxims are so efficient and persuasive that they have been quoted more frequently than any other part of *Rasselas*. Taken out of context, they are very discouraging indeed. They convinced William Mudford that Johnson's "writings are more calculated to injure than benefit society, and ought to be sedulously withheld from the early perusal of inquisitive and candid youth." [14]

3. The ironist. Both Imlac and the narrator of *Rasselas* are capable of irony in several shades. This voice can be grim, tight-lipped, even baleful—

> and as those, on whom the iron gate had once closed, were never suffered to return, the effect of longer experience could not be known . . . [1.7]

or frankly sardonic—

> The emperour asked me many questions concerning my country and my travels; and though I cannot now recollect any thing that he uttered above the power of a common man, he dismissed me astonished at his wisdom, and enamoured of his goodness. [9.8]

It is the ironist who keeps track of the exact number of weeks and months and years Rasselas wastes in chapter 4. It is his dry voice, supremely disillusioned, that lists fearful political

14. *A Critical Enquiry into the Moral Writings of Dr. Samuel Johnson* (London, 1802), p. 105.

catastrophes in chapter 24 without batting an eyelash; he it is who (as in the periodical essays) narrates disappointment with supreme swiftness and economy, who casts a cold eye on Rasselas's optimism, and who, somewhat more obviously than usual, announces in the chapter headings what will *not* occur in chapters 15–19, 21, and 22: "The prince and princess leave the valley, and see many wonders"; "They enter Cairo, and find every man happy"; "The prince associates with young men of spirit and gaiety"; and so on. So far as I know, none of Johnson's contemporaries responded to this voice, and it tells us something about changes of taste in the eighteenth century that Swift, whose pessimism can dent the composure even of tough undergraduates in 1970, was known to his contemporaries as the "jovial Dean," but the pervasiveness of Johnson's irony in *Rasselas* seems to have gone unnoticed, at least in print, till recently. This voice is pessimistic in general tendency because it operates at the expense of the dramatis personae, diminishes them, and through them their aspirations to happiness or virtue.

4. The old man, and others. In the last pages of Rasselas, as the prince and his companions are strolling along the Nile by moonlight, limp from their efforts to understand and come to terms with diseases of the imagination in chapter 44, they meet an old man "whose years have calmed his passions, but not clouded his reason." With renewed hopefulness they consult him on the choice of life; his answer is bleak:

> Nothing is now of much importance; for I cannot extend my interest beyond myself. Youth is delighted with applause, because it is considered as the earnest of some future good, and because the prospect of life is far extended: but to me, who am now declining to decrepitude, there is little to be feared from the malevolence of men, and yet less to be hoped from their affection or esteem. Something they may yet take away, but they can give me nothing. Riches would now be useless, and high employment would be pain. [45.6]

This voice is both melancholy and matter-of-fact. Its theme is the futility and unimportance of human exertions. It speaks at least three times in *Rasselas,* most memorably here in chapter 45, but also in chapter 35 when Nekayah laments the loss of her dearest friend: "Since Pekuah was taken from me, I have no pleasure to reject or to retain. She that has no one to love or trust has little to hope. She wants the radical principle of happiness." Characteristically, this voice expresses loss or bereavement (mostly in negatives), not pain or grief. (Something like it can be heard in the "frigid tranquillity" of the last paragraph of the preface to the *Dictionary*.) Readers who listen specially for this voice might easily conclude with Mrs. Chapone that the effect of *Rasselas* is to "extinguish hope."

Depressing Events

It is time to restore these four gloomy voices to their context in plot or action, and turn to particular events in *Rasselas* that might justify a pessimistic reading of the book. Not every event does, of course, just as not every voice in these forty-nine chapters disposes us "to lie down in sloth and despondency." For the sake of clarity, however, I shall squeeze as much negativism out of *Rasselas* as I can before looking for messages of hope.

1. "Lilies that fester. . . ." The fact that the Happy Valley is both a paradise and a prison is hard to cope with. Are we being manipulated, as Swift might manipulate his readers? We are given a set of narrative signals that seems conventional, but betrays us; in effect we watch a full-color earthly paradise—very like the golden age as depicted in the allegories in the *Rambler* and related in some way to a long succession of magical gardens going back to Genesis and Homer—watch this demi-paradise turn gray before our eyes and dwindle to a trap.

Johnson has keyed his description of the Happy Valley on "verdure and fertility," but has not confined himself to natural advantages like these:

> From the mountains on every side, rivulets descended that filled all the valley with verdure and fertility, and formed a lake in the middle inhabited by fish of every species, and frequented by every fowl whom nature has taught to dip the wing in water. . . .
>
> The sides of the mountains were covered with trees, the banks of the brooks were diversified with flowers; every blast shook spices

from the rocks, and every month dropped fruits upon the ground. All animals that bite the grass, or brouse the shrub, whether wild or tame, wandered in this extensive circuit, secured from beasts of prey by the mountains which confined them. On one part were flocks and herds feeding in the pastures, on another all the beasts of chase frisking in the lawns; the sprightly kid was bounding on the rocks, the subtle monkey frolicking in the trees, and the solemn elephant reposing in the shade. All the diversities of the world were brought together, the blessings of nature were collected, and its evils extracted and excluded. [1.5–6]

I count six, perhaps seven, significant traits in Johnson's Abyssinian sanctuary: inaccessibility, isolation, and security; year-round fruitfulness (with some suggestion that fruit and flower coincide); spicy breezes; plenitude with respect to birds, fishes, and herbivores (every species represented); peacefulness in the animal kingdom, achieved by excluding carnivores; and a generic presentation of certain animals (kids, monkeys, elephants)—significant because, taken all together, they suggest that the Happy Valley was intended to be something more than the remote dormitory for heirs to the throne of Abyssinia mentioned by Father Lobo and other travelers, something more than the verdant retreats celebrated by so many poets between *Cooper's Hill* and Pope's "Verses on a Grotto." [15] Perfect inaccessibility is appropriate to holy *places,* and perpetual fruitfulness of the earth may be the natural emblem of a holy *time,* or of the mythic piety of its inhabitants, a Golden Age, or Eden before the Fall. By excluding "beasts of prey" Johnson, somewhat deviously perhaps, legislates natural harmony and peace, as Ovid does by excluding lawyers, judges, soldiers, and sailors from the Age

15. See Gwin J. Kolb, "The 'Paradise' in Abyssinia and the 'Happy Valley' in *Rasselas,*" *MP* 56 (1958): 10–16. Professor Kolb's article may be relied upon as a summary of and guide to earlier work on the Abyssinian backgrounds of *Rasselas;* more recent studies include D. M. Lockhart, " 'The Fourth Son of the Mighty Emperor': The Ethiopian Background of Johnson's *Rasselas,*" *PMLA* 78 (1963): 516–28; A. J. Weitzman, "More Light on *Rasselas,*" *PQ* 48 (1969): 42–59. For verdant retreats, see Maren-Sofie Røstvig, *The Happy Man* (Oslo and New York, 1954, 1958).

of Saturn, or as Milton does by surrounding Adam and Eve with friendly beasts:

> About them frisking play'd
> All Beasts of th' Earth, since wild, and of all chase
> In Wood or Wilderness, Forest or Den;
> Sporting the Lion ramp'd, and in his paw
> Dandl'd the Kid; Bears, Tigers, Ounces, Pards
> Gamboll'd before them, th'unwieldy Elephant
> To make them mirth us'd all his might, and wreath'd
> His Lithe Proboscis.
>
> [*Paradise Lost,* bk. 4, lines 340–47]

Definite articles preceding the names of animals give this picture a starched, academic quality; the beasts seem mounted in cardboard as in a crèche, and they seem to represent their species, as if to say that any other lion or kid or elephant (or monkey, in *Rasselas*) would do the same under the same circumstances.[16] In Milton and in Spenser the presence of all kinds of plants or animals fills out the tableau of an ultimate source of life, Nature's womb. Plenitude elsewhere is simply a commonplace indicating richness of decor, as spicy gales are a commonplace of sumptuousness and delightfulness.

We are in danger of allowing echoes to drown out the original sound: the Happy Valley may be unnaturally peaceful, fertile, diversified, and secure, but it is too carelessly sketched for us to take it seriously as a sacred place, whatever Johnson's half-conscious recollections may have been. As paradises go, it is perfunctory, and curiously unconnected to human beings. No one takes more than half hearted advantage of "the blessings of nature" here "collected." It is as if Johnson's imagination, having fashioned an earthly paradise,

16. Pope's translation of *Odyssey* 7.114–32 (the Gardens of Alcinous; lines 142–75 in the English) seems to call attention to the conjunction of fruit and flowers, underlines spiciness in the breezes, uses definite articles with animals, and ends up sounding much more like the Happy Valley than Homer does. On descriptions like this as a reflection of "the order and variety" of a cosmos governed by God, see *The Poems of Alexander Pope,* Twickenham ed., vol. 1 (London, 1961), pp. 133–34; William Youngren, "Generality in Augustan Satire," *In Defense of Reading,* ed. R. Brower and R. Poirier (New York, 1962), pp. 214, 226–34.

was unable to realize its own incredible fiction, and simply allowed it to run down. The "rainy season" of chapter 7, "which . . . made it inconvenient to wander in the woods," seems out of place in a valley where, only a few pages before, "every blast shook spices from the rocks, and every month dropped fruits upon the ground."

As a dwelling place for human beings, the Happy Valley leaves something to be desired. Our suspicions may be wakened when we are told in the third sentence of *Rasselas* that the prince was "confined" there, and further aroused by the suggestion that this retreat was designed and initiated not by "wisdom" but by "policy." Despite the luxury of their surroundings, the inhabitants of the Happy Valley are unhappy enough to need new entertainments every year, "to fill up the vacancies of attention, and lessen the tediousness of time" (1.7). Those who flock to be admitted are shown to be acting on "the *appearance* of security and delight" (my italics); the lucky ones who gain entrance "always desired that [their residence there] might be perpetual; and as those, on whom the iron gate had once closed, were never suffered to return, the effect of longer experience could not be known. Thus every year produced new schemes of delight, and new competitors for imprisonment" (1.7). Unobtrusively—the ironist is at work here—a shadow has fallen on this bower of pleasure. If it were as agreeable as it pretends to be, one could not think of residence therein as "imprisonment," and the management would not need to prevent all communication between inmates and the outside world. Surely the Happy Valley is being exposed as "a scheme of merriment," elaborately advertised but not therefore less "hopeless" (*Idler* 58); it is an expectation of happiness, a human desire magnificently institutionalized, but not therefore less vain. The prince has only to venture on a few "solitary walks" to find himself shadowed by an alert Sage, anxious to herd him gently but firmly back into the flock of captive voluptuaries.

Later, after Rasselas has dragged hopefully through almost four years of dissatisfaction, when he has just discovered Imlac (an intellectual oasis in this desert of fun), as he is about to sit down thirstily to hear Imlac's history, he is dragged off to "a concert" (7.5)—certain pleasures, it would seem, are compulsory. Especially musical ones: it is "the sound of musick" announcing dinner that concludes the prince's conversation with the Sage (4.1); and remember that the mechanist who tries to build wings had successfully installed in the ladies' grove a bucolic form of Muzak, "instruments of soft musick," "some played by the impulse of the wind, and some by the power of the stream" (6.1). "Every art was practised to make [the inhabitants of the Happy Valley] pleased with their own condition," even the art of prevarication, for "the sages who instructed them, told them of nothing but the miseries of publick life" (2.1).

2. *Dupes and dolts.* If the Happy Valley is a well-appointed jail, Rasselas's discontent may at first seem admirable, but not after the ironist (voice number 3 above) has worked him over. This happens very early: in chapter 2 we listen to Rasselas inform some goats that man is nobler than they but more unhappy; we are told that he spoke

> with a plaintive voice, yet with a look that discovered him to feel some complacence in his own perspicacity, and to receive some solace of the miseries of life, from consciousness of the delicacy with which he felt, and the eloquence with which he bewailed them. He mingled cheerfully in the diversions of the evening, and all rejoiced to find that his heart was lightened. [2.8]

It is difficult to feel sympathy for a person whose troubles are so easy to cure, and indignation, or another response appropriate to "angry" satire, would also be out of place; in this paragraph Rasselas becomes a comic figure (though there can be no guarantee that he will stay one).

Accordingly, in chapter 3 an aged Sage catches Rasselas's attention by discoursing on "the miseries of the world," and the prince plunges into twenty months of "visionary bustle." Don Quixote earns our respect for his sense of style, and perhaps for his durableness; Walter Mitty is the hero of countless flabby Americans; but Rasselas's daydreams do not reach full growth. The spectacle of a twenty-seven-year-old king's son panting resolutely in pursuit of an imaginary "orphan virgin" and her captor is ludicrous—a fact of which the prince becomes conscious only when physically obstructed from running further by "the foot of the mountain." He stops to think, and is deflected by his own self-consciousness into a string of "sorrowful meditations" whose general tendency is to go in circles: "he past four months in resolving to lose no more time in idle resolves." The chance remark of a scullery maid breaks this second trance, but locks him into a state of mind in which he "for a few hours, regretted his regret." Johnson has made something like a comedy of mechanism out of the mechanics of procrastination. The statistics here are satirical. It has taken the prince twenty-four months and "a few hours" to settle down to business.

Many of the questions that Rasselas addresses to Imlac are spectacularly naïve, in an unobtrusive way:

> "Surely, said the prince, my father must be negligent of his charge, if any man in his dominions dares take that which belongs to another." [8.4]

> "Why, said the prince, did thy father desire the increase of his wealth, when it was already greater than he durst discover or enjoy?" [8.8]

> "Stop a moment, said the prince. Is there such depravity in man, as that he should injure another without benefit to himself?" [9.4]

At least in the first half of the book Rasselas falls into almost every trap that appearances set for him. And yet he is not only the object but also the instrument of satire. With some assistance from Nekayah, he is responsible for the fresh light which in *ingénu* satire the naïve hero casts on our tired vices; it is his innocence and idealism and reasonableness that bring into sharp perspective the specious unreasonableness of ordinary people living in the world outside the Happy Valley.

During the eighteenth century, the point of view and many of the techniques of *ingénu* satire filtered into what we now distinguish as the novel. Tom Jones is less naïve than Parson

Adams, and Amelia still less unworldly, despite her virtue, than Tom Jones, but all Fielding's novels in some degree submit innocence to the trials of experience for purposes of satire and as a criticism of contemporary manners and morals. In Smollett's early novels, the hero is likely to be less naïve than, for example, Rasselas; he nevertheless suffers at the hands of far more knowledgeable rogues than himself. Of course, even before Rasselas sets out on his quest he is allowed to listen to the history of a former *ingénu,* a history that might dent the enthusiasm of an ordinary traveler. Imlac is "plundered upon false pretences" during his first caravan journey and shamefully neglected when he returns to Ethiopia twenty years later. He concludes that "there is so much infelicity in the world, that scarce any man has leisure from his own distresses to estimate the comparative happiness of others," and that "human life is every where a state in which much is to be endured, and little to be enjoyed." Imlac's travels do not anticipate Rasselas's in detail, nor do they make the quest superfluous; but they strongly imply that the quest will fail.

Where Imlac's history leans toward satire—at no point does it lean very far—it takes the form of a complaint, and narrates events analogous to some of those in the periodical-essay fiction. Imlac's swift disenchantment with the beauties of nature (chapter 9) parallels the experiences of Euphelia and Dick Shifter (*Rambler* 42 and *Idler* 71); his homecoming, impatiently anticipated, proves as barren and lonesome as Serotinus's (*Rambler* 165).[17] In *Rasselas,* however, conversation about these events and discussion of what they mean are essential events in and of themselves; this is not merely a "picture of life" (as Johnson describes his fictions, in *Rambler* 208) but a story about how people respond to life.

As Imlac's narrative draws to a close, Rasselas formulates the terms of the quest: "I am resolved to judge with my own eyes of the various conditions of men, and then to make de-

17. Other parallels: with Imlac's unsuccessful courtship, compare the one in *Rambler* 120; great knowledge also fails to impress the workaday world in *Idler* 75; well-meaning heroes are cheated in *Idler* 71 and *Adventurer* 41.

liberately my *choice of life*"—on the absurd assumption that "if I had the choice of life, I should be able to fill every day with pleasure" (12.15 and 12.1). To the extent that it is a hunt for a ready and easy formula for happiness, the choice of life is a pretty silly undertaking. In practice it becomes a survey of misery and folly, not of happiness—false appearances, consciously or unconsciously preserved, and false theories, blindly maintained. We are warned in chapter 16 that everyone who seems happy is likely to be stupid or hypocritical; that, in effect, happiness is a possession of being well-deceived; chapters 17, 19–21, 23–29 present us with a succession of fools among knaves.

The two theoreticians who lie in wait for Rasselas (chapters 18 and 22) deal in false appearances constructed out of "rhetorical sound," "polished periods and studied sentences," the jargon of philosophy. They are selling exotic recipes for happiness, which are refuted by the mere presence of real hardship (chapter 18), if they have not already refuted themselves by evolving into obvious nonsense (chapter 22).

In chapters 16–22 Johnson's method is to exaggerate in such a way as to widen the gulf between appearance and reality. The country gentleman of chapter 20 enjoys an estate more like Vauxhall Gardens than like suburban Egypt,[18] equipped—fantastically—with "youths and virgins dancing in the grove," and with all the civilized amenities, even "chearful" "domesticks." Such wealth, with a little ingenuity, could probably secure him from his enemies as effectively as it has adorned his estate, but if he is really at the mercy of the Bassa and local princes, as he claims to be, his happiness act, so elaborately staged, is ridiculous (not necessarily improbable). Likewise, since the hermit of chapter 21 is announced as a man of "age and virtue," who has "filled the whole country with the fame of his sanctity" (19.1), and since the piety of his conversation "soon gained the esteem of his guests," his frank confession of "vice" and "folly" is incongruous (if, again, not improbable).

18. *Rasselas, Poems, and Selected Prose,* ed. Bertrand Bronson (New York, 1958), p. 548 n. 11.

One way of exaggerating a promising appearance is to let it raise hopes; the *un*promising reality that lies beneath the surface will then be most clearly revealed if those hopes are disappointed not in tragic catastrophe but in muted farce. Contrasts between the mechanic's enthusiasm and the narrator's dour irony in chapter 6 are sharp and pleasing:

> In a year the wings were finished, and, on a morning appointed, the maker appeared furnished for flight on a little promontory: he waved his pinions a while to gather air, then leaped from his stand, and in an instant dropped into the lake. His wings, which were of no use in the air, sustained him in the water, and the prince drew him to land, half dead with terrour and vexation. [6.11]

Irony here, of course, depends on our seeing that these wings, designed for air, perform satisfactorily only in water, and that the mechanist is in more danger ("half dead") from "terrour and vexation" than from any great altitude he shall rise to. This episode is comic as well as ironical; we are made witnesses not of the much-heralded and long-awaited sublimity of flight, but of a pratfall. Another example of muted farce is the sequel to the hermit's painfully frank confession of failure as a hermit. "They heard his resolution with surprise, but, after a short pause, offered to conduct him to Cairo. He dug up a considerable treasure which he had hid among the rocks, and accompanied them to the city, on which, as he approached it, he gazed with rapture" (21.10). That "short pause" is a vaudeville double-take, underplayed but unmistakable; that "considerable treasure" throws a new, perhaps unflattering light on the hermit's fifteen years of solitude.

In chapter 30, Imlac drags his royal charges off to see the pyramids, interrupting the quest—it was losing momentum anyway—in order to study history. The reader alert for comedy may find some of the narrative in the next four chapters interestingly stilted, as if the joints of the travelers, who are responding dutifully to Imlac's observation that "while you are making the choice of life, you neglect to live," were stiff and creaky. Imlac's sententiousness, Rasselas's big-footed earnestness, and in chapter 36 Nekayah's highly colored exhibition of sorrow come in for a measure of gentle satire. As for "The adventures of the lady Pekuah," they do not fulfill their promise as melodrama, and have been identified as "a deflated romance." [19] Given the facts—"Lovely Maid of Honor Abducted by Haughty Arab Chief"—one might expect romantic motives to emerge from behind them, passionate love, undying hate, heroic pride. Pekuah's chronicle, however, is one of avarice and boredom; the Arab is a hardheaded businessman, his harem a group of silly girls, and his castle merely a residence, unfurnished with mermaids or tritons.

This episode may remind us of anticlimax and didactic comedy in *The Female Quixote,* the sprightly antiromance for which Johnson had written a chapter in 1752. In *Rasselas* Johnson seems to equate our hopes of happiness and our expectations of future good with the hallucinations of a Don Quixote. If that sounds like too harsh a way of putting it, think back to chapter 4, when the prince "feigned to himself an orphan virgin robbed of her little portion by a treacherous lover, and crying after him for restitution and redress," and galloped off in pursuit of this wholly imaginary villain. How is Rasselas's fantasy different from the madness of the astronomer in chapters 41–44, except that it is more literary and shorter-lived?

3. Futility and despair. The quest resumes in chapter 40, but with a difference: neither the astronomer nor the old man is a fool; both are presented in such a way as to earn our respect. Earlier encounters with potentially happy conditions or people had been limited to one chapter each; the astronomer takes four, and makes such an impact that he is adopted and befriended, and becomes one of the prince's party. The general tone of the quest has changed; there is nothing laughable about madness or about the apathy and disgust of the old man. We are permitted to smile at Pekuah when she sets her cap at the astronomer (she is conscious of and confident in her therapeutic powers: 46.3, 5), and perhaps at the facility with which

19. Alvin Whitley, "The Comedy of *Rasselas,*" *ELH* 23 (1956): 54 n. 4.

the travelers explain away the old man's despair (45.10), but from this point of view the choice of eternity (48.19) represents the failure of the choice of life, and chapter 49 is not a joke at all.

The very title of chapter 49 casts doubt on the validity of the quest. If after all this activity "nothing is concluded," surely nothing *can* be concluded in the choice of life, and, as Imlac argued back in chapter 16, "he who would fix his condition upon incontestable reasons of preference, must live and die inquiring and deliberating." Furthermore, the "various schemes of happiness which each of them had formed" seem to have been determined without reference to past experience, and in defiance of what the quest might have taught them. Imlac and the astronomer frankly abandon the quest, root and branch. Nevertheless, even a decision not to decide is not safe, since "of these wishes that they had formed they well knew that none could be obtained." The return to Abyssinia, whether or not to the Happy Valley, seems to represent defeat, *and* a foolish unwillingness to admit defeat. The last chapter of *Rasselas* seems to confirm the message of the old man of chapter 45, as if Johnson did not really care any longer what happened to his travelers.[20]

The inconclusiveness of chapter 49 derives in part from our sense of having seen it all happen before, over and over again. Rasselas wants to escape from his boredom into "the miseries of the world" (3.4); Imlac, fleeing from the miseries of the world, settles for boredom (he "bid farewell to hope and fear," 12.7), but he is quite willing to join Rasselas in tunneling out of their confinement again into the "sea foam-

20. "I was so well pleased with the laudable active spirit which brought Rasselas out of the deplorable 'happy valley,' and promised myself so fine a moral from the superior happiness I supposed he was to find even in hardships, wants, and dangers, when engaged in right pursuits, to what he had experienced from the vain efforts of luxurious idleness, that I was scandalized above measure when I found that all his reasoning and experience were to end in his returning again to the rattles and babies he had been tired of even in early youth. And that his maturity and old age were to be spent in the balls and concerts he had learnt to despise soon after twenty" (*The Works of Mrs. Chapone,* 1 : 109–10).

ing with tempests" that he envisages outside. Retreating from a "world full of snares, discord, and misery," the hermit of chapter 21 "rejoiced like a tempest-beaten sailor at his entrance into the harbour," for a while, but he too welcomes the opportunity to return to society (21.8–9). One of the sages of chapter 22

> thought it likely, that the hermit would, in a few years, go back to his retreat, and, perhaps, if shame did not restrain, or death intercept him, return once more from his retreat into the world: "For the hope of happiness, said he, is so strongly impressed, that the longest experience is not able to efface it. Of the present state, whatever it be, we feel, and are forced to confess, the misery, yet, when the same state is again at a distance, imagination paints it as desirable. But the time will surely come, when desire will be no longer our torment, and no man shall be wretched but by his own fault."

If Johnson had been able to "make his choice and be content" he would have been a rather different person, and presumably the characters in his fiction would not swing like pendulums from retirement to action and back again. Nekayah hints at the idea of a pendulum when she acknowledges that "those conditions, which flatter hope and attract desire, are so constituted, that, as we approach one, we recede from another" (29.14). In chapter 35 she resolves "to retire from the world with all its flatteries and deceits, and . . . hide" herself in the "solitude" of a convent (35.4). Not long after she has been rescued from this rash resolve, she finds herself at loose ends again, asking to "see something to morrow which I never saw before" (47.3), and Rasselas brings out "a new topick"—monasticism, institutionalized retirement. It seems that Nekayah still intends to withdraw, since her brother turns to the astronomer when this conversation is over and asks (is his question quietly sarcastic?) "whether he could not delay her retreat, by shewing her something which she had not seen before" (47.10); the astronomer suggests a visit to the catacombs, itself a final withdrawing place and scene of the last retreat of "the earliest generations" of Cairo.

No wonder that by the time chapter 49 arrives we derive no satisfaction from the convent of Pekuah, the college of

Nekayah, and the "little kingdom" of the prince. From our present point of view, *Rasselas* ends on a cynical note. Mankind "in ignorance sedate" does seem to "roll darkling down the torrent of his fate," as by the same metaphor Imlac and the astronomer are "driven along the stream of life without directing their course to any particular port"; their three companions are more ignorant and more bemused than they.

Beacons of Hope

1. "In these fruitless searches he spent ten months. The time, however, passed chearfully away . . ." (5.3). Darkness and gloom, however, seem faintly ridiculous in the face of the actual experience of the travelers; they are not suffering as profoundly as, speaking with the confident voice of the teacher of true pessimism, they seem to wish to think they are. If Rasselas had been alert he would have noticed that the activity of bewailing his miseries, eloquently performed, gave him pleasure (2.8), that he "rejoiced" at the prospect of seeing the outside world (4.2), and that while he was actively searching for an escape route, "the time . . . passed chearfully away":

> in the morning he rose with new hope, in the evening applauded his own diligence, and in the night slept sound after his fatigue. He met a thousand amusements which beguiled his labour, and diversified his thoughts. [5.3]

The "novelty and instruction" Imlac imparts to the prince "entertained" him and gave him "pleasure" (7.4); the friendship they share removes much of his uneasiness, even in the Happy Valley (13.2). Well before the choice of life has got under way, the prince's experience has demonstrated that happiness *is* somewhere to be found, in small doses. What actually occurs as the story unfolds continues to subvert the doctrines of the pseudo-oriental sage, if not of the confident teacher of true pessimism (just as, more obviously, experience refutes the theories of hopeful fools like Rasselas and of pedants like the stoic sage of chapter 18).

The relation between story and statement in *Rasselas* seems different from that relationship in the periodical essays. In the *Rambler* and its sequels experience is almost always painful; only in paragraphs of straight expository prose is pain justified, hope renewed, and faith strengthened. *Idler* 58 gives three examples of the hopelessness of "schemes of merriment": first, a banquet where everyone is ready "to laugh and to applaud," transformd by mutual discontent into "general malignity"; then a traveler who expects "shade and sunshine at his disposal," "tables of plenty," "looks of gaiety," but meets instead a dusty road, sultry air, a brutal postilion, a crowded inn; and finally the traveler's arrival in his "native province," where he is coldly received. It is only in the last sentence of *Idler* 58 that consolation is offered: "yet it is necessary to hope, tho' hope should always be deluded, for hope itself is happiness, and its frustrations, however frequent, are yet less dreadful than its extinction." This is a statement of faith; there is no "picture of life" to support it, no anecdote to illustrate it, no story to confirm it. Moreover, six periodical essays (*Ramblers* 42, 65, 101, 141; *Idlers* 71, 75) that narrate events closely analogous to these three episodes are less comforting even than *Idler* 58. Solace for these and similar discouragements is scattered through the periodical essays in passages of pure exposition, not in fiction, and often in the form of an exhortation to religion. It looks as though, in the periodical essays, pain is a matter of experience, and the consolation for pain a matter of faith.

In *Rasselas* we are privileged for perhaps the only time in Johnson's fiction to watch people "make the happiness they do not find." The futility and destructive irony of some parts of the last five chapters, in particular the "Conclusion in which nothing is concluded," force us to question how skillfully they perform this portentous task; and yet, at the same time, the structure of *Rasselas*—what happens to major characters at what point in the narrative—forces us to acknowledge that the voices of gloom are not telling the whole truth.

2. *Choosing life.* The problem with *Rasselas*'s structure is not that it presents one gleaming seamless surface but that its various parts overlap, and even the shorter sections are interrupted in various ways; hence several different pictures of its

structure are valid.[21] It seems to me crucial, however, to recognize that in chapter 30 when "Imlac enters, and changes the conversation," the whole direction of the narrative changes also. If *Rasselas* ended with chapter 29, we would find it far more pessimistic and negativistic than we do now. The action up to that point is one almost uninterrupted succession of failures and disappointments. Imlac, whose own life history was disillusioning, functions here as the confident teacher of true pessimism, and at a number of points seems to doubt whether the quest is worthwhile. When Rasselas hesitates over what to do next, he confers with Imlac, but is "answered by him with new doubts, and remarks that gave him no comfort" (23.1). In Nekayah's opinion, "Imlac favours not our search, lest we should in time find him mistaken" (23.2).

Not that the choice of life is ultimately a waste of time. Behind it is a peculiar form of spiritual restlessness, which sufficiently distinguishes man from goat; the "discontent of Rasselas in the happy valley," though it traps him in comical visions and revisions, is more than a local itch, it is a permanent aspect of the human condition.[22] If, moreover, the Happy

21. Gwin J. Kolb, "The Structure of *Rasselas*," PMLA 66 (1951): 698–717, divides *Rasselas* into two parts, one that demonstrates the unhappiness of people who have "all the material ingredients for happiness" (the Happy Valley), another that "discloses the same condition in the outside world" (p. 702). *Rasselas* is therefore constructed as "an exhaustive survey of the kinds of places where happiness might be found" (p. 703). F. W. Hilles, "*Rasselas*, an 'Uninstructive Tale,'" *Johnson, Boswell, and Their Circle* (Oxford, 1965), pp. 111–13, divides the book into three parts, the Happy Valley, the world of men, and, after the pyramid, a section when "the observers become participants." Emrys Jones, "The Artistic Form of *Rasselas*," *RES*, n.s. 18 (1967): 396–400, points out that the structure of *Rasselas* is symmetrical; it can be divided into three equal parts of sixteen chapters each, variously and cunningly interrelated, with ch. 49 as a coda. W. K. Wimsatt, "In Praise of *Rasselas*," divides the story into six parts: (1) chs. 1–6, unrest; (2) chs. 7–15, story of Imlac; (3) chs. 16–22, exploratory; (4) chs. 23–29, conversation; (5) chs. 30–39, adventures; (6) chs. 40–49, somber experiences. This is, he points out, not structure in the Aristotelian sense, but "accumulation, something like . . . a series of laboratory reports" (pp. 115–17). Four parts are outlined by Mary Lascelles, "*Rasselas:* A Rejoinder," *RES*, n.s. 21 (1970): 49–56.

22. John Locke (*An Essay Concerning Human Understanding*, ed. A. C. Fraser [Oxford, 1895], 1 : 330ff.) makes "uneasiness" the determiner of the will; we do not act except from a sense of privation or pain.

Valley is an earthly paradise, however tainted, to renounce it is to opt for humanity; the voluntary rejection of even a gilt-and-tinsel Eden signifies a commitment to this world.

The quest for happiness, like the Happy Valley, is carefully shaped to prove or demonstrate something about the impulse it represents: four travelers are turned loose in the world under circumstances that permit them the broadest possible freedom of choice, so that readers may conclude that if happiness is attainable, these travelers will find it. Rasselas's naïveté is therefore a necessary condition of the quest, not just an amusing foible. If his enthusiasm were quenchable, he might quit the search before exhausting all possibilities. In another sense, his innocence and eagerness also represent general human nature; as Johnson puts it in *Rambler* 67, "hope begins with the first power of comparing our actual with our possible state, and attends us through every stage and period" of our lives.

Nevertheless, failure of the quest is the major event of the first half of *Rasselas,* and the fact that this failure has a completed dramatic shape of its own gives to the narrative a finer articulation, and deepens the contrast between chapters 1–29 and what happens later. After the six unsuccessful interviews of chapters 17–22, the prince and his sister strike out for themselves. They compare the results of their researches in a long conversation one evening "in a private summerhouse on the bank of the Nile" (chapters 25–29). One by one, various categories of public and private life are examined and rejected; youth disputes with age, parents with children, husband with wife. Rasselas asks, "What then is to be done? the more we enquire, the less we can resolve," and chides Nekayah for "gloom" and "the common errours of exaggeratory declamation." She replies with more gloom still.

> "You seem to forget, replied Rasselas, that you have, even now, represented celibacy as less happy than marriage. Both conditions may be bad, but they cannot both be worst. Thus it happens when wrong opinions are entertained, that they mutually destroy each other, and leave the mind open to truth."
>
> "I did not expect, answered the princess, to hear that imputed to falshood which is the consequence only of frailty." [28.6–7]

The purpose of this argument is to work Rasselas and Nekayah into a straitjacket of doubt. According to Sextus Empiricus, the skeptic, the first step in achieving contentedness is *isosthenia,* the marshaling of one *logos* or dogma against another, so that they cancel each other out: here, different species of wretchedness are balanced against each other, and all this unhappy experience against the assumption that there *is* any such thing as happiness; all dogmas so far have failed. Stage two is *epoké,* a stalemate ("the more we enquire, the less we can resolve"), a state of suspended judgment. The narrative of chapters 23–29 seems roughly parallel to these two stages of classical skepticism: [23] the prince and his sister, by the end of chapter 29, have succeeded in arguing themselves into a corner ("when wrong opinions are entertained, . . . they mutually destroy each other"). It is worth noticing that this is the only occasion in *Rasselas* when any of the travelers expresses annoyance or irritation. A hint of the direction this discussion is taking appears at the end of chapter 28, in Rasselas's suggestion that "You surely conclude too hastily from the infelicity of marriage against its institution; will not the misery of life prove equally that life cannot be the gift of heaven?" To ask this question, for a mind as ardent as Johnson's, is to stand at the brink of an abyss. Chapters 23–29 develop in a mounting atmosphere of doubt and distrust.

3. The choice of eternity. But in chapter 30, "Imlac enters, and changes the conversation" by proposing that "while you are making the choice of life, you neglect to live." His program for "living," a visit to the great pyramid and a lecture on history, is swept aside in chapter 33 by the disappearance of Pekuah, and quite suddenly the travelers are living in earnest, transformed from observers to participants. In the first half of *Rasselas* they had examined the actions and sufferings of others; now they act and suffer themselves. Imlac's role in the

23. Sextus Empiricus, *Outlines of Pyrrhonism* (LCL, 1933) 1 : 3–19, esp. pp. 6–7. The parallel is striking, but not philosophically significant. It furnishes the reader with a *logical* procedure for exhaustive inquiries into happiness (see Kolb on structure as cited n. 21), and it works out nicely as a *dramatic* means of preparing for the change of weather in ch. 30.

new dispensation is no longer to plant doubts, but to raise up hope and to nourish faith.

As the chances of recovering Pekuah diminish, Nekayah sinks "down inconsolable in hopeless dejection," and reproaches herself bitterly for letting Pekuah out of her sight.

"Great princess, said Imlac, do not reproach yourself for your virtue, or consider that as blameable by which evil has accidentally been caused. Your tenderness for the timidity of Pekuah was generous and kind. When we act according to our duty, we commit the event to him by whose laws our actions are governed, and who will suffer none to be finally punished for obedience. . . ." [34.8]

This last sentence has a distinctive ring to it: its piety, its weariness, and the way it backs into an affirmation by way of negatives of elimination, scrupulously marking out an asylum of the very last resort, remind us of the unnamed sage of chapter 22, who trusts and believes that "the time will surely come, when desire will be no longer our torment, and no man shall be wretched but by his own fault." Imlac, in other words, has discarded the confident voice of the teacher of true pessimism, and speaks here in an affirming voice, closer to pathos than to irony, very moving, very potent.[24]

In chapter 46, Imlac finds himself drawn into a new relation with the astronomer, once that shy scholar's acquaintance has been successfully cultivated by Pekuah; he takes on the role of healer: "Imlac was delighted to find that the sage's understanding was breaking through its mists, and resolved to detain him from the planets till he should forget his task of ruling them, and reason should recover its original influence" (46.11). His disquisition on diseases of the imagination concludes with words resonant and positive, like a blessing: "Your learning and virtue may justly give you hopes" (47.2).

Therefore, ground has been prepared for eschatological seriousness and an open concern with religious issues in chap-

24. Other examples of this voice: 22.3, 34.8, 47.7. Something very like this voice occurs in the last paragraphs of *Ramblers* 41, 52, 190, *Adventurers* 84, 107, 120, *Idler* 41. On the theological context of a longing not to be "tormented" by desire, see Chester F. Chapin, *The Religious Thought of Samuel Johnson* (Ann Arbor, Mich., 1968), pp. 101–04.

ters 47 and 48 (by comparison, the first twenty-two chapters of *Rasselas* seem rather light-weight). The subject of monasticism arises when Nekayah calls for a new entertainment, and Rasselas remembers how well the monks of St. Anthony get along without variety or luxury; they are "less wretched in their silent convent than the Abissinian princes in their prison of pleasure" (47.3–5). Monasticism was not a popular institution in eighteenth-century England;[25] and yet Johnson sets Imlac to talking of religious retirement as if it were a choice of life everyone considered: "Those retreats of prayer and contemplation have something so congenial to the mind of man, that, perhaps, there is scarcely one that does not purpose to close his life in pious abstraction with a few associates serious as himself" (47.7). Thus, dexterously, in a few paragraphs the choice of life becomes the choice of eternity. Chapter 48 begins with a sightseer's question, but reasons backward through the metaphysics of spirit and matter to first principles, our sense of having been created, our creatureliness:

> "But the Being, said Nekayah, whom I fear to name, the Being which made the soul, can destroy it."
>
> "He, surely, can destroy it, answered Imlac, since, however unperishable, it receives from a superiour nature its power of duration. That it will not perish by any inherent cause of decay, or principle of corruption, may be shown by philosophy; but philosophy can tell no more. That it will not be annihilated by him that made it, we must humbly learn from higher authority." [48.16–17]

A few sentences later, the princess makes her celebrated dismissal of the choice of life: it has become "less important" to her now; she hopes "hereafter to think only on the choice of eternity" (48.19).

25. Monasteries crop up occasionally in eighteenth-century romances as the last hiding place for misanthropists (e.g., *Plain Dealer* 3; Sarah Fielding, *David Simple* [1744], bk. 4, ch. 2). Richardson toyed with the idea of convents as a solution for certain female problems; see *Sir Charles Grandison* (Oxford, 1931), 3 : 383. For Johnson's real-life plans to retire, 1783–84, to the cell reserved for him at the English Benedictine Convent in Paris, see James M. Osborn, "Dr. Johnson and The Contrary Converts," *New Light on Dr. Johnson*, ed. F. W. Hilles (New Haven, 1959), pp. 297–307. *Rambler* 28, fourth-to-last paragraph ("the necessity of setting the

If at this point we feel that we have come to rest, briefly, in a faith that rises above the doubts, disappointments, and misfortunes of preceding chapters, it is partly because the structure of *Rasselas* comes to a quiet climax in this penultimate chapter, logically and aesthetically: logically because the "desire distinct from sense" of chapter 2, the "unextinguishable curiosity" of chapters 4, 5, and 8, various anxieties of chapters 17–29, the "hunger of imagination" of chapter 32, and the "despotick . . . fictions" of chapters 40–46 have here an ultimate source and justification; aesthetically because we have completed a symbolic journey from childhood to old age, from the valley of eternal spring to the valley of the shadow of death, from the source to the mouth of the Nile. Rasselas contriving his escape from the Happy Valley is a human being struggling to be born; when they emerge into the world, Imlac pampers his royal charges like children; their travels take them to the city of man, "where travellers and merchants assemble from all the corners of the earth" (16.1), to the great pyramid, a testimony to "industry and power before which all European magnificence is confessed to fade away," interpreted here as "a monument of the insufficiency of human enjoyments" (30.3, 32.5), and conclude in catacombs, "the habitations of the dead" (47.13).

Travel and Talk

I think it is fair to say that though *Rasselas* makes somber fun of the quest for a secular *summum bonum,* it tells or implies a good deal about *areté,* the activity proper to mankind, the particular enterprises most satisfying and suitable to human nature. Among others that give delight and hurt not, during these forty-nine chapters, one set of activities seems specially privileged, the kind of travel that encourages talk, and the kind of talk that thrives on travel. Travel, in this extended sense, is more than transportation from one place to

world at a distance from us, when we are to take a survey of ourselves, has sent many from high stations to the severities of a monastick life"), and *Idler* 38, par. 11, suggest that the Imlac of chapter 47 is not merely suffering from an "enthusiastic fit" like that of chapter 10.

another, and talk, which might more aptly be called conversation, is more than trading words; both must be linked with history and the acquisition of knowledge, with curiosity, the pursuit of novelty, friendship, sociableness, and the city.[26]

Imlac's experience provides most of these links. His education was "a continual course of gratifications" because "every hour taught me something new" (8.11). When he reaches the age of twenty his travels begin:

> "We laid our money upon camels, concealed in bales of cheap goods, and travelled to the shore of the red sea. When I cast my eye on the expanse of waters my heart bounded like that of a prisoner escaped. I felt an unextinguishable curiosity kindle in my mind, and resolved to snatch this opportunity of seeing the manners of other nations, and of learning sciences unknown in Abissinia.
>
> "I remembered that my father had obliged me to the improvement of my stock, not by a promise which I ought not to violate, but by a penalty which I was at liberty to incur; and therefore determined to gratify my predominant desire, and by drinking at the fountains of knowledge, to quench the thirst of curiosity." [8.13–14]

Curiosity is thirst in this second paragraph; it was an "unextinguishable" fire which "kindled" Imlac's imagination in the first. Cities give Imlac the finest opportunities to indulge his curiosity in "tracing human nature through all its variations" (9.11); "in a city, populous as Cairo, it is possible to obtain at the same time the gratifications of society, and the secrecy of solitude" (12.3). Imlac, after all, is less a philosopher than a man of great practical experience (see 13.5, 33.3, 37.2–3) who has traveled widely. He advertises himself as a poet, but the only production of his muse mentioned in this narrative is devoted to "the various conditions of humanity" and "scenes of life" (7.4); moreover, his digression upon poetry, requiring a poet to "range" mountains and deserts, to "observe," to "wander," to "watch" and to "study" (10.3), strikes even

26. For a discussion of the special significance of travel in the eighteenth century, complementary to mine, see Paul Fussell, *The Rhetorical World of Augustan Humanism* (Oxford, 1965), ch. 11, esp. pp. 262–74. See also Donald Greene, *Samuel Johnson* (New York, 1970), pp. 33–36, for Johnson "In Society," talking and traveling.

Rasselas as unreasonably encyclopedic.[27] Imlac, though learned, is a man of the world compared to the astronomer. "Men of *various* ideas and fluent *conversation* are commonly welcome to those whose thoughts have been long fixed upon a single point . . . I delighted him with my remarks, he smiled at the narrative of my *travels*" (40.2; my italics).

Rasselas itself feels like a travel book, in places. When the prince and his companions throw over the choice of life in chapter 30, Imlac takes them to visit the pyramids; his idea of real living is a tour of historical monuments; and his discourse in chapter 32 has the shape, though something more than the conventional style and content, of the set speech of a professional guide. Pekuah takes over as travel-guide in the narrative of her "adventures" in chapters 38 and 39. Whatever dangers and excitements she lived through are played down; as soon as her commercial value as a hostage has been established, the Arab chief goes out of his way to show her "places . . . worthy the notice of a passenger." "I amused myself with observing the manners of the vagrant nations, and with viewing remains of ancient edifices with which these deserted countries appear to have been, in some distant age, lavishly embellished" (38.10 and 11). Here again, stimulating conversation is more important than mere change of place. Pekuah runs a great risk of being detained indefinitely by the Arab, a man "hungry for knowledge," who is reluctant "in an intellectual famine, to lose such a banquet as Pekuah's conversation" (39.11). Similarly, Imlac and the astronomer become friends when they find themselves "enamoured" of each other's conversation (40.6). "As each knew much which the other was desirous of learning, we exchanged our notions with great delight" (40.3). The astronomer, victim of an imagination diseased by solitude (like the hermit of chapter 21), recovers his sanity under the combined ministrations of "familiar friendship," conversation, "projects and pleasures" (46.10–13).[28]

27. In this context the "hint on pilgrimage" of ch. 11 is not a digression, since pilgrimages ("long journeys in search of truth") are a specialized form of travel.

28. Another sightseeing tour ocurs in chs. 47–48, the visit to the catacombs. Johnson surmised that Swift traveled on foot, or in a wagon,

This network of associations is not something peculiar to *Rasselas*. Gentlemen, and those who aspired to gentility, traveled to prepare themselves for full participation in society (i.e., the conversation of educated men and sociable women) and politics (i.e., recent history applied to problems of government). "Certainly," says *Spectator* 364, "the true End of visiting forreign Parts, is to look into their Customs and Policies, . . . and wear off such awkard [*sic*] Stiffnesses and Affectations in our Behavior, as may possibly have been contracted from constantly associating with one Nation of Men, by a more free, general, and mixed Conversation." Swift told the young lady to whom he wrote a "Letter . . . on her Marriage" (1723) that "you must get a Collection of History and Travels . . . and spend some Hours every Day in reading them. . . . You must invite Persons of Knowledge and Understanding to an Acquaintance with you, by whose Conversation you may learn to correct your Taste and Judgment." It was generally agreed that "*Travel* and *Polite* Conversation are . . . the chief Parts of a liberal Education" (*Universal Spectator* 50).[29] At the same time, travel literature during the first half of the eighteenth century gradually assimilated many of the duties and privileges of history: simple narrative took up less and less space, whereas discourses on local history, politics, economics, geography, antiquarian topics, architecture, social history, and so on and so forth claimed a larger and larger share in the whole—travel books evolved toward general history.[30] In this context Imlac's

perhaps because of "his desire of surveying human life through all its varieties" (*Lives,* 3 : 6). See also Mary Lascelles, "Some Reflections on Johnson's Hebridean Journey," *The New Rambler,* June 1961, pp. 2–13; and, for a detailed discussion of points of contact between Johnson and the literature of travel, see Thomas Michael Curley, "Samuel Johnson and the Age of Travel" (Ph.D. dissertation, Harvard University, 1970).

29. Swift, *Prose Works,* ed. H. Davis, vol. 9 (Oxford, 1948), p. 90. See also Herbert Davis, "The Augustan Art of Conversation," *Jonathan Swift* (1957; rpt. New York, 1964), pp. 260 ff.; Peter Gay, *The Enlightenment: An Interpretation,* vol. 1 (New York, 1966), pp. 176–78.

30. Louis L. Martz, *The Later Career of Tobias Smollett* (New Haven, 1942), shows exactly how this happened, and points out specific relations between travel literature, the development of "l'esprit philosophique," general history, the encyclopedias, and the novel. For history as an aspect

abrupt transitions from "neglecting to live" to history to visiting the pyramids make sense, and the fact that all the major symbols in *Rasselas* are historical-geographical landmarks seems appropriate and right.

The key to travel motifs in *Rasselas* is not so much motion as freedom to move and access to novelty. It is possible to live at one address in Cairo and yet enjoy "a mixture of all nations" (12.3), but amid all the flowery meadows and ingenious amusements of the Happy Valley the prince finds "one day and one hour exactly like another" (3.3). Conversely, the prince and his companions encounter as hazards along their way a series of enclosures, literal and metaphorical. Rasselas meditating his escape from the Happy Valley is "impatient as an eagle in a grate" (5.1). Imlac declares that "when I cast my eye on the expanse of waters my heart bounded like that of a prisoner escaped" (8.13). The hermit in his commodious cavern longs for "the counsel and conversation of the good" (21.9), and Pekuah in the Arab's fortress finds the "Conversation" of his women tedious; "they ran from room to room as a bird hops from wire to wire in his cage" (39.8, 6). "If I am accidentally left alone for a few hours," says the astronomer, "my inveterate persuasion rushes upon my soul, and my thoughts are *chained down* by some irresistible violence, but they are soon disentangled by the prince's conversation" (46.13; my italics).

Philosophic Fiction

The studied impotences of chapter 49 seem to undermine whatever has been accomplished up to that point; if *Rasselas* had concluded with chapter 48, we would have put the book

---

of culture and a liberal art, not a scientific discipline, and for connections between history and conversation, see J. B. Black, *The Art of History* (New York, 1926), pp. 1–28. See also R. W. Frantz, *The English Traveller and the Movement of Ideas 1660–1732* (Lincoln, Nebr., 1934) for a detailed summary of the influence of travel books on current controversies in religion, morals, government: the age of heroic adventure was over; only three exploring expeditions left England 1660–1732, but hundreds of travelers reported their findings "not so much to startle the world as to enlighten it" (p. 13).

down in a chastened mood but with a sense of having been consecrated to the choice of eternity and to preparation for judgment by "the Being whom I fear to name, the Being which made the soul." As it is, every reader must come to terms with anticlimax and futility in "The conclusion, in which nothing is concluded." [31]

Notice, however, that Imlac and the astronomer do not form "schemes of happiness," and that their program, humdrum or not, may be exempt from the frustrations predicted in the last paragraph ("of these wishes that they had formed they well knew that none could be obtained"), because it isn't a wish: "Imlac and the astronomer were contented to be driven along the stream of life without directing their course to any particular port" (49.6). This is a good deal less blasé than it looks: not only does it admit the possibility of contentedness (two dark and violent lines from *The Vanity of Human Wishes,* "Must helpless man, in ignorance sedate, / Roll darkling down the torrent of his fate?" make a striking contrast based on the same metaphor); it also dignifies Imlac and the astronomer with a complex and satisfying relation to one of the controlling metaphors of *Rasselas.* "Do not suffer life to stagnate," says Imlac to Nekayah; "it will grow muddy for want of motion: commit yourself again to the current of the world" (35.8). Isolation, enclosure, ignorance, and grief cause stagnation, leave the mind "torpid," or "stupid" (11.11, 12.9, 19.3). To be driven along the stream of life implies a commitment to life, to friendship, travel and talk, learning, variety; implies also an acceptance of "continual flux" (35.8) as a condition of existence. Rasselas laments twenty months wasted in the Happy Valley:

"In this time the birds have left the nest of their mother, and committed themselves to the woods and to the skies: the kid has forsaken the teat, and learned by degrees to climb the rocks in quest of

31. Hawkins (*Life of Samuel Johnson,* p. 372) and Mrs. Chapone (*Works,* 1 : 111) were reassured by hearing that Johnson planned a sequel. Ellis Cornelia Knight, *Dinarbas. Being a Continuation of Rasselas* (London, 1790) is the result of one reader's total inability to live with the ending as written.

independant sustenance. I only have made no advances, but am still helpless and ignorant. The moon by more than twenty changes, admonished me of the flux of life; the stream that rolled before my feet upbraided my inactivity. I sat feasting on intellectual luxury, regardless alike of the examples of the earth, and the instructions of the planets." [4.10]

Not to commit oneself is to remain unnaturally a child, imprisoned within one's own mind.

Those who are "driven along" seem more passive than those who "commit themselves to" the *stream* of life; both are more contemplative and peaceful than sailors on the *ocean* of the world, "a sea foaming with tempests, and boiling with whirlpools" (12.14). It is impossible, moreover, to participate in life even as observer without taking some risks: the mechanick artist of chapter 6 wants to watch what's going on but not get his hands dirty; he promises Rasselas the pleasures of Lucretius's philosopher—"how must it amuse the pendent spectator to see the moving scene of land and ocean, cities and desarts! To survey with equal security the marts of trade, and the fields of battle; mountains infested by barbarians, and fruitful regions gladdened by plenty, and lulled by peace!" "All this, said the prince, is much to be desired, but I am afraid that no man will be able to breathe in these regions of speculation and tranquility" (6.5–6), which is figuratively as well as literally true.[32] As if to make sure that the point of this metaphor comes across, Johnson repeats it in chapter 18, where Rasselas thinks he has found a man "who, from the unshaken throne of

32. "The world is a Comedy . . . I know no securer box, from which to behold it, than a safe *solitude*. And it is easier to feel than to express the pleasure which may be taken in standing aloof, and in contemplating the reelings of the multitude, the excentrick motions of great men, and how fate recreats itself in their ruine" (Sir George Mackenzie, *A Moral Essay, Preferring Solitude to Publick Employment* [1666], p. 81, cited by Røstvig, *The Happy Man*, 1 : 317). The Epicurean pleasure of watching others act and suffer from a safe elevation (Lucretius, *De rerum natura* 2.1–16) is second cousin to the Lucianic pleasure of surveying the folly and petty knavery of mankind from an absurd height ("Icaromenippus," LCL, 2 : 287–97); both must be distinguished from the Augustan survey, which examines the various scenes of human life to gain wisdom through broader perspectives.

rational fortitude, looks down on the scenes of life changing beneath him"; perfect detachment and security are denied him also, and he too must live as a man, though he speaks like an angel.

If our eyes have been peeled for symbols in *Rasselas,* we shall see more meaning in the next-to-last paragraph of chapter 49 than, perhaps, Johnson did himself, he underplays it so. The river of life is a favorite image elsewhere; its effectiveness here is enhanced by readers' memories of the Nile winding its way in and out of the narrative, a symbolic leitmotif. Rasselas and Imlac were both born near the source of the Nile; the first sight that greets them when they have broken out of the Happy Valley is "the Nile, yet a narrow current, wandering beneath them" (14.4); the quest proper never strays far from the Nile, and comes to rest in its capital city, Cairo. A number of the grandest speeches in *Rasselas* call on the "Father of Waters." It is by no means impossible that Johnson knew of the tradition which "regarded the Nile as one of the four great rivers of the garden of Eden." [33]

"Contented to be driven along the stream of life without directing their course to any particular port": if figuratively this spells commitment, it is literally a rather noncommittal brand of commitment, tentative, free from dogma. To explain why the inconclusiveness of chapter 49 seems to me just as meaningful as its "conclusions," I must here make two large associative leaps, from *Rasselas* to its contexts, first in British empiricism, then in that multinational phenomenon in the history of ideas known as the Enlightenment.

> Nullius addictus jurare in verba magistri
> Quo me cunque rapit tempestas deferor hospes.

Or, in Pope's version:

> Sworn to no Master, of no Sect am I:
> As drives the storm, at any door I knock.

33. O. F. Emerson, Introduction, *History of Rasselas* (New York, 1895), p. xxiii. References to the Nile: 1.2, 6.5, 8.3, 19.1 (the hermit lives near the lowest cataract), 21.1, 25.4 (where the dialogue of chs. 25–29 takes place), 29.14, 39.2 (the Arab's castle), 41.3 (the astronomer's delusions of power), 42.5 (madness), 43.2, 45.1, 49.1, 2, 7.

These two lines from Horace's *Epistle* 1.1 were the motto of *The Rambler.* They supplied also the motto of the Royal Society: *in verba nullius*—take no one's word for anything. Imlac's and the astronomer's reluctance to direct their course to any particular port corresponds to the refusal of British empiricists to attach themselves to any one dogma or sect or authority. Both Horace and Imlac yield to the tide of circumstance described in one case as a storm, in the other as a river. In *Idler* 51, written a few months after *Rasselas,* Johnson put it more bluntly: "a man who has duly considered the condition of his being, will contentedly yield to the course of things." Pope quoted one of Horace's lines to amplify his idea of a man "above all parties of men": "It seems to me," he wrote to Swift, "that you value no man's civility above your own dignity, or your own reason . . . Nullius addictus jurare in verba magistri." [34] Horace's hexameters appeared at the head of *Free-Thinker* 2 (1718), which includes a Character of the Free-thinker: "He takes nothing upon Trust . . . He is listed into no Party, nor tied down to any Profession: He is confined to no Places and (like a *Denizen* of the World) thinks himself at home Everywhere: neither is he a Slave to Modes and Customs." What all these passages have in common, and what we can, I think, confidently read into Imlac's and the astronomer's inconclusive behavior, is an ideal of disinterestedness. In each of these passages someone renounces a teacher or an authority or a faction—or the choice of life—to gain less obstructed access to truth.

Disinterestedness in chapter 48 of *Rasselas* takes the form of positivism, a refusal to believe more than what we know for sure, that distrust of hypotheses which was most effectively formulated by Isaac Newton, and which later strengthened important planks in some of the best-known platforms of the French Enlightenment. In chapter 48, a very compact piece of argument, Imlac attacks the hypotheses of the astronomer;

34. Swift, *Correspondence,* ed. Harold Williams (Oxford, 1963; rpt. with corrections 1965), 3 : 182. The sentence just quoted from *Idler* 51 may clarify what it means to be driven along the stream of life, and may also suggest what Johnson was feeling at the time: see Lascelles, "*Rasselas:* A Rejoinder."

Johnson is pitting Newton against Locke,[35] using the rigorous positivism of the scientist to demolish question-begging suppositions that may be found in the philosopher. In 48.5, 8, 10 the astronomer alludes to Locke's opinion on the nature of the soul: "some yet say, that it may be material, who, nevertheless, believe it to be immortal." God may have attached to matter "qualities with which we are unacquainted"; we should not "too arrogantly limit the Creator's power." Locke underlined more than once the impossibility of knowing how matter and spirit are related to each other, but he insisted that "God can, if he pleases, superadd to matter *a faculty of thinking*," however incomprehensible to human understandings such a thing may be, and thereby left it open to heterodox thinkers (including Voltaire and Priestley) to refine the materialist psychology implicit in this possibility.[36]

At this point Imlac figuratively kicks the stone:

> "He who will determine, returned Imlac, against that which he knows, because there may be something which he knows not; he that can set hypothetical possibility against acknowledged certainty, is not to be admitted among reasonable beings." [48.9]

I know of no better expression of what E. A. Burtt calls "scientific positivism"; it is, moreover (and therefore), much closer

35. Or rather, Newton's positivism, as defined in his *Rules of Reasoning*, against Locke's embryonic or potential materialism. The controversy over the nature of the soul was more complex than I allow here; at some points in the *Essay Concerning Human Understanding* Locke sounds more like Imlac than like the astronomer: "sensation convinces us that there are solid extended substances; and reflection, that there are thinking ones: experience assures us of the existence of such beings . . . But beyond these ideas . . . our faculties will not reach" (1 : 414). On the other hand, see 1 : 418; and the crucial paragraph, bk. 4, ch. 3, par. 6 (2 : 191–98), which was, according to Locke's editor, A. C. Fraser, "the text of a large part of the controversy with Stillingfleet, and also between Clarke and Dodwell, and between Clarke and Collins" (2 : 198 n. 3). I quote a clause from this paragraph in my text three sentences below.

36. See Voltaire, *Elémens de la philosophie de Newton* (1738), in *Oeuvres* (Paris, 1828), 41 : 85–95; *Traité de metaphysique* (1734?), in *Mélanges* (Bibliothèque de la Pléiade, 1961), ch. 5; Joseph Priestley, *Disquisition relating to Matter and Spirit* (London, 1777), sect. 1, which quotes Newton's *"rules of Philosophizing,"* just as I am about to do.

to the cautious empiricism of Isaac Newton than to modern theories of scientific method, with their mathematical hunches and dissolving paradigms. Compare the principle of simplicity, as defined in Newton's first *Rule of Reasoning in Philosophy:*

> We are to admit no more causes of natural things than such as are both true and sufficient to explain their appearances. To this purpose, the philosophers say, that nature does nothing in vain, and more is in vain when less will serve; for nature is pleased with simplicity, and affects not the pomp of superfluous causes.

Newton, like Imlac, rejects the seductive uncertainties of "hypothetical possibility": his fourth rule illustrates this dislike and also shows the "tentative, positivistic" quality of his approach:

> In experimental philosophy we are to look upon propositions collected by general induction from phenomena as accurately or very nearly true, notwithstanding any contrary hypotheses that may be imagined, till such time as other phenomena occur, by which they may either be made more accurate, or liable to exceptions. This rule we must follow, that the argument of induction may not be evaded by hypotheses.[37]

We are engaged in hunting down useful contexts for *Rasselas:* it is reasonable to jump from Newton to Voltaire, and from British empiricism to the European Enlightenment. Johnson was certainly an empiricist; but a statement about the nature of Johnson's participation in the Enlightenment, an intellectual phenomenon subversive and irreligious in some of its most characteristic phases, must be carefully hedged. I shall be emphasizing aspects of the Enlightenment that Johnson *could* participate in.[38] In many respects Johnson resisted the current of Enlightenment. A crusading and progressive

37. Cited by E. A. Burtt, *The Metaphysical Foundations of Modern Physical Science* (1924; rev. 1932; rpt. Garden City, N.Y., 1954), pp. 218–19, from *Mathematical Principles,* trans. Motte (London, 1803), 2 : 160ff.

38. As does Robert Shackleton in his useful article, "Johnson and the Enlightenment," *Johnson, Boswell, and Their Circle,* pp. 76–92. Voltaire's *contes* were widely available in England: see J. A. R. Séguin, *Voltaire and the Gentleman's Magazine: 1731–1868* (New York, 1962), Items 50, 68, 74, 80, 92, 96.

spirit, the grand confidence of Voltaire (consciously intent to "renverser le colosse," dedicated to a grand mission with Hume and Bolingbroke as allies) or of Paine ("I have no notion of yielding the palm of the United States to any Grecians or Romans that were ever born")[39] is impossible to match in Johnson. His fear of death and hell and his sense of sin lean backward toward an older Christian tradition, Pauline and orthodox, not forward to the "modern paganism" most obviously rising in France.

The Enlightenment as an international phenomenon, however, was very diverse—moralistic in Germany, libertine and elegant in France, revolutionary in America. In Britain, political and scientific revolutions had already been staged, peacefully, in the seventeenth century: the anglophilia of the philosophes suggests that in their view Britain *was* enlightened, and did not need to "renverser le colosse." Johnson, of course, approved of the Glorious and scientific revolutions, and his toleration in religious matters extended to Catholics and dissenters, though not to unbelievers. His own references to "these enlightened days" (*Adventurer* 115) and to "our age, which true policy has enlightened beyond any former time" (*Idler* 38) seem to associate enlightenment with the spread of knowledge and the advancement of civilization.[40] Enlightenment from this point of view is the opposite not just of ignorance but of rudeness or lack of polish, and the Enlightenment of the middle of the eighteenth century differs only in

39. H. H. Clark, *Thomas Paine* (New York, 1944), p. civ. F. L. Ford proposes as two of "four attitudes" characteristic of and essential to the Enlightenment, (1) a sense of liberation, and (2) "the conviction that basic changes were occurring in man's condition, that more would occur in the future, and that an effort to control the nature and direction of such changes was not only intellectually respectable but indeed imperative" ("The Enlightenment: Towards a Useful Redefinition," *Studies in the Eighteenth Century,* ed. R. F. Brissenden [Toronto, 1968], pp. 24–26); these are certainly not Johnsonian attitudes. See also Gay, *The Enlightenment,* vol. 2, ch. 1.

40. Other uses of the word: *Idler* 6, par. 5 (ironic); *Adventurer* 115, par. 12; *Rambler* 104, par. 11; *Lives,* 3 : 310; *Essay on Epitaphs,* par. 17. A precise analysis of the limits of Johnson's toleration: Chapin, *The Religious Thought of Samuel Johnson,* ch. 8, esp. pp. 118–21.

degree from, for example, that of the Renaissance (which Johnson referred to as "the revival of letters"). If "the regular progress of cultivated life is from Necessities to Accommodations, from Accommodations to Ornaments," we can expect "enlightenment" as the by-product of certain recurring historical changes.

From another point of view Johnson was conscious that the spread of knowledge in his own lifetime had worked unprecedented changes. "That general knowledge which now circulates in common talk was in [Addison's] time rarely to be found" (*Lives,* 3:146). Johnson, in other words, did recognize certain distinctive qualities in the European Enlightenment of the eighteenth century. It was, he felt, an "age of enquiry and knowledge, when superstition is driven away, and omens and prodigies have lost their terrours" (*Idler* 11).[41] It was also an age of improving technology, when the curious gadgets of virtuosos might be put to work, eventually, "to drain fens, or manufacture metals, to assist the architect, or preserve the sailor" (*Rambler* 83). Diderot went to great lengths to record the best available information on the mechanical arts in the *Encyclopédie;* Johnson was persistently fascinated by technology, and much more closely in touch with scientific thinking of the time than, say, Boswell, who seems in some other respects more up-to-date than his older friend. A serious interest in artisans and manufacturing seems in Diderot and d'Alembert to reflect a scale of priorities that at least begins where Johnson's does, with the necessary, with the recognition that adequate food, clothing, shelter must precede any attempts at higher excellences. Johnson's humanitarianism is founded on the same hierarchical arrangement of values that puts fiction so entirely in the service of truth (see chapter 1 above), and humanitarianism was very much a part of the European Enlightenment.

41. For Johnson on superstition and on the "gradual progress" of empirical knowledge, see *The False Alarm,* par. 1; *Lives,* 1 : 208–9; *Rambler* 9, par. 7–8; *Rambler* 129, par. 13; *Rambler* 41, par. 5; *Rambler* 71, par. 11. See also Richard B. Schwartz, *Samuel Johnson and the New Science* (Madison, Wis., 1971), pp. 30–58.

Another measure of Johnson's participation in the Enlightenment is the fact that he worked extensively in enlightened literary forms.[42] The periodical essays were intended to bring philosophy down to the coffee houses; the *Encyclopédie* and Johnson's *Dictionary* were popularizations, of a different order. The essay form, which Bacon referred to as "Knowledge broken," played a substantial role in the German Enlightenment. The Johnsonian survey relies on an encyclopedic structure, in *The Vanity of Human Wishes,* in the quests of the *Rambler,* and in *Rasselas.* Johnson wrote more introductions and prefaces to dictionaries and compilations of various kinds than any other writer of genius I know; they seemed to suit his talents and tastes. All these forms forwarded the Enlightenment's goal of a general increase of knowledge, and profited by the Enlightenment's retreat from genres heroic and sublime; but none is so characteristic of the Enlightenment as the philosophic voyage.[43]

In its most diluted and sometimes parodistic form, the philosophic voyage can be said to overlap with the Fielding-Smollett-Sterne tradition of comic narrative. Philosophic travelers ramble observantly or scurry disconsolately through many of the best and most interesting fictions of the eighteenth century. A number of the Cervantic heroes alluded to in chapter 1 above have some pretensions to philosophy (e.g., Parson Adams and the Vicar of Wakefield). The eighteenth century rewrote *Don Quixote* as a quest for truth or happiness; in some cases, to put it rather crudely, seeds from *Don Quixote* sprouted from the soil of the Enlightenment as Bildungs-

42. Enlightenment "consists less in certain individual doctrines than in the form and manner of intellectual activity in general"—Ernst Cassirer, *The Philosophy of the Enlightenment* (1932; rpt. Boston, 1955), p. 163.

43. Bacon, *Advancement of Learning,* bk. 2, sect. 17, par. 7. For the importance of encyclopedic forms in the Enlightenment, see Paul Hazard, *European Thought in the Eighteenth Century* (New Haven, 1954), part 2, ch. 7. "To 'know' a manifold of experience is [for the Enlightenment] to place its component parts in such a relationship to one another that, starting from a given point, we can run through them according to a constant and general rule" (Cassirer, *The Philosophy of the Enlightenment,* p. 23).

roman, and Bildungsroman in the eighteenth century is often philosophic: "mores hominum multorum vidit" (which could be translated, "he has surveyed the customs of many nations") is the title-page motto of *Tom Jones,* though Tom himself is not much of a philosopher. Pope's Odysseus, like Rasselas and Imlac, went "Wand'ring from clime to clime, observant stray'd, / Their Manners noted, and their States survey'd." [44]

Travelers who may more seriously claim to be "philosophic," in an Enlightenment sense of the word, are those who go to some trouble to establish themselves as disinterested. "Rica et moi sommes peut-être les premiers parmi les Persans que l'envie de savoir ait fait sortir de leur pays, et qui aient renoncé aux douceurs d'une vie tranquille pour aller chercher laborieusement la sagesse." [45] Rasselas renounces tranquillity too, the "tasteless tranquillity" of the Happy Valley, in order "to judge with my own eyes of the various conditions of men." He may not be shrewd, but he is objective, and Imlac by studious travels has formed himself into a fine specimen of the citizen of the world, at home in every civilized nation, cosmopolitan. This is the quality in Bayle (often cited as a precursor of the Enlightenment) that Johnson appreciated; Bayle painted the historian as "a citizen of the world," "not in

44. The Latin motto of *Tom Jones* is Horace's translation of the opening of the *Odyssey,* in *Ars Poetica,* line 142. See Robert Fagles, "Pope's *Odyssey,*" in *The Poems of Alexander Pope,* Twickenham ed., vol. 7 (London, 1967), pp. ccvii–ccxiv. Fénelon's *Télémaque* was enormously influential as moral-philosophical narrative in the eighteenth century. Fielding, Author's Preface to *The Journal of a Voyage to Lisbon* (1755), mentions the *Odyssey* as a travel book. It is hard to say exactly when the practice of observing the manners of men, so very popular in the eighteenth century, becomes philosophical. For a few of the very many relevant texts, see La Bruyère, *Les caractères* (4th ed. 1689), "Des ouvrages de l'esprit" no. 34 ("le philosophe consume sa vie à observer les hommes . . ."); Robert Alter on Gil Blas (*Rogue's Progress* [Cambridge, Mass., 1964], p. 17) as a "critical observer of *moeurs*"; *Essay on Man,* Ep. 1, lines 1–16 ("catch the manners living as they rise").

45. "Rica and I are perhaps the first among the Persians whom the desire for knowledge has made to leave their country, and who have renounced the pleasures of a tranquil life to go to search laboriously for wisdom" (Montesquieu, *Lettres Persanes* [1721], ed. P. Vernière [Paris, 1960], p. 12. See also pp. 21–22).

the service of the Emperor, nor in that of the King of France, but only in the service of Truth. She is my queen; to her alone have I sworn the oath of obedience."[46] And when Johnson explains that "Free-Thinking" in Ambrose Philips's periodical means simply "freedom from unreasonable prejudice" (*Lives,* 3:322), he is distinguishing between *sapere aude* and Deism, between the critical spirit that developed as one of the most powerful forces (creative and destructive) in the Enlightenment, and impiety, irreligion.[47] Philips's Free-Thinker, as we have seen, is described in a paraphrase of the verses from Horace's *Epistle* 1.1 that seem to me a suggestive analogue for the next-to-last paragraph of *Rasselas:* he is "listed into no Party, nor tied down to any Profession: He is confined to no Place, and (like a *Denizen* of the World) thinks himself at home Everywhere: neither is he a Slave to Mode and Custom." The most influential periodical of the eighteenth century makes a point of being an objective *spectator* of manners and morals. The imaginary club in *Spectator* 2 and later essays was intended to bring together various points of view, thereby offering the reader (at least in theory) a disinterested choice among them; Johnson's numerous real-life clubs were composed of sociable people from many different walks of life. Samuel Richardson and Catherine Talbot—who may be counted among the more devout and respectable of Johnson's friends—testify to the strength and popularity of disinterestedness as an ideal. Charles Grandison is "in the noblest sense, a Citizen of the World." Miss Talbot defends the French from the strictures of Elizabeth Carter, feeling herself "indebted to them for many excellent books. This is a reason why, as citizens of the world, we should love even French folks, and judge

46. Quoted by Cassirer, *The Philosophy of the Enlightenment,* pp. 208–09. For Johnson on Bayle, see Boswell, 5 : 287 and 288 n. 3.

47. *Sapere aude* (dare to know): "the motto of the enlightenment," according to Immanuel Kant, "What is Enlightenment?" (1783). For a wide-ranging analysis of the critical spirit, see Gay, *The Enlightenment,* 1 : 127–58; compare Cassirer on "analysis," *The Philosophy of the Enlightenment,* ch. 1. Cassirer does not feel the Enlightenment was basically irreligious; Hume and Holbach seem to him anomalies (ibid., pp. 65–73, 134–36, 182).

with candour of whatever they would introduce." And yet Diderot, *encyclopédiste,* and Hume, questioner of miracles, preened themselves on being citizens of the world also. The phrase was applied by Cicero and Plutarch to Socrates, by Seneca to the wise man of the Stoics, and by Lucian to a scurrilous cynic—in each case as a way of praising a disinterested man.[48]

The way to become disinterested is to free oneself from provincialities by surveying the manners and morals of many nations or kinds of men. This is one of the things it means to be "philosophic" in the eighteenth century. Pope's major philosophic poem, *An Esaay on Man,* promises to "Expatiate free o'er all this scene of Man." Gay, writing a set of fables for the education of a prince, tells us that he will "in these tales mankind survey." Goldsmith in an essay of 1760 sets out to "survey the various customs" of the world. Even Laurence Sterne, in a characteristic variation on the same formula, arranges his *Sentimental Journey* so that "through the different disguises of customs, climates, and religion," he may "find out what is good" in the hearts of men (and women), "to fashion my own by." The most obvious procedures by which one surveys manners and morals are travel and talk.[49]

Within this general context we can return to *Rasselas* as a philosophic tale of the European Enlightenment, and revive to some purpose the well-worn comparison between *Rasselas* and *Candide.* Similarities between them were obvious from the beginning. Boswell seemed a little stunned by the likenesses; Johnson seemed to accept them with what I read as something bordering on complacence. The French philosophic tale, wrote Boswell, is "wonderfully similar in its plan and

48. Richardson, *Grandison* (Oxford, 1931), 6 : 11; Elizabeth Carter, *A Series of Letters between Mrs. Elizabeth Carter and Miss Catherine Talbot,* ed. Montagu Pennington (London, 1809), 1 : 327 (February 4, 1750); Diderot to Hume, February 22, 1768 (cited from *Correspondence,* 8 : 16 by Gay, *The Enlightenment,* 1 : 13); Hamilton Jewett Smith, *Oliver Goldsmith's Citizen of the World* (New Haven, 1926), pp. 29–31 n. 14.

49. *Essay on Man,* Ep. 1, line 5; John Gay, Fable 1, line 2; Goldsmith, *Works,* ed. Arthur Friedman, 3 : 69; *A Sentimental Journey,* ed. Ian Jack (New York, 1968), p. 84.

conduct" to the English, "insomuch, that I have heard Johnson say, that if they had not been published so closely one after the other that there was not time for imitation, it would have been in vain to deny that the scheme of that which came latest was taken from the other."[50] Voltaire's narrative, structurally, is Johnson's turned backward: in the first twenty-one chapters, Candide suffers and gathers experience; in the last nineteen chapters, Candide observes (he is searching for Cunégonde, but in the process he rambles over half of Europe, keeping an eye out for "le meilleur des mondes possibles"), and has his hopes systematically punctured. Both heroes are irrepressibly hopeful, and rich enough for all purposes; a skeptical sage escorts them on their travels, which include a mountain-encircled utopia not quite good enough to detain them from the quest for happiness. In both stories naïveté is a comic surrogate for philosophic disinterestedness, and survives repeated disillusionment by making a commitment to the world. The way fact subverts theory, the manner in which bubbles of expectation are blown—and then popped—is similar in some parts of *Rasselas* and *Candide* (see chapter 2 above, and compare Voltaire's Pococurante with the Country Gentleman of chapter 20 or the Old Man of chapter 45). To be driven along the stream of life is not the same as to cultivate one's garden, but both are a species of disengagement that is not withdrawal or retreat, and both imply a strong sense of the limits of human endeavor. Both stories are more

50. Boswell, 1 : 342. See for chronology and further discussion, ibid., n. 2, and J. L. Clifford, "Some Remarks on *Candide* and *Rasselas," Bicentenary Essays on Rasselas,* pp. 7–10. Among others who have compared *Rasselas* and *Candide:* Sir Walter Scott, *Lives of the Novelists* (Oxford, 1906), pp. 161–62; Martha Conant, *The Oriental Tale* (New York, 1908), pp. 144–51; Joseph Wood Krutch, *Samuel Johnson* (New York, 1944), pp. 181–84.

Other analogues besides *Candide:* see Geoffrey Tillotson, " 'Rasselas' and the 'Persian Tales,' " *Times Literary Supplement,* August 29, 1935, p. 534; Ian Jack, "The 'Choice of Life' in Johnson and Matthew Prior," *JEGP* 49 (1950): 523–30; Lascelles, *Rasselas* Reconsidered," *Essays and Studies by Members of the English Association,* n.s. 4 (1951): 40–44, for John Kirkby's *Automathes* (1745); J. W. Johnson, "Rasselas and his Ancestors," *N&Q,* n.s. 6 (1959): 185–88.

expressive than mimetic.[51] In both *Candide* and *Rasselas* a certain measure of complexity derives from inconsistencies of one sort or another. "Le monde offre à Voltaire un spectacle qui ne cesse d'être affreux que pour paraître ridicule." [52]

Many critics, however, have seemed to wish to argue that despite such likenesses there is no essential kinship between *Rasselas* and *Candide*. And it is true that whereas the attack on optimism in *Rasselas* reinforces, eventually, our reliance on Providence, in *Candide* it undermines our belief in a providential ordering of the universe: Johnson is wise and compassionate; Voltaire's snowballs have rocks in them. But in terms of the way they transcribe experience into narrative, *Rasselas* and *Candide* are first cousins at least; formal similarities are a clue to the fact that, however their philosophies may differ, they go at the important business of being philosophic in roughly the same way. The Enlightenment, taken as an international event in the history of ideas, helps us understand what this means in *Rasselas:* disinterestedness, commitment to the secular river of life, a tireless interest in travel and talk, and an insatiable appetite for surveys of mankind.

Not that Voltaire and Johnson were basically alike; but in these two works philosophy, pessimism, a realistic appreciation of the damage life can inflict on people, and an ironic spirit of comedy combine to produce similar narratives. To state it in these terms illuminates some of the distinctive qualities of

51. Voltaire's characters "are not alive because they do not need to be alive, because Voltaire is alive" (Ira O. Wade, *Voltaire's Micromegas* [Princeton, 1950], p. 106). Everyone in *Rasselas* speaks with Johnson's voice, writes Mary Lascelles, "and so they should; for it is not the diversity of several views that they were created to express, but the complexity inherent in one" ("*Rasselas* Reconsidered," p. 45).

52. "The world offers Voltaire a spectacle that ceases to be appalling only to appear ridiculous" (Philippe Van Tieghem, Introduction, Voltaire, *Contes et Romans* [Paris, 1930], p. xx). See also J. G. Weightman, "The Quality of *Candide,*" Voltaire, *Candide,* ed. Robert M. Adams (New York, 1966), p. 155. Some readers found *Candide* blasphemous, others comic: the variety of responses to Voltaire's tale corresponds roughly to the variety of reactions to *Rasselas,* except that no one so far as I know emphasizes the "wisdom" of *Candide;* see *Voltaire's Correspondence,* ed. T. Besterman (Geneva, 1965), 35 : 136–37, 142, 236–38.

Rasselas: consider Johnson's pessimism, which is basically psychological, as one vector, his sense of comedy as another, his vitality and dogmatism as a third (or as a third and a fourth?); the resultant is a renewal of religious humility, complicated by our memory of the harmonies, dissonances, and simple concussions set up and detonated when these forces met from various angles and in various contexts earlier in the book. The choice of life is the arena in which these forces interact to produce, finally, an act of self-submission which is not final, for Johnson; the whole is to do again—another reason for the conclusion in which nothing is concluded. And yet I for one would rather be driven along the stream of life with Imlac than labor thoughtlessly in Candide's garden. The sense of life embodied in *Rasselas* is very different from that in *Candide;* it is heroic, it is also bleak and caustic, pious and melancholy, inquisitive and pedestrian sometimes, like any tourist guidebook—impossible to define in any one sentence or paragraph, *Johnsonianissimus.*

This last, of course, can be reduced to platitude. *Rasselas* is very Johnsonian. Yet I am confident (and my analysis of this platitude, breaking it up into distinct aspects and voices and components, has intended to show) that to be truly Johnsonian is to be both complex and profound. Some, but by no means all, of this complexity and depth derives from what we think *Rasselas* means. In spite of the strenuous ambiguities of the last chapter, Nekayah's decision to leave to heaven the measure and the choice lingers in our minds. And we cannot rule out the possibility that Imlac and the astronomer will go on surveying all sorts and conditions of men (after chapter 49), that their choice of life is to continue to make the choice of life—having already made, in some fashion that the history of Rasselas does not clearly define, the choice of eternity.

Summing Up

The denunciation of romance in chapter 11 of book 9 of *The Female Quixote* is more uncompromising than most such documents. It does break into print as a chapter in a novel, however. Antiromance, which has almost as voluminous and interesting a history as romance, and which was intimately involved in the rise of the novel, provides a good context not only for Johnson's opinions on fiction but also for the stories he himself wrote. Fiction, in Johnson's critical writings, though always subordinate to truth (what is necessary always takes precedence over what is merely useful, or only a luxury), may add savor to "the insipidity of truth"; and such is the weakness of human nature that fiction may become necessary, as a respite from stern reality. Johnson is not hostile to fiction in any simple or uncomplicated way; but he marks off the limits of the domain of fiction more strictly than do most neoclassical authors.

Chapter 5, in another version of this book, might have served as a preliminary essay, showing that major conventions of periodical-essay fiction before 1750 do have repercussions in *The Rambler* and its successors. Johnson's most characteristic strengths and limitations appear in sharper focus when projected through the medium of alien modes of narrative. The prestige of the voice of Addisonian humour attracted him into a number of halfhearted or unsuccessful fictions, and he adopted episodes from the Catonist and the Man of Sentiment, with mixed results.

The principle of decorum helps to account for variations in the prose style of Johnson's fiction. There is a good deal more variety in the language of *The Rambler* than Johnson has been given credit for. Satirical narratives like *Rambler* 12 descend to very homely idioms and very short sentences. Some introductory paragraphs in the oriental tales, on the other hand, rise to a pitch of splendor and verbal magnificence well above the ordinary stateliness of *The Rambler.* The quality of this splendor is worth particular notice; there had been nothing quite like it in English prose before 1750; no one combines, as Johnson does, Hebraisms and prose rhythms from the King James Bible with emblematic and pictorial locutions reminiscent of neoclassical history-painting; no one achieves such rich and stilted specimens of the rhetorical sublime. Although the separation of styles in Johnson's fiction is orthodox, the use of a periodical essay as the generic vehicle for experiments in sublime prose is not; the slovenliness of the language of oriental tales before 1750 and scattered examples of excessively gorgeous prose immediately after 1750 suggest that these few passages may have had an influence out of proportion to their length.

The peculiar virtues of Johnson's fiction appear most convincingly as virtues—not as mere peculiarities—within the world of problems and priorities established by "the choice of life," a dominating theme. The narrative form that most efficiently dramatizes the choice of life is the quest, because it allows the main character more than one choice and therefore inflicts on him more than one disappointment. The manner in which these disappointments occur is very distinctive, as the inevitable anticlimax of burgeoning hopes schematically arranged, like experiments in moral philosophy. Those who obstruct the choice of life and those who assume they *can* make a meaningful choice of life become the butts of satirical comedy. The self-conscious irony of the portraits of some of Johnson's idlers exposes—whether in character, author, or persona, or all three is not always perfectly clear—incompetence in the choice of life.

Allegories like *Rambler* 33 outline the conditions under which the choice of life must be made: the golden age has dwindled to iron, the gods have departed, life has evolved into the ambiguous state familiar to all of us in which (for example) neither the luxuries of Rest nor the solid benefits of Labor are durable. Here not only the rhetoric but also the action is pictorial, unfolding in static scenes, not in a chain of mic events; the elaborate pictorialism of some of John- writings has not been adequately appreciated. Allegories 'The Vision of Theodore" illustrate the impossibility of making a good choice of life except as a corollary of the choice of eternity; even the path of reason and religion is difficult and dangerous. The picture of human life in Johnson's allegories, like that in complaint, confession, and quest, is more strikingly pessimistic than moralistic.

We need not condescend to the periodical-essay narratives; they are our guide to Johnson's imagined world, in which almost every human aspiration is balked. They teach us something also about relationships between imagination and reason in Johnson's writings. At the *end* of an essay, reason may rescue the reader—battered and disillusioned by his encounters with the world of Johnson's imagination—and hand him over to religion; instantly the curtain falls. That is, where consolation for the harsh realities of the kind of experience we find in the fiction is offered, it comes as a replay of "The Vision of Theodore, Hermit of Teneriffe." Obvious parallels between the moral essays and the fiction may serve to remind us that for Johnson, in a secular context, experience comes first and precept follows: his moral essays were not reasoned together in a vacuum, but are based on vividly imagined, real experiences, including those we can learn about in the fictions. Johnson's fictions were, after all, fact, so far as he was concerned, Truth dressed in a loose and changeable robe. And if Johnson's fictions are in this sense natural and true, then for him mimesis *is* expression. The more obviously these "pictures of life" violate the reader's standards of reality, the more value they may have as the relics of a very unusual human being.

Johnson, of course, entitled his book "The Choice of Life" before he had decided on the name Rasselas for his protagonist. In this longer fiction the choice of life is given a larger significance, and some of the same narrative machinery we encountered in the periodical essays is refined and subordinated to larger purposes. The golden age establishes itself in a mountain valley in Abyssinia, and proves as visionary as any of the long-expected boons in *The Rambler;* Rasselas rejects it in order to make the choice of life, and for twenty-nine chapters he tumbles down a staircase of predictable comic disappointments. If he had given up at this point, when his systematically unsuccessful canvassing of the varied scenes of human life had left him and his sister bewildered, angry (so far as it is possible for two such courtly personages to show anger), and quite at a loss, he would *exemplify* the vanity of human wishes in much the same way numerous correspondents of *The Rambler* do. But his history transcends exemplum, especially as it develops in the last twenty chapters; it *embodies* a positive set of values and attitudes; it transforms the failure of the choice of life into a complex and compelling affirmation subsuming irony, hunger for new scenes and social comforts, disillusion, pessimism, and religious faith. The presence of several interacting main characters and forty-nine chapters in which to expatiate allows Johnson not merely to integrate fictional modes from the periodical essays into a more sophisticated narrative, but also to break free from self-imposed constraints into a new kind of fiction.

The new freedom of *Rasselas* is in part a matter of form: similarities between this oriental tale and the most famous of all *contes philosophiques* help us understand how in *Rasselas* Johnson is being philosophic. A relish for disinterested surveys of the various lots of man, whether through travel or talk, from a vantage point neither so detached as to be inhuman nor so closely involved as to be overwhelmed by every storm that breaks, was not restricted to extreme radicals of the European Enlightenment. The new freedom and expressiveness of *Rasselas* is in part a matter of content. We can applaud at least one indisputable success in the struggle to make the happiness one does not find, the healing of the astronomer. It is no accident, I think, that Pekuah's relation with the astronomer —one of the irreducibly human transactions in *Rasselas;* she treats him with an entirely feminine mixture of patronage, flattery, and respect—has some analogies with the relation between Arabella and the pious priest in Johnson's chapter of *The Female Quixote,* and with crucial episodes in Johnson's personal history; Pekuah's role anticipates that of Mrs. Thrale and Fanny Burney, among others. Imlac's counsel to the princess ("commit yourself again to the current of the world") applies as well to Rasselas and to anyone whose choice of life has failed; it justifies the quest, anticipates the healing of the astronomer, and sanctions—obliquely, figuratively—the final decision of Imlac and the astronomer "to be driven along the stream of life."

Johnson's achievement in *Rasselas* cannot be measured simply in terms of the persuasiveness of its moral teachings, nor in terms of the aptness with which it exemplifies certain ideas. Its interest is, I think, enhanced by the affinities it shows with enlightenment philosophic tales; but whether these affinities are assessed in terms of the history of ideas or in terms of narrative form, they serve primarily to illuminate Johnson's tremendous individuality. In its own odd, cyclical, and unfinished way *Rasselas* is an artistic trumph. It is also a personal triumph and an earned affirmation; the better we know it the more likely we are to regard *Rasselas* as Boswell, summing up, regarded its author, "with admiration and reverence."

Index

Novels are entered under the names of their authors; periodical essays are listed by title, with the names of the authors/editors where pertinent. SJ = Samuel Johnson.